Marlowe

Tamburlaine the Great
Edward the Second
and
The Jew of Malta

A CASEBOOK

EDITED BY

JOHN RUSSELL BROWN

MACMILLAN

Selection, editorial matter and Introduction
© John Russell Brown 1982

First published 1982 by
THE MACMILLAN PRESS LTD
Houndmills, Basingstoke, Hampshire RG21 2XS
and London
Companies and representatives
throughout the world

ISBN 0–333–28364–3

A catalogue record for this book is available
from the British Library.

Reprinted 1989, 1991, 1994

Printed in Hong Kong

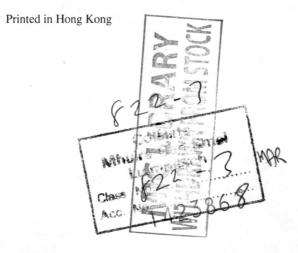

CASEBOOK SERIES

JANE AUSTEN: *Emma* (Revised) David Lodge
JANE AUSTEN: *'Northanger Abbey'* & *'Persuasion'* B. C. Southam
JANE AUSTEN: *'Sense and Sensibility'*, *'Pride and Prejudice'* & *'Mansfield Park'*
B. C. Southam
BECKETT: *Waiting for Godot* Ruby Cohn
WILLIAM BLAKE: *Songs of Innocence and Experience* Margaret Bottrall
CHARLOTTE BRONTE: *'Jane Eyre'* & *'Villette'* Miriam Allott
EMILY BRONTE: *Wuthering Heights* (Revised) Miriam Allott
BROWNING: *'Men and Women'* & *Other Poems* J. R. Watson
CHAUCER: *The Canterbury Tales* J. J. Anderson
COLERIDGE: *'The Ancient Mariner'* & *Other Poems* Alun R. Jones & W. Tydeman
CONRAD: *'Heart of Darkness'*, *'Nostromo'* & *'Under Western Eyes'* C. B. Cox
CONRAD: *The Secret Agent* Ian Watt
DICKENS: *Bleak House* A. E. Dyson
DICKENS: *'Hard Times'*, *'Great Expectations'* & *'Our Mutual Friend'* Norman Page
DICKENS: *'Dombey and Son'* & *'Little Dorrit'* Alan Shelston
DONNE: *Songs and Sonets* Julian Lovelock
GEORGE ELIOT: *Middlemarch* Patrick Swinden
GEORGE ELIOT: *'The Mill on the Floss'* & *'Silas Marner'* R. P. Draper
T. S. ELIOT: *Four Quartets* Bernard Bergonzi
T. S. ELIOT: *'Prufrock'*, *'Gerontion'* & *'Ash Wednesday'* B. C. Southam
T. S. ELIOT: *The Waste Land* C. B. Cox & Arnold P. Hinchliffe
T. S. ELIOT: *Plays* Arnold P. Hinchliffe
HENRY FIELDING: *Tom Jones* Neil Compton
E.M. FORSTER: *A Passage to India* Malcolm Bradbury
WILLIAM GOLDING: *Novels 1954–64* Norman Page
HARDY: *The Tragic Novels* (Revised) R. P. Draper
HARDY: *Poems* James Gibson & Trevor Johnson
HARDY: *Three Pastoral Novels* R. P. Draper
GERARD MANLEY HOPKINS: *Poems* Margaret Bottrall
HENRY JAMES: *'Washington Square'* & *'The Portrait of a Lady'* Alan Shelton
JONSON: *Volpone* Jonas A. Barish
JONSON: *'Every Man in his Humour'* & *'The Alchemist'* R. V. Holdsworth
JAMES JOYCE: *'Dubliners'* & *'A Portrait of the Artist as a Young Man'* Morris Beja
KEATS: *Odes* G.S. Fraser
KEATS: *Narrative Poems* John Spencer Hill
D.H. LAWRENCE: *Sons and Lovers* Gamini Salgado
D.H. LAWRENCE: *'The Rainbow'* & *'Women in Love'* Colin Clarke
LOWRY: *Under the Volcano* Gordon Bowker
MARLOWE: *Doctor Faustus* John Jump
MARLOWE: *'Tamburlaine the Great'*, *'Edward II'* & *'The Jew of Malta'* J. R. Brown
MARLOWE: *Poems* Arthur Pollard
MAUPASSANT: *In the Hall of Mirrors* T. Harris
MILTON: *Paradise Lost* A. E. Dyson & Julian Lovelock
O'CASEY: *'Juno and the Paycock'*, *'The Plough and the Stars'* & *'The Shadow of a Gunman'* Ronald Ayling
EUGENE O'NEILL: *Three Plays* Normand Berlin
JOHN OSBORNE: *Look Back in Anger* John Russell Taylor
PINTER: *'The Birthday Party'* & *Other Plays* Michael Scott
POPE: *The Rape of the Lock* John Dixon Hunt
SHAKESPEARE: *A Midsummer Night's Dream* Antony Price
SHAKESPEARE: *Antony and Cleopatra* (Revised) John Russell Brown
SHAKESPEARE: *Coriolanus* B. A. Brockman

CONTENTS

Part One: *Comments and Criticism before 1900*

Part Two: *Modern Studies and Accounts of Performance*

1 Marlowe's Style

ACKNOWLEDGEMENTS

The editor and publishers wish to thank the following who have kindly given permission for the use of copyright material:

John Russell Brown, 'Marlowe and the Actors' from *Tulane Drama Review*, VIII, IV (1964), by permission of the editor; J. S. Cunningham and Roger Warren, 'Tamburlaine the Great Rediscovered' from *Shakespeare Survey*, vol. 31 (1978), by permission of the authors and Cambridge University Press; Stephen J. Greenblatt, essay 'Marlowe and Renaissance Self-Fashioning' from *Two Renaissance Myth-Makers: Christopher Marlowe and Ben Jonson*, Selected Papers from the English Institute (1975–6), New Series, No. 1, edited by Alvin Kernan, reprinted by permission of the author and the Johns Hopkins University Press; Clifford Leech, 'Power and Suffering in Edward II' from *Critical Quarterly*, 1 (1959), by permission of Mrs Gabriela Leech; Harry Levin, 'More of the Serpent' from *The Overreacher: A Study of Christopher Marlowe* by permission of Faber and Faber Limited; Johnstone Parr, extracts from 'Tamburlaine's Malady' in *PMLA*, 59 (1944), by permission of the author and the Modern Language Association of America; Irving Ribner, extract from *The English History Play in the Age of Shakespeare* (1957; reissued 1979 by Octagon Books), by permission of Mrs Roslyn Ribner; unsigned review in *The Times* (2 Oct. 1964), of the play *The Jew of Malta*, by permission of Times Newspapers Limited; Eugene M. Waith, extract from *The Herculean Hero in Marlowe, Chapman, Shakespeare and Dryden* (1962), by permission of the author and Chatto & Windus Limited; Judith Weil, chapter from *Christopher Marlowe: Merlin's Prophet* (1977), by permission of the author and Cambridge University Press; David Hard Zucker, extract from *Stage and Image in the Plays of Christopher Marlowe* (1972), by permission of the editor, Institute for English Language and Literature, University of Salzburg.

GENERAL EDITOR'S PREFACE

The Casebook series, launched in 1968, has become a well-regarded library of critical studies. The central concern of the series remains the 'single-author' volume, but suggestions from the academic community have led to an extension of the original plan, to include occasional volumes on such general themes as literary 'schools' and genres.

Each volume in the central category deals either with one well-known and influential work by an individual author, or with closely related works by one writer. The main section consists of critical readings, mostly modern, collected from books and journals. A selection of reviews and comments by the author's contemporaries is also included, and sometimes comment from the author himself. The Editor's introduction charts the reputation of the work or works from the first appearance to the present time.

Volumes in the 'general themes' category are variable in structure but follow the basic purpose of the series in presenting an integrated selection of readings, with an Introduction which explores the theme and discusses the literary and critical issues involved.

A single volume can represent no more than a small selection of critical opinions. Some critics are excluded for reasons of space, and it is hoped that readers will pursue the suggestions for further reading in the Select Bibliography. Other contributions are severed from their original context, to which some readers may wish to turn. Indeed, if they take a hint from the critics represented here, they certainly will.

A. E. DYSON

INTRODUCTION

In 1587, Sir Francis Drake sailed into Cadiz harbour and attacked the Spanish galleons that were preparing to land a huge army on English shores. The power of Philip II of Spain had been reinforced by the Pope who proclaimed a Holy Crusade against England and promised huge sums of money to finance the projected invasion. Drake's raid could only postpone a major conflict. Strict measures were enforced for defence of the realm and, after many delays, Elizabeth I gave approval for the execution of Mary Queen of Scots who had a rival claim to the throne. Royal proclamations announced measures against seditious rumours (6 February) and against corruption of the coinage (12 October). By November 1587, people living on the coast were instructed to keep to their own homes. In the following year, the Spanish Armada did sail and it was repulsed by English ships and stormy seas. But before that event all the odds were stacked against the small island country; 1587 was a crucial year, in which England put itself into a posture of defiant and watchful defence.

The new public theatres of London reflected the spirit of this time. The year 1587 marked also the first performances of *Tamburlaine the Great, Part One*. Its author, Christopher Marlowe, was only twenty-three years of age, son of a shoemaker of Canterbury and a recent graduate of the University of Cambridge. Its hero, the unbeaten conqueror of the known world, was almost certainly played by Edward Alleyn, son of an innkeeper and, at twenty-one, even younger than its author. By 1590, two years after the defeat of the Armada, *Tamburlaine, Parts One and Two* were published with a title-page announcing that these 'tragical discourses' had been 'sundry times showed upon stages in the City of London'. Both plays were reprinted four times by 1606: a record for those days, implying that they were the first successes from the public theatres to gain additional popularity in print.

Marlowe's triumph was shared by Alleyn and the company of players called the Admiral's Men. From records that have survived, we know that on 28 August 1594, at a revival of *Part One* of *Tamburlaine*, Philip Henslowe, theatre-owner and manager, took £3 11s od from receipts at the doors, more than twice the usual amount. Between this day and 13 November, *Part One* was performed fifteen times and *Part Two* seven. As late as 1633, Thomas Heywood, the dramatist, remembered the 'peerless' achievement of the star performer. The plays had become a byword: Tamburlaine's cry to the captive kings as he forces them to pull his chariot – 'Holla, ye pampered jades of Asia!' – was quoted by Ancient Pistol in *Henry IV, Part Two* and by many braggarts and mockers before and since. By the sixteen-thirties, Ben Jonson, a dramatist of conscious art and high ambition, would condemn the 'scenical strutting and furious vociferation' of Marlowe's hero, but in so doing he testified to its long-lasting influence from what was already 'the late age'.

Tamburlaine was Marlowe's first great success and it made him renowned and criticised by other writers. The first to record in print the young dramatist's reputation was Robert Greene, a playwright six years his senior and another Cambridge graduate. Opinion had only one voice: Marlowe's gifts were heavenly and his use of them successful, bold, dangerous, 'mad' or, even, 'hellish'. After 1598, when he was stabbed to death in a tavern brawl at Deptford, near London – modern research has shown that this was the outcome of espionage work among English catholics in Europe undertaken immediately after graduation – Marlowe also became an example of how God punishes evil-doers and blasphemers. Not only did the plays show an atheist defying God, a king of England obsessed with 'perverted' love, a scholar selling his soul to the Devil, and a Jew triumphing, until the very last moment, over a crowd of Christians almost all as corrupt and mercenary as himself, but Thomas Kyd, a play-wright with whom Marlowe had shared a lodging, testified to the authorities that his companion had been heretical in his beliefs. Marlowe was also reputed to be 'lewd' and drunken. But even his detractors and those to whom his death was a moral warning all acknowledged, with his admirers, a sense of loss both personal and theatrical. Shakespeare in *As You Like It* (c. 1599) made one of his very rare references to a contemporary writer:

> Dead shepherd, now I find thy saw of might:
> 'Whoever lov'd that lov'd not at first sight?'   [III v 80–1]

To his contemporaries, Christopher Marlowe was, in his life as in his work, like a torch that burned brightly and fiercely, and was soon extinguished.

After the death of Elizabeth, only *Dr Faustus, Edward II* and *The Jew of Malta* seem to have survived in occasional performances and, after the closure of the theatres for the Civil War, the next production seems to have been a revival of *The Jew* in 1818; it had been cut and altered to provide a star-vehicle for the romantic and dynamic actor, Edmund Kean. (An account of his portrayal and the treatment of the text is reprinted in this volume from *Blackwood's Magazine*.) But as seventeenth-century editions of all the major plays testify, Marlowe's influence continued through the printed word without a break. *The Jew* and *Edward II* were also reprinted in the eighteenth century, and 1826 saw the first *Collected Works* in three volumes edited by G. Robinson. Alexander Dyce published a new collection in 1850, revising it in 1858 and 1865. The Mermaid one-volume edition of *The Best Plays of Christopher Marlowe*, edited by Havelock Ellis and first published in 1887, brought the texts within every reader's reach and prepared the way for many other editions of both single plays and complete works. Stage productions followed more slowly, but since the 1939–45 war all the major plays – *Tamburlaine, Edward II, The Jew of Malta* and *Doctor Faustus* – have become part of the repertoire of British theatre, and *Faustus* has been filmed. The last to establish themselves as complete and viable works for the modern theatre were the two parts of *Tamburlaine*; after several productions in shortened forms, these were staged almost in their entirety as the opening productions of the Olivier Theatre of the National Theatre, London, in 1976.

The retrieval of Marlowe's reputation dates from the Romantic period, at about the same time as the revival of *The Jew of Malta*. Charles Lamb, writing in 1808, had been almost as dismissive as Thomas Warton in his *History of English Poetry* (1781), but in 1820 William Hazlitt recognised 'a glow of the imagination' in the dramatic verse and described Marlowe as a doomed, heroic iconoclast:

his thoughts burn within him like a furnace with bickering flames; or throwing out black smoke and mists that hide the dawn of genius, or like a poisonous mineral corrode the heart.

Hazlitt faults the plays for their construction, characterisation and sensationalism, but singles out *Edward II* for its 'historic truth' and argues that the death of the king 'is certainly superior' to that in Shakespeare's *Richard II*. Here criticism begins to distinguish Marlowe from his great contemporary by a recognition of the pathos of a single scene, the power of dramatic illusion. By 1844, Leigh Hunt was arguing that Marlowe was a truly original poet, like Edmund Spenser: he had recreated 'ancient fabling' and risen to 'modern rapture'. In this view, as in some earlier comments, Marlowe is praised more for his 'poetry' than his plays, as if he were a literary artist writing in an unpropitious theatrical form. This dichotomy has survived as a significant strand in criticism to much later times, as in A. P. Rossiter's *English Drama from Early Times to the Elizabethans* (1950) and J. B. Steane's *Marlowe: A Critical Study* (Cambridge, 1964).

A development of the Romantic and personal understanding of Marlowe is Edward Dowden's assessment in *The Fortnightly Review* for January 1870. This begins auspiciously by marking a polar difference between Shakespeare and Marlowe: the former is a realist whose plays spring from an understanding of character and action; the latter an idealist, like Milton, whose plays express a passion or an idea. From this concept Dowden proceeds to a reconsideration of the plays: he finds a 'unity' in *Tamburlaine*'s 'multitude of scenes', a vivid revelation of avarice in *The Jew of Malta* which obliterates conventional responses to a miser, and a 'pliable' – rather than thunderous – strength in much of the dialogue after *Tamburlaine*. Slowly Marlowe's distinctive voice and dramatic skill were being appraised in their own right. A. W. Ward was primarily an historian which may be one reason why his *History of English Dramatic Literature* (1875) pays careful attention to the various political portraits in *Edward II* and leads to a new appreciation of Marlowe's dramatic intelligence. John Addington Symonds, who wrote extensively about Italian renaissance art, probed wider still, recognising Marlowe's originality as a dramatic poet. He responded equally to the 'vastness of design and scale' and to what, following Dowden, he conceived to be a 'simplicity and certainty of purpose'. Symonds rephrased Hazlitt's romantic concept, relating it to the plays rather than their author and showing in the dramatic achievements of each work how all may be considered as treatments of the one motive of '*L'Amour de l'Impossible*–the love or lust of unattainable things'.

The twentieth century has seen the fruits of careful scholarship and a basic reappraisal of Marlowe's distinctive achievements. The chronology of Marlowe's writings is not wholly settled, but most scholars would accept the following:

1585–6   *Dido, Queen of Carthage*. (But it may have been among Marlowe's later works; it was published in 1594, as a collaboration between Marlowe and Thomas Nashe.)
1587–8   *Tamburlaine the Great, Parts One and Two.*
1589–90   *The Jew of Malta*
1590–2   *The Massacre at Paris*
1592–3   *Doctor Faustus*
1591–3   *Edward the Second*

For an up-to-date understanding of the qualities of Marlowe's plays a significant starting point is an essay of 1919 by the poet, T. S. Eliot.[1] Here Marlowe is still considered as poet rather than dramatist, but now his verse is judged in its historical context as the unique achievement of a very conscious artist. In Eliot's praise of the 'driving power' of Marlowe's blank-verse and of a developing 'intensity' in his soliloquies there is also a recognition of essentially dramatic virtues. Eliot's brief essay heralds the more serious and sustained scholarly investigations that in sixty years have established Marlowe as a learned, intelligent, passionate, witty and resourceful dramatist. As Irving Ribner pointed out in 1964, Marlowe has become 'our contemporary' in a very precise sense: only since 1920 'have either the man or his works come to be seen for what they really are'.[2]

Several main streams of criticism and research may be distinguished. The attitudes of his own contemporaries, and of Hazlitt and J. A. Symonds, still inform some writing about Marlowe. Una Ellis-Fermor's *Christopher Marlowe* (1927) values the plays for their evocation of a Renaissance pursuit of power, pleasure and understanding at the risk of heresy and isolation. More recently, L. C. Knights has argued, in *Further Explorations* (1965), that 'in some important respects Marlowe's creative fantasy did not meet sufficient resistance – the kind of resistance that is necessary for the production of the highest kind of energy, which is at once affirmation, growth and understanding'.[3] In this tradition Eugene M. Waith studied Tamburlaine as a Herculean hero (1962), and in a later book (1971) considered Marlowe as a writer concerned with drama as a means of exploring Greatness.[4]

But recent critics who respond to the glowing images of Marlowe's aspiring fantasies have also developed a further contrasting theme and have argued that Marlowe was also a restless sceptic and independent thinker. Harry Levin's study, called *The Overreacher* (1952), claims that Marlowe was seriously concerned with atheism, Machiavellianism and Epicureanism as alternative ways of life to the scholastic Christianity in which he had been brought up at Canterbury and Cambridge: 'no other poet has been, so fully as Marlowe, a fellow traveller with the subversive currents of his age'.[5] Paul H. Kocher has documented this freethinking aspect very fully in his *Christopher Marlowe: A Study of his Thought, Learning and Character* (1946).

Yet another contrasting view sees Marlowe as an orthodox Christian who wrote exemplary plays about the wages of sin. This was first presented with elaborate scholastic support by R. W. Battenhouse in *Marlowe's Tamburlaine* (1941) and later by Douglas Cole in *Suffering and Evil in the Plays of Christopher Marlowe* (1962). These scholars argued that Marlowe's heroes transgress orthodox morality so thoroughly and so precisely that their eventual deaths must be received as a just judgement on their sins. Only modern moral laxity and an ignorance of scholastic literature could interpret them in any other way. The hero of *Dr Faustus* is taken off to hell, so that case does not need the same subtlety of argument as does the case of *Tamburlaine*, who dies

convinced that the gods mean to raise him 'Above the threefold
astracism of heaven' (2: IV iii 61–2). But Tamburlaine does
become ever more cruel, more dependent on others (until his son
has to stand in his place) and more at the mercy of his body; and
so the notion that Marlowe condemned him for his overweening
ambition can be shown to have textual and structural grounding.
Independent articles have argued the same thesis: Johnstone
Parr's on 'Tamburlaine's Malady' (1944), Michael Quinn's on
'The Freedom of Tamburlaine' (1960), and Alexander Leggatt's
on 'Tamburlaine's Sufferings' (1973). A recent book in this
tradition, that covers all the plays, is Judith Weil's *Christopher
Marlowe: Merlin's Prophet* (1977). Professor Weil shows that much
of the rhetoric and dramatic action exploits paradox, in the
tradition of Erasmus's *Praise of Folly*:

> The allusions, analogies, and emblematic shows in more satiric plays
> based on a Christian foundation never fully prepare us for the disasters
> which match so precisely the errors of the characters. . . . For
> Marlowe, the mythical figures of Icarus and Phaeton seem to have
> symbolised a tragic conflict between self-centred idealism and the
> objective, heliocentric triumphs of time. Speed and obliquity in the art
> of his plays force the audience to experience this conflict as a profound
> disturbance in the seasons of its own understanding.[7]

The contrasting views of Marlowe as sceptic and Marlowe as
orthodox moralist have often been held, as if in suspension,
within a single critique of the plays. Clifford Leech's article on
'Marlowe's Humor' (1962) is one example, and the same
author's essay on *Edward II* (1964) – excerpted in Part Two
below – is another.[8] Professor Leech argued for the objectivity of
Marlowe's art, which presents human action clearly for the
audience to make its own judgement. Molly M. Mahood in *Poetry
and Humanism* (1950) had earlier reconciled the two views by
arguing that Marlowe becomes progressively more disillusioned
with a Renaissance glorification of man, so that his heroes
dwindle from the titanic to the puny.

In a wider view of the plays, and one that is not dependent on a
questionable chronology or on issues of personal morality as
viewed within a received and established tradition, Stephen J.
Greenblatt (1977) has seen Marlowe as a man of his age daring to

question the validity both of world and of self. Whereas Levin had seen Marlowe exploring new ideas, Professor Greenblatt shows a Marlowe who questioned all ideas and his own identity:

Marlowe's heroes must live their lives as projects, but they do so in the midst of intimations that the projects are illusions. Their strength is not sapped by these intimations . . . . Rather, they derive a tragic courage from the absurdity of their enterprise, a murderous, self-destructive, supremely eloquent courage.[9]

One further line of Marlowe criticism remains to be distinguished: a new attempt to see Marlowe's dramaturgy in its historical context and in its originality: a spectacular and extraordinarily varied invention that can provide both a large-scale show and an intense, prolonged focus on a single mind. F. P. Wilson's clear-headed *Marlowe and the Early Shakespeare* (1954) helped to place his works in perspective; and David M. Bevington's *From 'Mankind' to Marlowe: Growth of Structure in the Popular Drama of Tudor England* (1962) provided precise knowledge about devices such as the doubling of roles and the use of stage-properties. The issue of the *Tulane Drama Review* published in 1964 – which contained the articles of that date by Leech and by Ribner previously mentioned – included five articles about Marlowe's stagecraft and had considerable influence on later investigations.

Nicholas Brooke's chapter in the collective volume *Elizabethan Theatre* (1966) is boldly entitled 'Marlowe the Dramatist' and argues that the dramatist's attitudes to his subject-matter can best be discerned in dramatic structure, not in eminently quotable individual lines: 'his plays are not the carelessly half-written throw-outs of poetic genius, but successive experiments in different dramatic forms'.[10] Professor Brooke argued that this theatrical view bypasses the difficulty of imagining Marlowe to be an ingenious and covert intellectual writing puzzles with dark and hidden meanings: 'rather, it supposes imaginative opportunism [which] might well produce a result more complex than the intention'. David Hard Zucker's *Stage and Image in the Plays of Christopher Marlowe* (Salzburg, 1972) built on these beginnings and established Marlowe as a writer who enjoyed and relied on the very tangible three-dimensional and living image of the theatre.

In addition to scholarly and critical investigation, the staging of plays in the theatre has had its own effect on understanding. A prime example is *The Jew of Malta* which surprised many dramatic critics when it was revived in celebration of the four-hundredth anniversary of its author's birth. N. W. Bawcutt, editor of the Revels Plays text (1978), has acknowledged the effect of this and other productions, observing (at p. 37):

My own feeling is that the comedy (which is theatrically very effective, as modern productions show) is a harsh and disturbing comedy, near to ridicule, not the cheerful laughter which relaxes and heals. It should not distract us from the play's seriousness, but intensify it. . . . The play may seem at times a parody of normal human behaviour; even so, it is the kind of parody that is uncomfortably close to reality . . . producers have seized on it as a play with exciting and unexplored possibilities.

In selecting articles and chapters of books for reprinting in this Casebook, I have had three main concerns. First, I have provided examples of the main streams of criticism of Marlowe's plays. Secondly, I have presented studies of *Tamburlaine, Edward II* and *The Jew of Malta* as fully as possible, so that students of these individual plays may be provided with fully informed and varied views, including some sense of the life they have in performance. There is no stage-centred discussion of *Edward II*, but Clifford Leech's study springs directly from his reactions to one of its most praised productions. Thirdly, I have included general articles on Marlowe's style and sense of tragedy that should illuminate the reading of any of his plays, including *Doctor Faustus*. In this way the present Casebook is a complementary volume to John Jump's earlier one on *Doctor Faustus*; this printed no criticism published after 1966, at which date the study of Marlowe was just getting into its later twentieth-century stride.

References to other plays, *The Massacre at Paris* and *Dido, Queen of Carthage*, occur in several of the chapters of this book and are intended as further means to a view of Marlowe's whole career as a dramatist.

NOTES

1. T. S. Eliot, 'Notes on the Blank Verse of Christopher Marlowe' (1919), collected in *The Sacred Wood: Essays on Poetry and Criticism* (London, 1920).

2. Irving Ribner, in *Tulane Drama Review*, VIII, 4 (1964), p. 211.

3. L. C. Knights, op. cit., p. 97. For the context of this argument, see the excerpt from Knights's essay in the Casebook on *Dr Faustus*, pp. 204–7.

4. Eugene M. Waith, *Ideas of Greatness: Heroic Drama in England* (New York, and London, 1971).

5. Harry Levin, op. cit., p. 18: first published in 1952 in the United States as *The Overreacher: A Study of Christopher Marlowe*, the book's British edition (London, 1954) was entitled *Christopher Marlowe: The Overreacher*. The long excerpt from it in the Casebook on *Dr Faustus* (pp. 134–64) in part treats of the argument referred to here.

6. Johnstone Parr, in *PMLA*, LIX (1944), pp. 696–714; Michael Quinn, in *Modern Language Quarterly*, XXL (1960), pp. 315–20; and Alexander Leggatt, in *Yearbook of English Studies*, III (1973), pp. 28–38.

7. Judith Weil, op. cit., pp. 170–1.

8. Clifford Leech, in the collective volume, Richard Hosley (ed.), *Essays on Shakespearean and Elizabethan Drama in Honor of Hardin Craig* (Columbia, Miss., 1962), and in *Tulane Drama Review*, VIII, 4 (1964), pp. 32–46.

9. Stephen J. Greenblatt, in Alvin Kernan (ed.), *Two Renaissance Mythmakers* (Baltimore, Md, and London, 1977), p. 63.

10. Nicholas Brooke, in J. R. Brown and B. Harris (eds), *Elizabethan Theatre, Stratford-upon-Avon Studies*, 9 (London, 1966), p. 104.

NOTE ON TEXTS

In this Casebook, all references to Marlowe's works are systematised with *The Complete Plays* edited by J. B. Steane in the Penguin English Library (Harmondsworth, 1969).

Alternative one-volume editions are by L. Kirschbaum (Cleveland, Ohio and New York, 1962), I. Ribner (New York, 1963) and Roma Gill (London and New York, 1971).

The Complete Works of Christopher Marlowe, edited by Fredson T. Bowers in two volumes (Cambridge, 1973), is in old spelling and has a full textual collation.

Single-play editions are noted in the Select Bibliography, page 230, below.

References to Shakespeare's *Works* are systematised with Peter Alexander's edition(London and Glasgow, 1951).

PART ONE

Comments and Criticism
before 1900

Robert Greene   (1588, 1592)

I

. . . I keep my old course, to palter up something in prose, using mine old poesie still . . . although lately two gentleman poets made my two mad men of Rome beat it out of their paper bucklers and had it in derision, for that I could not make my verses jet upon the stage in tragical buskins, every word filling the mouth like the faburden of Bow-Bell, daring God out of heaven with that Atheist Tamburlaine or blaspheming with the mad priest of the sun. But let me rather openly pocket up the ass at Diogenes' hand than wantonly set out such impious instances of intolerable poetry, such mad and scoffing poets that have prophetical spirits as bold as Merlin's race . . . . I think either it is the humour of a novice that tickles them with self-love, or too much frequenting the hot house . . . hath sweat out all the greatest part of their wits. . . .[1]

II

. . . Wonder not – for with thee will I first begin – thou famous gracer of tragedians, that Greene, who hath said with thee (like the fool in his heart), 'There is no God', should now give glory unto his greatness: for penetrating is his power, his hand lies heavy upon me, he hath spoken unto me with a voice of thunder and I have felt he is a God that can punish enemies. Why should thy excellent wit, his gift, be so blinded that thou shouldst give no glory to the giver? Is it the pestilent Machiavellian policy that thou hast studied? O peevish folly! What are his rules but mere confused mockeries, able to extirpate, in small time, the generation of mankind? For if *Sic volo, sic iubeo*, hold in those that are able to command, and if it be lawfull *Fas et nefas* to do anything that is beneficial, only tyrants should possess the earth and they, striving to exceed in tyranny, should each to other be a slaughterman till, the mightiest outliving all, one stroke were left for Death, that in one age man's life should end.

The broacher of this diabolical Atheism is dead, and in his life had never the felicity he aimed at, but, as he began in craft, lived in fear and ended in despair. *Quam inscrutabilia sunt Dei iudicia?* This murderer of many brethren had his conscience seared like Cain; this betrayer of him that gave his life for him, inherited the portion of Judas; this Apostate perished as ill as Julian: and wilt thou my friend be his disciple? Look but to me, by him persuaded to that liberty, and thou shalt find it an infernal bondage. I know the least of my demerits merit this miserable death, but wilfull striving against known truth exceedeth all the terror of my soul. Defer not with me till this last point of extremity, for little knowst thou how in the end thou shalt be visited. . . .[2]

SOURCE: extract I from *Perimedes the Blacksmith* (1588), Preface; extract II from *A Groatsworth of Wit bought with a Million of Repentence* (1592), E4V–FI.

NOTES

1. Extract I: here Greene addresses his 'Gentleman readers' in imitation of Rabelaisian wit; he writes that 'I speak darkly'.
   The cynic Diogenes was told that people laughed at him and replied: 'And so very likely do the asses at them; but as they don't care for the asses, so neither do I care for them' (*Lives of Eminent Philosophers* by Diogenes Laertius, trans. R. D. Hicks (1958), ii 61).
   faburden refrain; *hot house* brothel.
2. Extract II: *Sic volo* &c. If I wish it so, I order it so; *Fas et nefas* Right and wrong; *Quam inscrutabilia* &c. How inscrutable are the judgements of God?

George Peele   (1593)

. . . unhappy in thine end,
Marley, the Muses' darling for thy verse,
Fit to write passions for the souls below,
If any wretched souls in passion speak.   . . .

SOURCE: *The Honour of the Garter* (1593), Prologue.

Joseph Hall   (1597–8)

. . .

One higher pitch'd doth set his soaring thought
On crowned kings that Fortune hath low brought,
Or some upreared, high-aspiring swain,
As it might be the Turkish Tamburlaine.
Then weeneth he his base drink-drowned spright,
Rapt to the threefold loft of heaven's height,
When he conceives upon his fained stage
The stalking steps of his great personage,
Graced with huff-cap terms and thund'ring threats,
That his poor hearer's hair quite upright sets.
Such soon, as some brave-minded hungry youth,
Sees fitly frame to his wide-strained mouth,
He vaunts his voice upon an hired stage,
With high-set steps and princely carriage:
Now sooping in side robes of royalty
That earst did scrub in lousy brokery.
There if he can with terms Italianate,
Big-sounding sentences and words of state,
Fair patch me up his pure iambic verse,
He ravishes the gazing scaffolders.   . . .

SOURCE: lines from *Virgidemiarum* (1597–8), I iii.

NOTES

huff-cap swaggering, drunken; *sooping* sweeping; *side* long, reaching
far down; *scrub* go poorly dressed (with quibble on *scrubbing* a floor);
brokery second-hand clothes; *scaffolders* i.e. playgoers.

Anonymous   (1598–1601)

...

JUDICIO   Marlowe was happy in his buskin'd muse,
Alas unhappy in his life and end.
Pity it is that wit so ill should dwell;
Wit lent from heaven, but vices sent from hell.
INGENIOSO   Our theatre hath lost, Pluto, hath got,
A tragic penman for a dreary plot.   ...

SOURCE: extract from *The Three Parnassus Plays*, ed. J. B. Leishman (London, 1949), pp. 242–3.

NOTES

buskin'd wearing high-soled boots of tragic actors – tragic, elevated; *dreary* bloody, dire.

Michael Drayton   (1627)

Neat Marlowe, bathed in the Thespian springs,
Had in him those brave translunary things
That the first poets had; his raptures were
All air and fire, which made his verses clear,
For that fine madness still he did retain
Which rightly should possess a poet's brain.   ...

SOURCE: lines from 'To my Most Dearly-loved Friend, Henry Reynolds Esquire, of Poets and Poesie' (1627), in Drayton's *Works*, ed. J. W. Hebel et al. (Oxford, 1931–41; 2nd edition 1962), III, p. 228.

NOTES

Neat elegant, fine; *Thespian* tragic (Thespis was the founder of Greek tragedy); *clear* glorious, illustrious; *still* ever; *retain* possess, continue to use.

Ben Jonson   (before 1635)

. . . The true artificer will not run away from nature, as he were afraid of her, or depart from life and the likeness of truth, but speak to the capacity of his hearers. And though his language differ from the vulgar somewhat, it shall not fly from all humanity with the Tamerlanes and Tamer-Chams of the late age which had nothing in them but scenical strutting and furious vociferation, to warrant them to the ignorant gapers. . . .

SOURCE: extract from *Timber: or, Discoveries; Made upon Men and Matter* (published posthumously, 1640); in Jonson's *Works*, ed. C. H. Herford, P. and E. Simpson (Oxford, 1925–52), VIII (1947), p. 587.

Thomas Warton   (1781)

. . . His tragedies manifest traces of a just dramatic conception, but they abound with tedious and uninteresting scenes, or with such extravagancies as proceeded from a want of judgment and those barbarous ideas of the time, over which it was the peculiar gift of Shakespeare's genius alone to triumph and predominate. . . .

Marlowe's wit and spriteliness of conversation had often the unhappy effect of tempting him to sport with sacred subjects, more perhaps from the preposterous ambition of courting the casual applause of profligate and unprincipled companions, than from any systematic disbelief of religion. His scepticism, whatever it might be, was construed by the prejudiced and peevish puritans into absolute atheism: and they took pains to represent the unfortunate catastrophe of his untimely death as an immediate judgment from heaven upon his execrable impiety. . . .

SOURCE: extracts from *The History of English Poetry* (1781), III, PP. 453–4.

Charles Lamb   (1808)

. . . The lunes of Tamburlaine are perfect 'midsummer madness'. Nebuchadnazar's [sic] are mere modest pretensions compared with the thundering vaunts of this Scythian Shepherd. He comes in . . . drawn by conquered kings, and reproaches these 'pampered jades of Asia' that they can 'draw but twenty miles a day'. Till I saw this passage with my own eyes, I never believed that it was anything more than a pleasant burlesque of Mine Ancient's [in Shakespeare's *Henry IV* (*2*: II iv 178)–Ed.]. But I assure my readers that it is soberly set down in a play which their ancestors took to be serious. . . .

Edward II . . . is in a very different style from 'mighty Tamburlaine'. The reluctant pangs of abdicating royalty in Edward furnished hints which Shakespeare scarce improved in his Richard the Second; and the death-scene of Marlowe's king moves pity and terror beyond any scene, ancient or modern, with which I am acquainted. . . .

Marlowe's Jew [of Malta] does not approach so near to Shakespeare's as his Edward II does to Richard II. Shylock, in the midst of his savage purpose, is a man. His motives, feelings, resentments, have something human in them: 'If you wrong us, shall we not revenge?' Barabas is a mere monster, brought in with a large painted nose, to please the rabble. He kills in sport, poisons whole nunneries, invents infernal machines. . . .

SOURCE: extracts from *Specimens of English Dramatic Poets who Lived about the Time of Shakespeare* (1808); reprinted (1835), I, pp. 19–45.

Anonymous   (1818)

. . . *The Jew of Malta* is, on many accounts, a very curious and interesting work. It is undoubtedly the foundation of Shakespeare's Jew. But it possesses claims to no common admiration for itself; for, besides the high poetical talent it exhibits, it may be considered as *the first* regular and consistent English drama; the first unassisted and successful attempt to embody that *dramatic unity* which had been till then totally neglected or overlooked. The dramatic poems which preceded the *Jew of Malta* could be considered as dramas only in so far as they *exhibited* events, instead of *relating* them. The poet, instead of telling a story himself, introduced various persons to speak their own thoughts and feelings, as they might be supposed to arise from certain events and circumstances; but his characters, for the most part, expressed themselves in a style and language moulded and tinctured by *his* particular habits of thinking and feeling.

Marlowe was the first poet before Shakespeare who possessed any thing like real *dramatic* genius, or who seemed to have any distinct notion of what a drama should be, as distinguished from every other kind of poetical composition. It is with some hesitation that we dissent from the opinion of an able writer in this Magazine, in thinking, that the *Jew of Malta* is Marlowe's best play. Not that we *like* it better than the *Faustus* or *Edward II*, but it is better as a *play*. There is more variety of character, and more of moral purpose, in the *Edward II*, and the *Faustus* exhibits loftier and more impassioned poetry; but neither of those plays possess, in so great a degree as the one before us, that rare, and when judiciously applied, most important quality, which we have called dramatic unity – that tending of all its parts to engender and sustain the same kind of feeling throughout. In the *Jew of Malta*, the characters are all, without exception, wicked, in the common acceptance of the term. Barabas, the Governor, Ithamore, the Friars, Abigail, to compass their own short-sighted views, all set moral restraint at defiance, and they are all unhappy – and their unhappiness is always brought about by their own guilt. We cannot agree with many persons in thinking, that this play is without a moral purpose; or that Barabas is a mere monster, and not a man. We cannot allow, that even Ithamore is *gratuitously* wicked. There is no such thing in nature – least of all in human nature, and Marlowe knew this. It is true that Ithamore appears to be so at first sight. He finds it a pleasant pastime to go about and kill men and women who have never injured him. But it must not be forgotten that he is a *slave*; and a slave should no more be expected to keep a compact with the kind from which he is cut off, than a demon or a wild beast. Who shall limit the effects of slavery on the human mind? Let those answer for the crimes of Ithamore who broke the link that united him to his species. . . .

The alterations in the *Jew of Malta*, as it has now been performed are chiefly confined to omissions . . . . The performance flags very much during the second and third acts, and is not likely to become a favourite with the public.

The whole weight of the play lies upon Mr Kean. No one else has a single line that can be made any thing of in the way of acting. The character of Barabas is, as far as it goes, well enough adapted to display some of Mr Kean's peculiar powers, but not those of the highest or rarest kind. In some parts, however – and those the very best – he made more of the character than the author has done. There was something very fine and sepulchral in his manner of delivering that admirable speech at the beginning of the second act, where he goes before daylight to seek for Abigail, who is to bring him the concealed remnant of his treasures.

> Thus like the sad presaging raven that tolls
> The sick man's passport in her hollow beak,
> And in the shadow of the silent night
> Doth shake contagion from her sable wings,
> Vex'd and tormented runs poor Barabas
> With fatal curses towards these Christians, . . . [II i iff.]

The next speech is still finer than this; and Mr Kean's manner of delivering was beautifully solemn and impressive.

> Now I remember those old womens' words,
> Who in my wealth would tell me winter's tales,
> And speak of spirits and ghosts that glide by night
> About the place where treasure hath been hid.
> And now methinks that I am one of those;
> For, whilst I live, here lives my soul's sole hope,
> And, when I die, here shall my spirit walk.   [II i 24–30]

Also, when Barabas recovers the gold he has concealed, nothing could surpass the absolute delirium of drunken joy with which he gives the speech – or rather the string of exclamations in the same scene, beginning 'Oh, my girl! my gold!' &c.

Upon the whole, Mr Kean's Barabas was as fine as the character would admit of its being made; but it bore no more comparison to that of Shylock than the play of the *Jew of Malta* does to the *Merchant of Venice*. . . .

SOURCE: extracts from an unsigned review in *Blackwood's Magazine* (May 1818). [The spelling of Marlowe's name is here revised to the modern convention –Ed.]

William Hazlitt (1820)

. . . There is a lust of power in [Marlowe's] writings, a hunger and thirst after unrighteousness, a glow of the imagination, unhallowed by any thing but its own energies. His thoughts burn within him like a furnace with bickering flames; or throwing out black smoke and mists, that hide the dawn of genius, or like a poisonous mineral, corrode the heart. . . .

I do not think *The Rich Jew of Malta* so characteristic a specimen of this writer's powers. It has not the same fierce glow of passion or expression. It is extreme in act, and outrageous in plot and catastrophe; but it has not the same vigorous filling up. The author seems to have relied on the horror inspired by the subject, and the national disgust excited against the principal character, to rouse the feelings of the audience: for the rest, it is a tissue of gratuitous, unprovoked, and incredible atrocities, which are committed, one upon the back of the other, by the parties concerned, without motive, passion, or object. There are, notwithstanding, some striking passages in it, as Barabas's description of the bravo, Pilia Borza; the relation of his own unaccountable villanies to Ithamore; his rejoicing over his recovered jewels 'as the morning lark sings over her young' [II i 64–6]; and the backwardness he declares in himself to forgive the Christian injuries that are offered him, which may have given the idea of one of Shylock's speeches, where he ironically disclaims any enmity to the merchants on the same account. It is perhaps hardly fair to compare the *Jew of Malta* with the *Merchant of Venice*; for it is evident, that Shakespeare's genius shews to as much advantage in knowledge of character, in variety and stage-effect, as it does in point of general humanity. . . .

Edward II is, according to the modern standard of composition, Marlowe's best play. It is written with few offences against the common rules, and in a succession of smooth and flowing lines. The poet however succeeds less in the voluptuous and effeminate descriptions which he here attempts, than in the more dreadful and violent bursts of passion. *Edward II* is drawn with historic truth, but without much dramatic effect. The management of the plot is feeble and desultory; little interest is excited in the various turns of fate; the characters are too worthless, have too little energy, and their punishment is, in general, too well deserved, to excite our commiseration; so that this play will bear, on the whole, but a distant comparison with Shakespeare's *Richard II* in conduct, power, or effect. But the death of Edward II, in Marlowe's tragedy, is certainly superior to that of Shakespeare's King; and in heart-breaking distress, and the sense of human weakness, claiming pity from utter helplessness and conscious misery, is not surpassed by any writer whatever. . . .

SOURCE: extracts from *Lectures on the Dramatic Literature of the Age of Elizabeth* (1820); quoted from Hazlitt's *Works*, ed. P. P.

Howe, 21 vols (1930–34): VI (1931), pp. 202, 209–11. [Hazlitt's spellings (Marlow, Shakespear) are here revised to the modern convention –Ed.]

Leigh Hunt (1844)

. . . If ever there was a born poet, Marlowe was one. He perceived things in their spiritual as well as material relations, and impressed them with a corresponding felicity. Rather, he struck them as with something sweet and glowing that rushes by; – perfumes from a censer, – glances of love and beauty. And he could accumulate images into as deliberate and lofty a grandeur. . . .

Marlowe, like Spenser, is to be looked upon as a poet who had no native precursors. As Spenser is to be criticised with an eye to his poetic ancestors, who had nothing like the *Faerie Queene*, so is Marlowe with reference to the authors of *Gorboduc* [1565]. He got nothing from them; he prepared the way for the versification, the dignity, and the pathos of his successors, who have nothing finer of the kind to show than the death of Edward the Second – not Shakespeare himself: – and his imagination, like Spenser's, haunted those purely poetic regions of ancient fabling and modern rapture, of beautiful forms and passionate expressions, which they were the first to render the common property of inspiration, and whence their language drew 'empyreal air'. Marlowe and Spenser are the first of our poets who perceived the beauty of words; not as apart from their significance, nor upon occasion only, as Chaucer did (more marvellous in that than themselves, or than the originals from whom he drew), but as a habit of the poetic mood, and as receiving and reflecting beauty through the feeling of the ideas. . . .

SOURCE: extracts from *Imagination and Fancy* (1844), pp. 136–41. [The spelling of Shakespeare's name is here revised to the modern convention – Ed.]

Edward Dowden   (1870)

The study of Shakspere[1] and his contemporaries is the study of one family consisting of many members, all of whom have the same life-blood in their veins, all of whom are recognisable by accent and bearing, and acquired habits, and various unconscious self-revealments as kinsmen, while each possesses a character of his own, and traits of mind and manners and expression which distinguish him from the rest. . . .

It is, however, amongst the pre-Shaksperians that we find the man who, of all the Elizabethan dramatists, stands next to Shakspere in poetical stature, the one man who, if he had lived longer and accomplished the work which lay clear before him, might have stood even *beside* Shakspere, as supreme in a different province of dramatic art. Shakspere would have been master of the realists or naturalists; Marlowe, master of the idealists. The starting-point of Shakspere, and of those who resemble him, is always something concrete, something real in the moral world – a character and an action; to no more elementary components than human characters and actions can the products of their art be reduced in the alembic of critical analysis; further than these they are irreducible. The starting-point of Marlowe, and of those who resemble Marlowe, is something abstract – a passion or an idea; to a passion or an idea each work of theirs can be brought back. . . . Marlowe worked, as Milton also worked, from the starting-point of an idea or passion, and the critic who might dissect all the creatures of Shakspere's art without ever having the honour to discover a soul, may really, by dexterous anatomy, come upon the souls of Marlowe's or of Milton's creatures – intelligent monads seated observant in the pineal gland. . . .

. . . There are critics who can more readily forgive any literary deficiencies or incapacities than sins of actual commission, who can bear with every evidence of dulness of poetical vision, languor of the thinking power, uncertainty of the shaping hands, but who have no toleration for splendid crimes, the sins of the sanguine temperament, extravagant fancies, thoughts that climb too high, turbulency of manner, and great swelling words of vanity. These have pronounced *Edward the Second* Marlowe's best play. And it is, doubtless, free from the violence and extravagance of the dramas that preceded it, from the vaulting ambition of poetical style, which 'o'erleaps itself, and falls o' the other'; but, except in a few scenes, and notably the closing ones, it wants also the clear raptures, the high reaches of wit, the 'brave translunary things', the single lines – each one enough to ransom a poet from captivity – which especially characterise Marlowe. The historical matter he is unable to handle as successfully as a subject of an imaginative or partly mythical kind; it does not yield and take shape in his hands as readily, and accordingly *Edward the Second*, though containing a few splendid passages, is rather a series of scenes from the chronicles of England than a drama. . . .

The subject of *Tamburlaine* – probably Marlowe's earliest work, certainly the first which made an impression on the public – if we would express it in the simplest way, is the mere lust of dominion, the passion of 'a mightly hunter before the Lord' for sovereign sway, the love of power in its crudest shape. This, and this alone, living and acting in the person of the Scythian shepherd, gives unity to the multitude of scenes which grow up before us and fall away, like the fiery-hearted blossoms of some inexhaustible tropical plant, blown with sudden and strong vitality, fading and dropping away at night, and replaced next morning by others as sanguine and heavy with perfume. There is no construction in *Tamburlaine*. Instead of two plays there might as well have been twenty, if Marlowe could have found it in his heart to husband his large supply of kings, emperors, soldans, pashas, governors, and viceroys who perish before the Scourge of God, or had he been able to discover empires, provinces, and principalities with which to endow a new race of rulers. The play ends from sheer exhaustion of resources. As Alexander was reduced to weep for another world to conquer, so Tamburlaine might have wept because there were no more emperors to fill his cages, no more monarchs to increase his royal stud. He does not weep, but what is much better, dies. . . .

Yet *Tamburlaine* is the work of a master-hand, untrammelled, if from some painting ill-composed, full of crude and violent colour, containing abundant proofs of weakness and inexperience, and having half its canvas crowded with extravagant grotesques which the artist took for sublime – if from such a painting one wonderful face looked out at us, the soul in its eyes and on its lips, a single desire possessing it, eager and simple as a flame, should we question the genius of the painter? And somewhat in this manner the single passion which has the hero of the piece for its temporary body and instrument looks out at us from the play of *Tamburlaine*. The lust and the pride of conquest, the ambition to be a god upon earth, the confident sense that in one's own will resides the prime force of nature, disdain of each single thing, how splendid soever, which the world can offer by way of gift or bribe, because less than the possession of all seems worthless – these are feelings which, though evidence from history that they are real is not wanting, are yet even imagined in a vivid way by very few persons. The demands which most of us make on life are moderate; our little lives run on with few great ambitions, and this gross kind of ambition is peculiarly out of relation to our habits of desire. But Marlowe, the son of the Canterbury shoemaker, realised in imagination this ambition as if it were his very own, and gave it most living expression. . . .

A grosser air is breathed throughout *The Jew of Malta*. The whole play is murky with smoke of the pit. Evil desires, evil thoughts, evil living, fill its five acts to the full. Nine-tenths of the picture are as darkly shadowed as some shadowy painting of Rembrandt; but, as might also be in one of Rembrandt's paintings, in the centre there is a head relieved against the gloom, lit by what strange light we do not know, unless it be the reflection from piles of gold and gems – a head fascinating and detestable, of majestic proportions, full of intellect, full of malice and deceit, with wrinkled brow, beak-like nose, cruel lips, and eyes that, though half-hooded by leathery lids, triumph visibly in the success of something devilish. Barabas is the dedicated child of sin from his mother's womb. As he grew in stature he must have grown in crooked wisdom and in wickedness. His heart is a nest where there is room for the patrons of the seven deadly sins to lodge, but one chief devil is its permanent occupier – Mammon. The lust of money is the passion of the Jew, which is constantly awake and active. His bags are the children of his heart, more loved than his Abigail, and the dearer because they were begotten through deceit or by violence. Yet Barabas is a superb figure. His energy of will is so great; his resources and inventions are so inexhaustible; he is so illustrious a representative of material power and of intellectual. Even his love of money has something in it of sublime, it is so huge a desire. He is no miser treasuring each contemptible coin. Precisely as Tamburlaine looked down with scorn at all ordinary kingships and lordships of the earth, as [Marlowe's] Faustus held for worthless the whole sum of stored-up human learning in comparison with the infinite knowledge to which he aspired, so Barabas treats with genuine disdain the opulence of common men. . . .

It has not seemed necessary here to dwell upon all that is worthless, and worse than worthless, in Marlowe's plays – on the midsummer madness of *Tamburlaine*, the contemptible buffoonery of *Dr Faustus*, and the overloaded sensational atrocities of *The Jew of Malta*. Such criticism every one but an Ancient Pistol does for himself. We all recognise the fustian of Marlowe's style, and the ill effects of the demands made upon him by sixteenth-century play-goers for such harlequinade as they could appreciate. A more important thing to recognise is that up to the last Marlowe's great powers were ripening, while his judgment was becoming sane, and his taste purer. He was escaping . . . from his 'Sturm und Drang' when he was lost to the world. *Tamburlaine* was written at the age of twenty-two, *Faustus* two or three years later. At such an age accomplishment is rare; we usually look for no more than promise. If Shakspere had died at the age when Marlowe died we should have known little of the capacity which lay within him of creating a Macbeth, a Lear, an Othello, a Cleopatra. Marlowe has left us three great ideal figures of Titanic strength and size. That we should say is much. In one particular a most important advance from *Tamburlaine* to *Dr Faustus* and the later plays is discernible – in versification. His contemporaries appear to have been much impressed by the greatness of his verse – Marlowe's 'mighty line'; and it was in the tirades of *Tamburlaine* that blank verse was first heard upon a public stage in England. But in this play the blank verse is like a gorgeous robe of brocade, stiff with golden embroidery; afterwards in his hands it becomes pliable, and falls around the thought or feeling which it covers in nobly significant lines.

SOURCE: extracts from *Fortnightly Review* (January, 1870); quoted from *Transcripts and Studies* (1888), pp. 431–53.

NOTE

1. [Ed.] Dowden's insisted-on spelling, Shakspere, is here retained.

A. W. Ward   (1875)

. . . The dramatic merits as well as the poetic beauties of *Edward II* are extremely great. The construction is upon the whole very clear, infinitely superior e.g. to that of Peele's *Edward I*. The two divisions into which the reign of Edward II naturally falls, viz. the period of the ascendancy of Gaveston and that of the ascendancy of the Spensers, are skilfully interwoven; and after the catastrophe of the fourth act (the victory of the King's adversaries and his capture) the interest in what can no longer be regarded as uncertain, viz. the ultimate fate of the King, is most powerfully sustained. The characters too are mostly well drawn; there is no ignobility about the King, whose passionate love for his favourites is itself traced to a generous motive; he is not without courage and spirit in the face of danger; but his weakness is his doom. Misfortune utterly breaks him; and never have the 'drowsiness of woe' (to use Charles Lamb's expression), and, after a last struggle between pride and necessity, the lingering expectation of a certain doom, been painted with more tragic power. The scene in Act IV, where the King seeks refuge among the monks of Neath Abbey, is of singular pathos; but it is perhaps even more remarkable how in the last scene of all the unutterable horror of the situation is depicted without our sense of the loathsome being aroused; and how pity and terror are mingled in a degree to which Shakspere himself only on occasion attains. For the combined power and delicacy of treatment, the murder of Edward II may be compared to the murder of Desdemona in *Othello*; for the fearful suspense in which the spectator is kept, I know no parallel except the *Agamemnon* of Aeschylus, but even here the effort is inferior, for in the English tragedy the spectator shares the suspense, and shares the certainty of its inevitable termination, with the sufferer on the stage himself. On the other characters I will not dwell; but they are not mere figures from the

Chronicle. It may be worth while to note the skill with which the character of young Edward (afterward King Edward III) is drawn, and how our goodwill is preserved for him, even though his name is put forward by his father's enemies. Gaveston's insolence is admirably reproduced; he is a Frenchman, and has a touch of lightheartedness to the last, when he expresses his indifference as to the precise *manner* of his death:

> I thank you all, my lords. Then I perceive
> That heading's one, and hanging is the other,
> And death is all.   [II v 30–2]

The imperious haughtiness of Young Mortimer is equally well depicted; in the character of the Queen alone I miss any indication of the transition from her faithful but despairing attachment to the King to a guilty love for Mortimer. The dignity of the tragedy is not marred by any comic scenes – which is well, for humour is not Marlowe's strong point; but there is some wit in the sketch of Baldock as an unscrupulous upstart, who fawns upon the great, and gains influence by means of his ability to find for everything reasons, or, as his interlocutor terms them, *Quandoquidems*.

SOURCE: *A History of English Dramatic Literature* (1875), I, 196–8.

NOTE

Quandoquidems 'Since indeeds'; i.e., pedantic considerations.

J. A. Symonds   (1884)

Marlowe has been styled, and not unjustly styled, the father of English dramatic poetry. . . . Before he began to write, various dramatic species had been essayed with more or less success. Comedies modelled in form upon the types of Plautus and Terence; tragedies conceived in the spirit of Seneca; chronicles rudely arranged in scenes for representation; dramatised novels and tales of private life; Court comedies of compliment and allegory; had succeeded to the religious Miracles and ethical Moralities. There was plenty of productive energy, plenty of enthusiasm and activity. Theatres continued to spring up, and acting came to rank among the recognised professions. But this activity was still chaotic. None could say where or whether the germ of a great national art existed. To us, students of the past, it is indeed clear enough in what direction lay the real life of the drama; but this was not apparent to contemporaries. Scholars despised the shows of mingled bloodshed and buffoonery in which the populace delighted. The people had no taste for dry and formal disquisitions in the style of Gorboduc [1565]. The blank verse of Sackville and Hughes rang hollow; the prose of [the comedies of John Lyly (c.1554–1606)] was affected; the rhyming couplets of the popular theatre interfered with dialogue and free development of character. The public itself was divided in its tastes and instincts; the mob inclining to mere drolleries and merriments upon the stage, the better vulgar to formalities and studied imitations. A powerful body of sober citizens, by no means wholly composed of Puritans and ascetics, regarded all forms of dramatic art with undisguised hostility. Meanwhile, no really great poet had arisen to stamp the tendencies of either Court or town with the authentic seal of genius. There seemed a danger lest the fortunes of the stage in England should be lost between the prejudices of a literary class, the puerile and lifeless pastimes of the multitude, and the disfavour of conservative moralists. From this peril Marlowe saved the English drama. Amid the chaos of conflicting elements he discerned the true and living germ of art, and set its growth beyond all risks of accident by his achievement.

When, therefore, we style Marlowe the father and founder of English dramatic poetry, we mean that he perceived the capacities for noble art inherent in the Romantic Drama, and proved its adaptation to high purpose by his practice. Out of confusion he brought order, following the clue of his own genius through a labyrinth of dim unmastered possibilities. Like all great craftsmen, he worked by selection and exclusion on the whole mass of material ready to his hand; and his instinct in this double process is the proof of his originality. He adopted the romantic drama in lieu of the classic, the popular instead of the literary type. But he saw that the right formal vehicle, blank verse, had been suggested by the school which he rejected. Rhyme, the earlier metre of the romantic drama, had to be abandoned. Blank verse, the metre of the pedants, had to be accepted. To employ blank verse in the romantic drama was the first step in his revolution. But this was only the first step. Both form and matter had alike to be transfigured. And it was precisely in this transfiguration of the right dramatic metre, in this transfiguration of the right dramatic stuff, that Marlowe showed himself a creative poet. What we call the English, or the Elizabethan, or better perhaps the Shakespearean Drama, came into existence by this double process. Marlowe found the public stage abandoned to aimless trivialities, but abounding in the rich life of the nation, and with the sympathies of the people firmly enlisted on the side of its romantic presentation. He introduced a new class of heroic subjects, eminently fitted for dramatic handling. He moulded characters, and formed a vigorous conception of the parts they had to play. Under his touch the dialogue moved with spirit; men and women spoke and acted with the energy and spontaneity of nature. He found the blank verse of the literary school monotonous, tame, nerveless, without life or movement. But he had the tact to understand its vast capacities, so vastly wider than its makers had divined, so immeasurably more elastic than the rhymes for which he substituted its sonorous cadence. Marlowe, first of Englishmen, perceived how noble was the instrument he handled, how well adapted to the closest reasoning, the sharpest epigram, the loftiest flight of poetry, the subtlest music, and the most luxuriant debauch of fancy. Touched by his hands the thing became an organ capable of rolling thunders and of whispering sighs, of moving with pompous volubility or gliding like a silvery stream, of blowing trumpet-blasts to battle or sounding the soft secrets of a lover's heart. I do not assert that Marlowe made it discourse music of so many moods. But what he did with it, unlocked the secrets of the verse, and taught successors how to play upon its hundred stops. He found it what Greene [1558–92] calls a 'drumming decasyllabon'. Each line stood alone, formed after the same model, ending with a strongly accented monosyllable. Marlowe varied the pauses in its rhythm; combined the structure of succeeding verses into periods; altered the incidence of accent

in many divers forms and left the metre fit to be the vehicle of
Shakespeare's or of Milton's thought. Compared with either of
those greatest poets, Marlowe, as a versifier, lacks indeed variety
of cadence, and palls our sense of melody by emphatic
magniloquence. The pomp of his 'mighty line' tends to monotony;
nor was he quite sure in his employment of the instrument which
he discovered and divined. The finest bursts of metrical music in
his dramas seem often the result of momentary inspiration rather
than the studied style of a deliberate artist . . .

About Marlowe there is nothing small or trivial. His verse is
mighty; his passion is intense; the outlines of his plots are large; his
characters are Titanic; his fancy is extravagant in richness,
insolence, and pomp. Marlowe could rough-hew like a Cyclops,
though he was far from being able to finish with the subtlety and
smoothness of a Praxiteles. We may compare his noblest studies of
character with marbles blocked out by Michel Angelo, not with
the polished perfection of 'La Notte' in San Lorenzo. Speaking of
Dr Faustus, Goethe said with admiration: 'How greatly it is all
planned!' Greatly planned, and executed with a free, decisive
touch, that never hesitates and takes no heed of modulations. It is
this vastness of design and scale, this simplicity and certainty of
purpose, which strikes us first in Marlowe. He is the sculptor-poet
of Colossi, aiming at such effects alone as are attainable in figures
of a superhuman size, and careless of fine distinctions or delicate
gradations in their execution. His characters are not so much
human beings, with the complexity of human attributes combined in living personality, as types of humanity, the animated
moulds of human lusts and passions which include, each one of
them, the possibility of many individuals. They 'are the embodiments or the exponents of single qualities and simple forces.' This
tendency to dramatise ideal conceptions, to vitalise character
with one dominant and tyrannous motive, is very strong in
Marlowe. Were it not for his own fiery sympathy with the
passions thus idealised, and for the fervour of his conceptive
faculty, these colossal personifications might have been insipid or
frigid. As it is, they are far from deserving such epithets. They are
redeemed from the coldness of symbolic art, from the tiresome-
ness of tragic humours, by their author's intensity of conviction.

Marlowe is in deadly earnest while creating them, believes in their reality, and infuses the blood of his own untamable heart into their veins. We feel them to be day-dreams of their maker's deep desires; projected from his subjectivity, not studied from the men around him; and rendered credible by sheer imaginative insight into the dark mysteries of nature. A poet with a lively sense of humour might, perhaps, have found it impossible to conceive and sustain passions on so exorbitant a scale with so little relief, so entire an absence of mitigating qualities. But it was precisely on the side of humour that Marlowe showed his chief inferiority to Shakespeare. That saving grace of the dramatic poet he lacked altogether. And it may also be parenthentically noticed as significant in this respect that Marlowe never drew a woman's character. His Abigail is a mere puppet. Isabella, in his *Edward II*, changes suddenly from almost abject fawning on her husband to no less abject dependence on an ambitious paramour. His Dido owes such power as the sketch undoubtedly possesses to the poetry of the Fourth Æneid.

It is no function of sound criticism to decoct a poet's work into its final and residual essence, deducing one motive from the complex efforts and the casual essays of a mind placed higher *ex hypothesi* in the creative order than the critic's own; or inventing a catch-word whereby some incommensurable series of achievements may be ticketed. And yet, such is the nature of Marlowe's work, that it imperatively indicates a leading motive, irresistibly suggests a catch-word. This leading motive which pervades his poetry may be defined as *L'Amour de l'Impossible* – the love or lust of unattainable things; beyond the reach of physical force, of sensual faculty, of mastering will; but not beyond the scope of man's inordinate desire, man's infinite capacity for happiness, man's ever-craving thirst for beauty, power, and knowledge. This catch-word of the Impossible Amour is thrust by Marlowe himself, in the pride of his youthful insolence and lawlessness of spiritual lusts, upon the most diffident and sober of his critics. Desire for the impossible – impossible not because it transcends human appetite or capacity, but because it exhausts human faculties in the infinite pursuit – this is the region of Marlowe's sway as poet. To this impossible, because unlimited, object of desire he adds another factor, suggested by his soul's revolt against the given order of the world. He and the Titanic characters into whom he has infused his spirit – even as a workman through the glass-pipe blows life-breath into a bubble, permanent so long as the fine vitreous form endures – he and all the creatures of his fancy thirst for things beyond man's grasp, not merely because these things exhaust man's faculties in the pursuit, but also because the full fruition of them has been interdicted. Thus Marlowe's lust for the impossible, the lust he has injected like a molten fluid into all his eminent dramatic personalities, is a desire for joys conceived by the imagination, floating within the boundaries of will and sense at some fixed moment, but transcending these firm limitations, luring the spirit onward, exhausting the corporeal faculties, engaging the soul itself in a strife with God. This lust assumes the shape of thirst for power, of thirst for beauty, of thirst for knowledge. It is chiefly thirst for power which animates this poet and his brood. . . .

. . . He framed one character in which the desire of absolute power is paramount; this is Tamburlaine. When the shepherd-hero is confronted with the vanquished king of Persia he pours himself forth in a monologue which voices Marlowe through the puppet's lips:

> The thirst of reign and sweetness of a crown,
> That caus'd the eldest son of heavenly Ops
> To thrust his doting father from his chair,
> And place himself in the imperial heaven,
> Mov'd me to manage arms against thy state.
> What better precedent than mighty Jove?
> Nature, that fram'd us of four elements
> Warring within our breasts for regiment,
> Doth teach us all to have aspiring minds.
> Our souls, whose faculties can comprehend
> The wondrous architecture of the world,
> And measure every wandering planet's course,
> Still climbing after knowledge infinite,
> And always moving as the restless spheres,
> Wills us to wear ourselves and never rest,
> Until we reach the ripest fruit of all,
> That perfect bliss and sole felicity,
> The sweet fruition of an earthly crown.   [*1*: II vii 12–29]

It is Nature herself, says Tamburlaine, who placed a warfare of the elements within the frame of man; she spurs him onward by an inborn need toward empire. It is our souls, uncircumscribed by cosmic circumstances, free to weigh planets in their courses and embrace the universe with thought, that compel men to stake their all on the most perilous of fortune's hazards. In this speech the poet, who framed Tamburlaine, identifies himself with his creation, forgets the person he has made, and utters through his mouth the poetry of his desire for the illimitable. . . .

. . . When Zenocrate [his queen] is dying, Tamburlaine pours forth a monody, which, however misplaced on his lips, gives Marlowe scope to sing the nuptial hymn of beauty unapproachable, withdrawn from 'loathsome earth', returning to her native station in the heavens. There, and there only, says the poet, shall the spirit mate with loveliness and be at peace in her embrace:

> Now walk the angels on the walls of heaven,
> As sentinels to warn th' immortal souls
> To entertain divine Zenocrate.
> . . .
> The cherubins and holy seraphins,
> That sing and play before the King of Kings,
> Use all their voices and their instruments
> To entertain divine Zenocrate;
> And in this sweet and curious harmony,
> The god that tunes this music to our souls
> Holds out his hand in highest majesty
> To entertain divine Zenocrate.
> Then let some holy trance convey my thoughts
> Up to the palace of th' empyreal heaven,
> That this my life may be as short to me
> As are the days of sweet Zenocrate.
>
> [2: II iv 15–17, 26–37]

In this rapturous and spiritual marriage-song, which celebrates the assumption or apotheosis of pure beauty, the master bends his mighty line to uses of lyric poetry, as though a theme so far above the reach of words demanded singing. . . .

. . . The last scene he wrote for Tamburlaine is impressive in its dignity; torrid with the heat of Asia's sun descending to the caves of night through brazen heavens. There are no more kingdoms left for Tamburlaine to conquer, and the Titanic marauder feels his strength ebbing:

> What daring god torments my body thus,
> And seeks to conquer mighty Tamburlaine?
> Shall sickness prove me now to be a man,
> That have been termed the terror of the world?
> Techelles and the rest, come, take your swords,
> And threaten him whose hand afflicts my soul.
> Come, let us march against the powers of heaven,
> And set black streamers in the firmament,
> To signify the slaughter of the gods.
>
> [2: v iii 42–50]

Alas! these are but idle vaunts, and Tamburlaine is now aware of it. Even for would-be deicides death waits.

> Ah, friends, what shall I do? I cannot stand.　　　[51]

This is the one solitary cry of weakness wrung from the death-smitten tiger. Pain racks him. His captains comfort him by saying that such pain as this must pass; it is too violent. Then he bursts into the most magnificent of all his declamations, pointing to the bony skeleton who followed like a hound upon his heels across so many battle-fields, and who, all-terrified, is lurking now to paralyse the hand which surfeited his jaws with slaughter:

> Not last, Techelles! No, for I shall die.
> See, where my slave, the ugly monster Death,
> Shaking and quivering, pale and wan for fear,
> Stands aiming at me with his murdering dart,
> Who flies away at every glance I give,
> And, when I look away, comes stealing on!
> Villain, away, and hie thee to the field!
> I and mine armies come to load thy bark
> With souls of thousand mangled carcasses.
> Look, where he goes! But, see, he comes again,
> Because I stay! Techelles, let us march,
> And weary Death with bearing souls to hell.
>
> [2: v iii 66–77]

After this, the scene proceeds upon a graver and more tranquil

note of resignation, abdication, and departure. Tamburlaine
retains his stout heart and high stomach to the end, but he bows
to the inevitable and divides his power among his sons. His body,
the soul's subject, though it break beneath the stress of those
fierce passions, shall survive and be his children's heritage:

> But, sons, this subject, not of force enough
> To hold the fiery spirit it contains,
> Must part, imparting his impressions
> By equal portions into both your breasts;
> My flesh, divided in your precious shapes,
> Shall still retain my spirit, though I die,
> And live in all your seeds immortally.   [169–75]

There is surely enough of absurdity and extravagance in the two
parts of *Tamburlaine*. Relays of captive monarchs, fattened on
raw meat and 'pails of muscadel', draw the hero's chariot. A king
and queen dash out their brains against the cage in which they
are confined. Virgins are ravished and mangled, kingdoms
overrun, and cities burned to satisfy a whim. Tamburlaine kills
one of his three sons because he is a coward, and rips up the flesh
of his own left arm to teach his other sons endurance. Blood flows
in rivers. Shrieks and groans and curses mingle with heaven-
defying menaces and ranting vaunts. The action is one tissue of
violence and horror. The language is truculent bombast, tempered with such bursts of poetry as I have prudently selected in
my specimens. Yet in spite of preposterousness, more than
enough in volume and monotonous variety to justify Mine
Ancient's huffing vein of parody, the vast and powerful conception of the Tartar conqueror redeems *Tamburlaine* from that
worst bathos, the bathos of involuntary caricature. Marlowe
knew well what he was after. He produced a dramatic poem
which intoxicated the audience of the London play-houses with
indescribable delight, and which inaugurated a new epoch.
Through the cloud-world of extravagance which made *Tamburlaine* a byword, he shot one ray of light, clear still, and excellent in
the undaunted spirit of the hero. . . .

SOURCE: extracts from *Shakspere's Predecessors in the English*

Drama (1884), pp. 585–9, 606–9, 611, 616, 626–8. [The spelling of Shakespeare's name in the text is here revised to the modern convention –Ed.]

PART TWO

Modern Studies
and Accounts of Performances

1. MARLOWE'S STYLE

John Russell Brown   Marlowe
and the Actors (1964)

Marlowe wrote his plays before Shakespeare's masterpieces had
been conceived; but we read him afterwards and in his successor's
light. This causes many critical misapprehensions and theatrical
mistakes. We stage Marlowe in a theatre accustomed to
Shakespeare, with actors, directors, and designers who have all
had experience of *his* plays: talents have been developed and
techniques evolved for Shakespeare's dialogue in all its revolutionary subtlety, for Shakespeare's kind of dramatic action
and characterisation. A careful dissociation is necessary before
reading and performing Marlowe for his own sake.

Marlowe had not been dead ten years before these difficulties
arose. By the end of the century, Pistol in *Henry IV, Part Two* was
discharging his 'high astounding terms', which mocked the
bragging language of Tamburlaine and other plays of that
period. Within three decades of his death, Marlowe was a
pedagogue's victim, so that Ben Jonson, only eight years his
junior, could write that a true poet:

will not run away from nature, as he were afraid of her, or depart from
life and the likeness of Truth; but speak to the capacity of his hearers.
And though his language differ from the vulgar somewhat, it shall not
fly from all humanity, with the Tamerlanes, and Tamer-Chams of the
late age . . . .[1]

A particular style of acting had become associated with *Tamburlaine* and with Edward Alleyn, the creator of its title role.[2] In a
pamphlet of 1597, a man who 'bent his browes and fetcht his
stations up and downe the rome', was said to do so 'with such
furious Jesture as if he had beene playing Tamberlane on a stage'.

It was violent, stalking, astounding acting, and by 1600 was considered out of date.

It would be easy, from this evidence, to dismiss the Marlovian style as tiresome barnstorming, and to suppose that we have progressed far beyond its simplicities. But this response would be to less than half the story. Alleyn, who created the Jew of Malta and Faustus, as well as Tamburlaine, was praised as extravagantly as Shakespeare's Richard Burbage; he was a Proteus, a Roscius; Thomas Nashe said that his very name on the common stage 'was able to make an ill matter good'. In writing a prologue for a revival of *The Jew of Malta* in 1632 or 1633, Thomas Heywood called him 'peerless', and added that Richard Perkins, who then acted Barabas, had no ambition to 'exceed or equal' the earlier interpretation, only to 'prove his best'. If Alleyn's style was soon old-fashioned, it continued to be in demand; he had retired from the stage in 1597, but was recalled in 1600 with the special support of a Privy Council letter which spoke of Elizabeth I's 'greate lykeinge and Contentment' from his playing and that of his company. Moreover Marlowe's plays remained in the repertories; *Tamburlaine* until the end of the century at least, *Edward II* till sometime between 1606 and 1617, *The Jew* in the revival of the 1630s, and *Faustus* until a year or two before the closure of the theatres for the Civil War in 1642. And even while Alleyn's acting was condemned it was also praised for its hold over an audience: so Joseph Hall's satire of 'some upreared, high-aspiring swain' like 'the Turkish Tamburlaine', adds that:

> When he conceives upon his fained stage
> The stalking steps of his great personage,
> Graced with huff-cap terms and thund'ring threats,

this sets 'his poor hearer's hair quite upright'. The point is made twice over:

> He vaunts his voice upon an hired stage,
> With high-set steps and princely carriage:
> Now sooping in side robes of royalty
> That earst did scrub in lousy brokery.
> There if he can with terms Italianate,
> Big-sounding sentences and words of state,
> Fair patch me up his pure iambic verse,
> He ravishes the gazing scaffolders.   . . .[3]

On this part of the evidence Marlovian acting becomes at once interesting: it was broad and violent, but it could compete with newer styles; it could command popular attention and at the same time give special pleasure at Elizabeth's court. When we read today of the Eumenides in Aeschylus's play throwing the audience into alarm, we envy an ability to appeal to the widely representative audience that filled the theatre of Dionysus at Athens, for the Greek tragedy is obviously responsible as well as popular; we should also envy Marlowe's actors, for they had a similar appeal. Their acting had the strengths as well as the limitations of a primitive art. Stories were told of them, as of the Eumenides; there were reports of:

the visible apparition of the Devill on the Stage at the Balsavage Play-house, in Queene Elisabeth's dayes (to the great amazement both of the Actors and Spectators) whiles they were there prophanely playing the History of Faustus (the truth of which I have heard from many now alive, who well remember it,) there being some distracted with that fearefull sight.[4]

Marlowe wrote his plays for acting that was 'violent, stalking, astounding', and also strong, clear, galvanic. It was a style that would be suitable for Aeschylus as well as Marlowe; for Seneca, whom the Elizabethans have often been blamed for admiring; for Artaud, who admired Seneca; for highly developed rituals; for Genet, for Peter Brook; for plays that are visual as well as intellectual, physical *and* metaphysical, responsible *and* popular. It was a style for this kind of theatre; and it was something of its own, for Marlowe was an original.

The most obvious demand that Marlowe makes upon his actors is to speak his grandiloquent poetry fittingly. He used words so confidently that in the first part of *Tamburlaine* he could leave two queens to speak together instead of bringing a full-scale battle on to the stage; so with no sense of anti-climax, Tamburlaine commands Zenocrate:

> . . . take thou my crown, vaunt of my worth,
> And manage words with her, as we will arms.
>
> [*1*: III iii 130–1]

In the same play, Mycetes speaks of a grief that 'requires a great
and thundering speech', and the hero is admired for his 'working
words'. Quote any long speech from almost anywhere in
Marlowe's plays and Hamlet's advice will seem out of place:
'Speak the speech, I pray you, as I pronounc'd it to you,
trippingly on the tongue . . . '. Yet all this is a trap for actors
schooled in Shakespeare: they are tempted to go to the opposite
extreme and indulge in the thundering speech. This is fatally
wrong: Marlowe can easily sound dull, and even weak. Of
Tamburlaine at the Old Vic, London, in 1951, various critics
reported:

How the rhetoric clangs and thunders, and how seldom and fitfully it
lightens into poetry.

It is even less a play than one supposed: ramshackle as a raree-show,
which the trumpetings of noble verse soon cease to irradiate.

This power, rarely used at less than full stretch, makes continuously for
high dramatic poetry and, now and then, brings it off.

An actor must not expect to live on the fat of Marlowe's words;
they are 'working' words, witty as well as brave, energetic like
Marlowe's sceptical thought. 'Trippingly on the tongue' is
inappropriate for his speeches, but not 'acutely', or even
'temperately' or 'discreetly', in the sense of 'with proper control'.

Marlowe was not fond of the rhetorical elaboration of Seneca,
Kyd or early Shakespeare:

> Oh eyes, no eyes, but fountains fraught with tears:
> Oh life, no life, but lively form of death;
> Oh world, no world, but mass of public wrongs
>   . . . [*Span. Tragedy*, III ii]

or

> I cannot leave to love, and yet I do;
> But there I leave to love where I should love.
> Julia I lose, and Valentine I lose;
> If I keep them, I needs must lose myself;
>   . . . [*Two Gent.*, II vi]

Marlowe did not pursue comparisons so nimbly, and seldom developed an intricate argument; he preferred to build, to progress by marked degrees, retaining each element within the final large impression. Tamburlaine, Gaveston, Edward, Faustus, Barabas are all presented this way. Barabas can tell his life-story phase by phase, to give a definite, forceful impression [*Jew*, II iii 179–205]. He argues by independent statements and questions; in the following speech the steps of his deliberations are marked by alternate roman and italic type:

> My gold, my gold, and all my wealth is gone!
> *You partial heavens, have I deserv'd this plague?*
> What, will you thus oppose me, luckless stars,
> To make me desperate in my poverty?
> *And knowing me impatient in distress,*
> *Think me so mad as I will hang myself,*
> That I may vanish o'er the earth in air,
> And leave no memory that e're I was.
> *No, I will live!* Nor loathe I this my life:
> *And since you leave me in the ocean thus*
> *To sink or swim, and put me to my shifts,*
> *I'll rouse my senses, and awake myself.*
> Daughter, I have it: *thou perceiv'st the plight*
> *Wherein these Christians have oppressèd me:*
> Be ruled by me, for in extremity
> We ought to make bar of no policy.   [I ii 264–79]

In this passage the progress of his thought is clear, but only a recognition of the distinctive characteristics of the successive elements of Marlowe's rhetoric will reveal the varied and rich responses that are drawn together, and hence the speech's ability to give an impression of a lively, self-contained mind. This kind of elaboration is as minutely controlled as Kyd's or Shakespeare's; perhaps more so, for it is not at the mercy of a repeated rhetorical pattern. Tamburlaine's address when Zenocrate is shown on her death-bed [*2*: II iv] has something of a rhetorician's parallelism; but its units are large and firmly marked by the refrain, so that the first dark and angry impressions are held together with the concluding revelation of Tamburlaine's harmony of soul as he considers his own death with his queen's. The careful, large-spanned verbal architecture is perhaps most noticeable when several characters speak in chorus to establish a situation and display its diverse aspects, as they do in the opening of the last scene of *Tamburlaine, Part Two*. But while the structure is not always obvious on the surface of the dialogue, it is basic. If an actor wishes to render the full interest of Marlowe's poetry, it must be understood – like an argument or diagram – and given emphasis by varying verbal techniques and physical embodiments.

The intellectual life of Marlowe's dialogue is clearly shown in his use of surprising single lines. One of these follows the long consideration of Zenocrate's sickness. After talk of the 'God that tunes this music to our souls' and the 'palace of the imperial heaven', the 'divine Zenocrate' of the refrain is humanised in a changed phrase:

> That this my life may be as short to me
> As are the days of *sweet* Zenocrate;

and then comes the simple and yet opposite:

> Physicians, will no physic do her good?   [*2*: II iv 38]

In contrast to all the other thoughts, in this one line Tamburlaine is almost hopeful, and obviously dependent on others. Earlier, Zenocrate is given two lines only with which to withstand the black and lengthy threats against Damascus:

> Yet would you have some pity for my sake,
> Because it is my country's, and my father's.
>   [*1*: IV ii 123–4]

Here the answer is equally brief, and this is followed by rapid movement:

> Not for the world Zenocrate, if I have sworn:
> Come bring in the Turk.   *Exeunt.*

Such sharpness – dramatic corners boldly turned in a line or two – gives edge to the dialogue and suggests a kinetic, a reserved power. It is well fitted to the asides of Barabas in his dealings with

Christians and Jews, and to the timeless certainties of
Mephistophilis. For Tamburlaine's first intimation of his own
fatal disease, a brief passage is placed at the end of a scene, so
throwing expectation forward. For Isabella's realisation that all
her plans for the return of Gaveston will still leave her 'for ever
miserable', an unrhymed couplet is placed at the end of a
soliloquy questioning its whole effect and so preparing the
audience for the later change in Edward's queen. Not only
individual performances and the life of the dialogue depend on
such devices, but also the structure of the drama.

Even passages that sound at first like bombast can reveal a
kind of precision. Tamburlaine's

> Our conquering swords shall marshal us the way
> We use to march upon the slaughtered foe,
> Trampling their bowels with our horses' hoofs, . . .
>
> [*1*: iii iii 148–50]

is a direct reply, hitting the nail on its point, to Bajazeth's boast:

> I have of Turks, Arabians, Moors and Jews
> Enough to cover all Bythinia.
> . . . .
> Thou know'st not, foolish-hardy Tamburlaine,
> What 'tis to meet me in the open field,
> That leave no ground for thee to march upon.
>
> [136–7, 145–7]

Through all the great and thundering words, the actor must
search for an intellectual energy and control.

Here is the main difference from Shakespeare, in whose plays
we look always for verbal and metrical expressiveness, for
implicit meaning and feeling. Behind the rhetorical design of
Shakespeare's earliest dialogue and behind the rhetoric's more
subtle manipulation in later work, we have learned how to find
psychological realism, a representation of the inner workings of
thought and emotion. This is conveyed by tone, choice of words,
linked associations, fleeting transitions of subject or mood,
syntactical variety, the pulse and irregularities of the metre. It is
this continual expressiveness that Marlowe lacks: when a stage-

direction says '*The king rageth*', the verse-lines and syntactical units continue to work easily together; the vocabulary is not simplified or changed in other ways:

> I'll not resign, but, whilst I live be king.
> Traitors, be gone, and join you with Mortimer!
> Elect, conspire, install, do what you will;
> Their blood and yours shall seal these treacheries!
>
> [*E. II*, v i 86–9]

The varied content, the weight or force of each separate utterance within the speech, represents feeling as well as cumulative meaning; but there is hardly any realistic impression of enraged utterance. When Marlowe resorted to prose for Zabina's grief [*1 Tam.*, v ii] he introduced a much more elaborate system of rhetorical repetition to give distinct phases to her distraction. When he shows Tamburlaine in the last agonies of his sickness, the verse-lines remain full and regular: the architecture of his dialogue is still firm; there is comparison and allusion – indeed precision and compounded effect are notable characteristics even in the death-struggle. Marlowe is capable of moments of pathetic simplicity, but within defined bounds: J. C. Trewin noted such a moment in the Old Vic *Tamburlaine*, in one line 'that shone suddenly from the gilded welter of words: the simple "Come down from Heaven, and live with me again"' [*2*: II iv 118]. Marlowe's expressiveness and psychological realism are ingredients in his poetic design, not a sustained quality that to some degree illuminates almost every line, as in Shakespeare's mature plays. This is not to say that his attempt to give an impression of actual thought and feeling is unimportant; it must usually be looked for in the design of his speeches, in the contrasts between their various elements. Rightly – that is clearly and cleanly – rendered, it has a large effect. Even a brief impulse idiomatically expressed, or a moment of pathetic simplicity, can hold the theatre, through Marlowe's magnifying glass of constrast.

While words fill the mind on reading one of Marlowe's plays, in performance its visual effects can dominate the verbal. There are

opportunities for spectacle, in which Marlowe seems to join hands
with Cecil B. de Mille: parades and processions, coronations and
funerals, pursuits, battles, and horrors, are found variously in
every play. But, again, here is a trap for modern actors and
directors: this is not an open invitation to cineramic extravagance. Marlowe's plays have something of the attraction of a film
like *Spartacus*; and something of the repulsion of Auschwitz in *The
Deputy*, or that of the tortures in Whiting's *The Devils*. But, as with
the words, indulgence is dangerous. Some of the reviews of Sir
Tyrone Guthrie's *Tamburlaine* discerned the devaluing effect of a
skill used for its own limited ends. *The Times* remarked:

. . . Tyrone Guthrie enjoys himself unobtrusively in arranging ways in
which the more picturesque and horrible sights incidental to barbaric
warrings and triumphs may be effectively displayed, and handles a big
cast with unfailing expertness.

In memory, the cast has left an impression of actors exerting
themselves with adolescent relish. *The Daily Telegraph* noted at
the time that Guthrie

. . . accomplishes his part . . . by filling the stage from apron to
backcloth with constant action, and by contriving a wonderful
collection of barbarous weapons and complicated machines.

Several points might be made here: Tamburlaine is arguably a
Renaissance hero, not a 'barbaric' one; Elizabethan theatre
companies were hard-worked and limited in size, and therefore
would have sought some kind of simplicity in stage management.
But a more important objection is that Marlowe did not speak of
'spectacles' but of 'shows', a then fashionable word implying a
highly developed Renaissance art in which thematic significance
was the organising principle. Bajazeth in his cage is called 'a
goodly show at a banquet', and elsewhere there is talk of 'stately
shows', 'pleasing shows', 'public shows', 'lascivious shows'; but
the meaningfulness of this visual art is also implied, most clearly
in Faustus's explicit: 'What *means* this show? Speak,
Mephistophilis' [i v 82]. Again: Marlowe is an intellectual
dramatist.

For Marlowe all kinds of stage-action could be significant.

When Theridamas has praised the 'working words' of Tamburlaine, he adds:

> But, when you see his actions top his speech,
> Your speech will stay, or so extol his worth.
>
> [*1*: II iii 26–7]

This is a quibble on the 'actions' that should 'suit the words' in Renaissance oratory and acting, and on the 'actions' or deeds of conquest that demonstrate Tamburlaine's power: 'I am a lord, for so my deeds shall prove' [*1*: I ii 34]. For Marlowe both words and actions were important. He was sometimes content with action and no words at crucial moments of his drama: Helen, who ravishes Faustus and 'sucks forth' his soul, only passes over the stage in silence. When Tamburlaine overhears Agidas urging Zenocrate to seek escape, he *'goes to her, and takes her away lovingly by the hand, looking wrathfully on Agidas, and says nothing'*. Nowhere in Shakespeare is meaning and emotion so entirely represented by visual means; this should warn actors of how much of Marlowe's drama may be in shows and actions.

In this respect critics who have studied earlier drama will often be good guides along part of the way, for some of the importance of show and gesture is symbolic, in the tradition of allegorical drama. The Old Man who remonstrates with Faustus and then withstands the assault of fiends speaks for the power of Good Counsel, and then demonstrates it in action. The Good and Evil Angels who appear at crises in Faustus's career are visual representations of his conflict of conscience, and finally contrive an entirely visual effect with the throne and hell-mouth which they introduce to represent his eternal situation in the last scene. When the Bishop of Coventry has his 'sacred garments rent and torn' [*E. II*, I ii 35], Edward II is part of a 'show' signifying that he places his own concerns before those of the church. A comparison with Marlowe's source sometimes directs attention to the introduction of visual devices. When Holinshed, in describing the capture of Edward II, has 'They used such diligence in that charge, that finally with large giftes bestowed on the Welchmenne, they came to understande where the King was', Marlowe invented a 'Mower'. At first Spencer only refers to him:

> . . . shrewdly I suspect
> A gloomy fellow in a mead below;
> 'A gave a long look after us, my lord,
>   . . . [IV vi 28–30]

And when this 'gloomy fellow' enters, guiding the king's pursuers, only the stage direction clearly identifies his trade in the printed text; but the audience will *see* it at once. He is a mower, a symbol of the harvest, perhaps of 'Time'; his silent presence tells the audience that a reckoning is about to be made, that always a harvest comes. This last point is made allusively in the dialogue which Marlowe invented for the end of the scene, at the general exeunt:

> RICE   . . . Will your lordships away?
> MOWER Your worship, I trust, will remember me?
> RICE   Remember thee, fellow? What else? Follow me to the town.
>   [v i 115–17]

The mower with his sickle follows.

But Marlowe used the old allegorical reliance on visual impressions for dramatic purposes which are not always allegorical. He marked the course of the action in *Edward II*, for example, by the sequence of a royal presence with Gaveston standing aside, another with Gaveston sitting in state with the king, and a third, in the open air after a journey, as Edward (presumably cloaked from the wind) waits for his friend at Tynemouth; there is a further visual transformation as the king appears ready for battle with his 'sword drawn' and presumably dressed in armour. Before appearing in the dirty and ragged garments of his prison, he tries the disguise – the 'fained weeds' – of the monks of Neath; as he seeks refuge in 'this life contemplative' the stage will present that refuge in the new anonymity and simplicity of his clothing, and in the gentle and perhaps ceremonial ways of the religious men. In all these 'shows', the visual impression is eloquent in defining the progress of the action.

And often it does more than this, by forming a constant support or foil to the words. The end of *Edward II* is an example of this interplay. Edward's young son orders his father's hearse to be brought before him and assumes his 'funeral robes'; this must take some time to effect, but only two and a half lines have been spoken before the hearse is announced. It must then enter to a dead march; and young Edward asks his nobles to mourn with him, so that with some grouped reaction the bloody head of Mortimer, which is also on stage, is 'offered up' to Edward's 'murdered ghost'. It is a solemn, macabre show, accompanied by the youth's tears, which gives point and contrast to his concluding words of 'grief and innocency'; against an inescapable visual presentation of treachery, pain, and loss, a clear voice alone affirms an affectionate loyalty.

Marlowe's words are often given fresh power by show and gesture if the director and actors are able to realise on the stage the whole elaborate picture which Marlowe has intended. It has often been said that Faustus's exploits at Rome are trivial and anti-climactic; but this is to notice only the witticisms and firecrackers. The stage direction:

Enter the CARDINALS *and* BISHOPS, *some bearing crosiers, some the pillars;* MONKS *and* FRIARS *singing their procession. Then the* POPE *and* RAYMOND, King of Hungary, *with* BRUNO *led in chains.*

is an important element in the scene. Mr Michael Benthall's production for the Old Vic on the large, open stage of the Assembly Hall Edinburgh in 1961 vindicated the whole episode. *The Times* commented:

Mr Benthall realises that if the trivial conjuring tricks are played in surroundings of much splendour they will gain enormously in importance. . . . When the Papal court has been gradually assembled from the side gangways, the scene is so impressive in its solemnity that almost any joke would seem tellingly out of place, and the final wrecking of all this grandeur by Faustus and Mephistophilis seems indeed a devilish outrage.

More than the one scene is transformed. The critic of *Punch* noted that:

the pageant of the interrupted papal meeting is staged with magnificence . . . [so that] the contrast between the fusty study and the riot of colour when he gets loose as a magician is extremely effective.

Visual elaboration, like the elaborate and lengthy poetry, should be used intelligently, not indulgently, so that it plays its important part in shaping the drama thematically and deepening the understanding of the characters and action.

Reliance on visual effect is perhaps most impressive in relation to individual characterisation, for, besides maintaining a typically Renaissance complication of meaning and situation, a 'show' implied a kind of density in character portrayal. It was not accidentally that Alleyn was famed for 'majestic' parts, as Fuller records, or became associated with 'high-set steps and princely carriage'. The actor of Tamburlaine, Faustus and Barabas had to be able to hold the centre of a large stage-picture and make a clear, physical statement; nervous subtleties or minute physical realism were required for neither words nor gestures. In Rowlands's *Knave of Clubs* (1609) it is said:

> The Gull gets on a surplis,
> With a crosse upon his breast,
> Like Allen playing Faustus
> In that manner he was drest. . . .

This tells us that in original performances the hero's early devotion to study and divinity was given visual presentation in the first scene, the cross and surplice marking the normal expectancy of Renaissance learning; and presumably these symbols were worn throughout the scene, when Faustus had ceased to 'be a Divine in show' and the ambitious self-centred mind had become apparent through the disguise. Such a presentation would be far from Mr Paul Daneman's Faustus at Edinburgh, as recorded by *The Guardian*; he was judged to begin:

in much too cavalier a manner; the entry into this dark world of ghostly temptation and deep doubt needs to be more subtle and awed. He dashed his books aside like a naughty schoolboy. The Latin he spouted seemed to mean nothing to him.

To live up to the scenes Marlowe has contrived, the actor must use every resource of word, gesture and costume; he needs to build up large, deep, even solid impressions, and mark the variety of response as clearly and fully as possible; he needs to reach subtlety through a carefully varied simplicity and strength, as in a primitive art. A general liveliness will serve as little as continuous nervous realism. Like many Renaissance writers in England, Marlowe reached back to the Middle Ages; when a scene goes wrong an actor's resource should be to simplify and mark out the extremes of thought and feeling.

Costumes should be strong, like the 'breeches of crymson vellvet' that Henslowe kept in his wardrobe for Tamburlaine. The dresses will make a subtle effect when they speak against a clearly contrary impression, like Faustus's ambition within his surplice, or Tamburlaine's appearance 'all in black, and very melancholy' which contrasts with the apparently untroubled ferocity of his verbal threats against the virgins of Damascus. The complexity of Marlowe is characteristically in the ensemble, the whole; individual elements must always be strong and clear.

I have emphasised the intellectual demands that Marlowe makes upon actors and directors. This is not because I wish to deny that his plays are richly physical and grandly, even loudly, eloquent: of course they are, pre-eminently. But I have tried to argue for their intellectual control because today we do not usually associate cineramic spectacle or massed trumpets and bugles with an intellectually responsible art. Our larger theatrical productions have to be cunningly varied, of course; but the cunning Marlowe requires is socially, morally, humanely responsible, beyond the limited difficulties of producing a successful or efficient show. His plays probe human consciousness and the nature of man and society.

Again, this is not effected in Shakespeare's way. Marlowe has no Lear or Hamlet or Prospero, whose passage through a play involves a deepening or chastening of the character's thought and feeling. His plays are more centred on their heroes than most of Shakespeare's as far as plot and theatrical focus are concerned; but the audience, even of *Faustus*, is not so fully involved with the progress of the hero's consciousness. (Andrew Bradley would have had a thin diet with Marlowe.) The play is always more significant than any of its characters can realise: the hero is viewed ironically or relatively.

This is most obvious in *Tamburlaine*. Produced as a character-play, even with a greatly gifted actor such as Sir Donald

Wolfit, there will come an anti-climax. *The Times* reported his performance of 1956 in sorrow rather than in anger:

The passages which appear dull are those in which [Tamburlaine] mourns for Zenocrate and resigns himself to die. Perhaps they are irredeemably dull. The first has some fine lines, but the grief is hollow, and by the time that Tamburlaine comes to die the play is ceasing to hold the stage.

The Daily Telegraph's critic was encouraged to see a Victorian-style portrait, but he found it inconsiderable:

Brutal and boastful, and endowed by Donald Wolfit with a most unattractive Mongolian make-up, Tamburlaine has no redeeming feature except in his habit of recording his feelings in matchless verse at complete variance with his character.

Mr Hope-Wallace, for *The Guardian*, had looked for an Ibsen-style hero:

Monotony is inevitable where there is such a total lack of psychological revelation or development in the character. . . . One comes away battered and blood-boltered, yet without the expected exaltation.

Those critics and members of the audience who were attracted by this production – and it must be reckoned a 'success' by the Old Vic standards of the time – were those who caught something, in spite of over-indulgent spectacle and sound, of the progressive revelation of the play as a whole. The critic of the *Telegraph* recognised this shaping power, but the production and chief performance did not encourage him to fasten on this experience; it seemed out of place in a character-centred play, in a play like one of Shakespeare's:

I had not clearly realised into what a bath of blood Marlowe had plunged his delighted contemporaries. . . . 'To ride in triumph through Persepolis' sounds a noble ambition, but when it is carried out in terms of kings kept in cages or made to draw chariots it seems a little different.

The actor, even of the 'majestic' star part, must allow the audience to know better than he does, to know and feel more deeply, wisely, excitedly than the character he represents.

In *Tamburlaine* the grotesque horrors occur with meaningful crescendo immediately before the last scene: Tamburlaine is dressed in 'vermilion' scarlet; he calls the atrociously 'pampered' jades a just 'figure of my dignity'; a pair of exhausted kings is unharnessed to be killed, and is immediately replaced by another pair; the Governor of Babylon is shot to death, hanging helplessly in chains; an order is given to drown thousands of women and children; books are burned; and on report of the mass drownings, Tamburlaine responds: 'Well, then, my *friendly* lords, what now remains?' [2: v ii 208]. The hero never associates this monstrous pile-up of horrors with his sickness, only with his 'success': 'I feel myself distempered suddenly.' But, managed as it is with surprise and the shock of contrast at the end of a scene, the audience will respond to the sudden deflection of narrative interest and need a reconciliation of its diverging reactions: some may recognise a judgement on egotism or inhumanity; others may notice the instability of success; others the courage of Tamburlaine's resistance to his physical weakness. This is the preparation for the final scene, with more ideas, questions, and undefined responses in the audience's mind than the *character* has 'thoughts to put them in, imagination to give them shape, or time to act them in'. And so in the death of Tamburlaine: he does not see that the map he calls for is like a miser's scrap of paper; he does not seem to notice that his son, mounting into his chariot, is so inadequate, or merely so different, from himself, in words and 'figure'; he does not realise how his own imaginary glory appears obviously circumscribed when he cannot assure his followers of his invincibility, or when he cannot die without the tangible and macabre evidence of Zenocrate's beauty. It is before an audience who hears and *sees* all this, that his unconquerable pride is manifested, in his last moments of physical weakness, with a speech to his son and the silent crowd of dependents:

> The nature of thy chariot will not bear
> A guide of baser temper than myself,
> More than heaven's coach the pride of Phaeton.
> . . .

> My body feels, my soul doth weep to see
> Your sweet desires deprived my company,
> For Tamburlaine, the scourge of God, must die.
>
> [*2*: v iii 243–9]

In his mind he is unconquered. Nothing new in his thoughts or feelings has been revealed in his last struggle; only the scale of his reactions is greater because of the greater adversary, Death. The new revelation comes to the audience, not to Tamburlaine: it will realise more fully the precarious nature and the privacy – the fantasy, we might say – of his greatness: he dies along with the map, the chariot and captive kings, the hearse of Zenocrate, his silent son and followers, his own weak body, signs of pain and feeble voices, great only in that isolated and dangerous world of his own mind. The realisation of this is the climactic and unjudging conclusion of the two-part tragedy. The actor of Tamburlaine must plan for this audience reaction, which is more than he is allowed to express directly. (This is not an 'alienation' effect, but a wider orientation; a question of perspective.)

The same conditions are true for minor characters. For all their individualisation, they are most memorable as, literally, 'parts' – parts of a full design. They must be simply and strongly and variously themselves, in silence and stillness as well as speech and movement, and so serve the whole wide perspective of the drama. Marlowe was an intellectual dramatist who conceived a great panorama of 'figures', each brightly and energetically itself. He created the dramatic and poetic means of presenting not merely the individual figures but his concepts and questions about the panorama, about the 'world' of men.

Today it is a theatrical cliché to say that if a part is acted from within, from the conscious and unconscious being of the character impersonated – if it is acted from 'the belly' – then the dramatist's fictions, be they as strange as the witches in *Macbeth* or the trolls in *Peer Gynt*, will work, will 'come across': costume, stage-management, even tempo seem secondary. But this will not serve for Marlowe; the 'belly' must be in each performance, but the full life of the dramatic experience comes from wider perceptions.

Even the star parts depend for their proper performance on being less than the play itself. Barabas declines in subtlety and resource from a near-potentate to a petty schemer disguised as a French musician; and he finishes his part caught in his own joke, absurdly yelling from a cauldron. Edward II is at last a figure in a hearse; and in his death-scene he is unaware even of the irony implicit in his disbelieving trust in Lightborn, the murderer who is dressed in the Italianate fashion of his first favourite. Nor can he show that he is aware of the appropriateness of being 'pressed to death'[5]; his last vocal response is a cry of pain and horror as physical sensations crown his life without leaving a mark upon his body. The next incident, properly small, is the death of Lightborn through false faith and security, killed by his supposed accomplices; this casts yet further reflections on Edward's death.

Even Faustus, whose last speech comes closest in immediacy to the Shakespearian style, is presented as part of a wide picture and with ironic comment. He seems to understand his situation wholly. He has considered the need of his fellows to 'save themselves'. He knows that heaven and hell are visually represented above and below him. He calls for time to stand still in words first memorably used in the pursuit of pleasure. He is tortured by his own mind, that element of his being that has led him to this extreme situation. He now seeks to become nothing, as a direct result of the boundless demands of his own ambition. His last words seem to recognise all this, as the audience does, in a cry of horror, pain, denial, sacrifice, acceptance:

> My God, my God, look not so fierce on me.
> Adders and serpents, let me breathe a while.
> Ugly hell, gape not, come not, Lucifer!
> I'll burn my books. Ah, Mephistophilis!
>
> [v ii 197–200]

But the play goes beyond this cry. Even here, there is a new clarity and intensity of knowledge – for which Marlowe extended his stylistic range – which makes its own unnoticed victory; it draws the audience into the mind of the hero and so sustains his eloquent dominance over every other character. Faustus is Marlowe's only hero to die alone and with a notable access of knowledge: and this is one development Faustus cannot express. Then, according to the 1616 text, his 'mangled limbs' are left for his fellow scholars to wonder at, a reminder that the physical embodiment is all that they are capable of wondering at. And then the Chorus calmly reminds the audience of Apollo's 'laurel bough', yet a third view of the hero that cannot be realised or expressed by the hero himself.

Marlowe's plays need intense realisation in each distinct element; but actors must be prepared, after the exhausting demands of such powerful and simplified playing, to allow the audience to view the whole, to transcend every character's consciousness, to respond to Marlowe's world not that of his heroes. The 'violent, stalking, astounding' performances must, in the last resort, be self-effacing.

SOURCE: essay in *Tulane Drama Review*, VIII, 4 (1964), pp. 155–73 (slightly revised here from the original).

NOTES

1. Jonson, *Discoveries* . . .(1640 in *Works*, ed. C. H. Herford, P. and E. Simpson, VIII (Oxford, 1947), p. 587.
2. Alleyn's style has been discussed by W. A. Armstrong and A. J. Gurr in *Shakespeare Survey*, VII (1954) and XVI (1963); both articles usefully quote contemporary assessments.
3. A longer excerpt from Hall's *Virgidemiarum* is given in Part One, above.
4. W. Prynne, *Histrio-Mastix* (1633), fo. 556.
5. Lightborn's request for a red hot spit [v v 32] may indicate that Marlowe intended the further torture described by Holinshed to be enacted on the stage as well:

. . . they came sodenly one night into the chamber where hee lay in bed fast asleepe, and with heavie feather beddes (or a table as some write) being cast upon him, they kept him downe, and withall put into his fundament an horne, and through the same they thrust up into his bodie a hote spitte (or as other have through the pype of a Trumpet, a Plumbers instrument or yron made verie hote) the which passing up into his entrayles, and being rolled to and fro, burnt the same, but so as no appearance of any wounde or hurt outwardly might bee once perceyved.

This would be a still more basic 'figure' of the physical appetite which has become an inescapable element in Edward's life and death.

Judith Weil   Marlowe's Prophetic
Style (1977)

Marlowe designed his plays as striking reversals which heap
disaster upon the protagonists they have seemed to celebrate. His
heroes endure exacting retributions which are carefully matched
with their particular failings. The catastrophes adjust plot to
character, trapping protagonists within a rigorously moral form.
Their appropriateness may invite critics to read the plays
backwards, discovering anticipations of these last judgements.
John Russell Brown, for example, has argued that a play by
Marlowe 'is always more significant than any of its characters
can realise: the hero is viewed ironically or relatively'. [See the
preceding essay.] This argument depends, I think, on the
privilege of hindsight. It fails to explain why an audience might
experience a final disaster with great surprise and shock.

Guided by the morality of Marlowe's catastrophes, the
audience does ultimately discover that a protagonist's fate has
always been implicit in the strong desires which move him.
Douglas Cole has shown that Marlowe's plots seem to provide
rationalisations of an Augustinian moral psychology: 'The soul is
weighed in the balance by what delights her, as St Augustine put
it, which is another way of saying that what a man loves tells most
about what that man *is*.'[1] By creating disasters which fulfil
mistaken desires and identify the characters with their loves,
Marlowe casts brilliant light on basic spiritual perversions. Surely
a process so intelligible in retrospect cannot be all that puzzling
when experienced scene by scene. But, in fact, it can be very
puzzling indeed. Few playwrights have been as willing as
Marlowe was to obscure disaster in the offing, to postpone the
resolution of ambiguities. Few have disguised self-deception so
well or exposed it so belatedly. We might expect that Marlowe
would have been anxious to guide the judgement of the audience.
We probably do *not* expect that he would have sought to suspend
our judgements and to let them go straying through the
dark.

Even when Marlowe's irony brightens in a more satiric play
like *The Jew of Malta*, it is subdued to the power of a protagonist

who is a plausible spokesman for his own position. Marlowe's protagonists move energetically through contexts and relationships which reinforce their vigour and potency. This potency may prevent the audience from seeing the protagonists 'ironically or relatively' until the end of the play approaches. It is doubtful that 'Marlowe's staged suffering clearly underlines the irony of the kind of human "fulfilment" to which his major characters aspire', or that 'the dream of the poetic word is consistently confronted with the reality of the dramatic action'.[2] Marlowe encourages his audience to dream with his characters. While he intimates the 'reality' held in reserve, he also tempts the audience to ignore it. Marlowe's dramatic strategy inhibits detachment. In its overall function and effect upon an audience it bears a strong resemblance to the rhetorical questions asked so frequently by his characters. Repeatedly they adopt this method of affirming their values:

> Who hateth me but for my happiness?
> Or who is honour'd now but for his wealth?
>
> [*Jew*, 1 i 114–15]
>
> Is 'to dispute well logic's chiefest end'?
> Affords this art no greater miracle?   [*Dr F.*, 1 i 8–9]
>
> What greater bliss can hap to Gaveston
> Than live and be the favourite of a king! [*E. II*, 1 i 4–5]

We might pause to answer such questions, were the questioners themselves less persuasive or the pace of the action less swift. Our attention moves onward, and we are disturbed, if at all, only by a suspicion that Marlowe's questioners cannot really be answered in the terms they employ.

The dramatic conventions which Marlowe adapts to his obliquely ironic purposes are traditional ones which he shares with other playwrights of his time. As they work together, these conventional methods reveal Marlowe's preoccupation with particular types of character and theme. Risking repetition and a logical circle, I will consider these preoccupations before the ironic use of conventions. Both have been widely misunderstood. A brief discussion of his basic concerns may help to make the subsequent survey of Marlowe's methods more pertinent.

In *An Apologie for Poetrie*, Sir Philip Sidney states a distinction which can be brought to bear on Marlowe's kind of irony. When he turns to those objections to poetry which might be put in a 'counter ballance' against his own defence, Sidney mentions first a group of 'Poet-haters' and anti-poets. He describes them as:

All that kinde of people who seek a prayse by dispraysing others, that they doe prodigally spend a great many wandering wordes in quips and scoffes, carping and taunting at each thing, which, by styrring the Spleene, may stay the braine from a thorough beholding the worthines of the subiect.[3]

Many of Marlowe's characters belong to this group. The cowards in both *Tamburlaine* plays, the scheming Machiavels in *The Jew of Malta*, *The Massacre at Paris* and *Edward II*, and the Bad Angel and Mephistophilis in *Doctor Faustus* all know how to 'seek a prayse'.

Sidney then distinguishes these jesters, who deserve only our ridicule, from a second, more serious group:

So of the contrary side, if we will turne *Ouid's* verse, *Ut lateat virtus proximitate mali*, that good lye hid in the neerenesse of the euill, *Agrippa* will be as merry in shewing vanitie of Science as *Erasmus* was in commending of follie. Neyther shall any man or matter escape some touch of these smyling raylers. But for *Erasmus* and *Agrippa*, they had another foundation [than] the superficiall part would promise.[4]

Marlowe's raillery seems to have been more sardonic than the 'smyling' version which Sidney commended in Agrippa and Erasmus. But like their raillery, Marlowe's does seem to have had 'another foundation than the superficiall part would promise'. We need not identify him with the clever scoffers in his plays. Sidney went on to observe that 'scoffing commeth not of wisedome'. When scoffers like Barabas and Faustus celebrate their wisdom they are actually praising their folly. Such paradoxical encomia may be highly persuasive, for, like Erasmus himself, Marlowe knew well how to 'stay the braine from a thorough beholding the worthines of the subiect'. His glorious fools are especially plausible when their exciting ideas and activities coincide with the ways of their worlds. That the pleasing spokeswoman of *The Praise of Folly* often has enough sense to understand such ways hardly recommends their value. Erasmus permits her to identify and satirise other fools, but he reminds us of her folly by suggesting now and again that her use of authorities and her reasoning are dubious. We will see that Marlowe uses a similar procedure in presenting his characters.

Through the allusions which occur in all of his plays, Marlowe reveals an abiding preoccupation with wisdom. We can discern, behind his mistaken praisers of wisdom, the shadow of that lady who praised herself in the books of Proverbs and Wisdom as the bride of God and mother of all creation. The Church Fathers chose to replace this mediating Wisdom figure with the second person of the Trinity, Christ. Nevertheless, she preserved a feminine identity congenial to Erasmus and to such Christian poets as Dante, Spenser and Donne.[5]

There appears to be a natural congruity between the darkness of Marlowe's ironic style and 'Wisdom's' shadowy life in literary convention. As a symbol for mediation and intuition, it is simply not in her character to support any literary 'foundation' too obviously. We will see that only Faustus and Tamburlaine, the boldest of overreachers, insist on giving wisdom a literal human shape. Many of Marlowe's allusions to wisdom appear to derive from the Hebraic sources of the wisdom tradition – the books of Job and Proverbs, and the 'ecclesiastical' books of Wisdom and Ecclesiasticus. In *The Jew of Malta* and *Doctor Faustus* he suggests a foolish distortion of wisdom through allusions to Christ – in St Paul's words, 'the power of God, and the wisdom of God' [1 Corinthians, i 24]. Perhaps these plays also make some reference to the distinction stated in the Epistle of St James [iii 13–18] between genuine and devilish wisdom. Other allusions to wisdom ultimately derive from classical sources but seem to have taken on a proverbial, topical character in the Renaissance. Marlowe could easily hint at the folly of a character by comparing him with Actaeon or Icarus.

Within their dramatic contexts, these allusions imply that Marlowe's characters pervert 'sapientia' – a knowledge of things human as well as things divine. Until more definitive studies of Marlowe's own Biblical learning have been made, it might be best to regard the wisdom which his characters abuse as eclectic and traditional in nature. Renaissance thinkers adapted the ancient wisdom tradition to their own attitudes and purposes.

These ranged from the mysticism of the Florentine neo-Platonists to the prudent virtue commended by Erasmus and Vives. Where Marlowe is concerned, there may be little point in attempting to define the tradition too rigidly. We will see that the resemblance between the ironic styles of Erasmus and Marlowe extends to their specific subject matter as well, particularly in *Doctor Faustus*. Therefore it might be suggested that, like Erasmus, Marlowe valued a wisdom more ethical than esoteric. The first principle of the moralised and humanistic wisdom to which Erasmus so frequently refers seems to have been, 'Know Yourself.' Even though Marlowe mentions the Delphic oracle only once, in *Doctor Faustus*, his idea of wisdom seems to depend largely upon the same principle.

Marlowe's use of allusions can be described as one of his essential ironic methods. But in studying this method as a dramatic technique, it is important to remember that spectators unfamiliar with his plays might fail to notice the allusions or to understand their significance. Again, if we abuse our privilege of hindsight, we will distort the quality of Marlowe's irony, which is dark or oblique. To judge his intentions we must consider not only the sources of the allusions and the diverse abilities of a popular audience, but also the exact manner in which the allusions are presented. Otherwise we are apt to identify responses to allusions by an Elizabethan audience with our own most recent discoveries about their sources. In that case we would not see that Marlowe has often made it difficult to recognise allusions to more familiar materials. The most learned spectator, theoretically responsive to his classical as well as to his Biblical references, might not grasp some of them unless he came to 'hear' a play several times.

Perhaps I can clarify this point by citing briefly two different approaches to a common problem – that readers who should have known the Bible well understood it poorly. In his Prologue to *The Ship of Fools*, Sebastian Brant gives as his general reason for writing, the ignorance of men who had had greater access to 'Holy Writ' through printed books but had not benefited from it.[6] In his address 'To the Reader' in *Of the Vanitie and Uncertaintie of Artes and Sciences*, Cornelius Agrippa observes:

I see many ware proude in Humane learning and knowledge, that

therefore they do despise and lothe the Sacred and Canonicall
Scriptures of the Holie Ghoste, as rude and rusticall, bycause they have
no ornamentes of wordes, force of sillogismes, and affectate persuasions,
nor the straunge doctrine of the Philosophers: but are simply grounded
upon the operation of Vertue, and upon bare Faith.[7]

Brant's solution is to provide a catalogue of follies simply
illustrated with woodcuts for the less literate readers:

> The viewer learns with certainty:
> My mirror leaves no mystery.[8]

Agrippa's solution implicitly repudiates Brant's. Certainty and
authority were among the intellectual attitudes this sceptic
questioned. He therefore approaches his readers by encouraging
them to discover their own ignorance. Although Agrippa does
occasionally pause to indicate that he is criticising the abuses,
rather than the uses of learning, he fills his critique with
distortions and confusions. The main concern of this 'rayler', as
Sidney called him, is the reader who gradually recognises that
almost every statement must be tested and then compared with
other statements.

Marlowe's method resembles Agrippa's rather than Brant's.
Of course, he emphasises the experience of his heroes more than
the learning of his audiences. But he does implicate his audiences
by veiling allusions which might have exposed the heroes, had he
presented them more directly. My references to 'dark' allusions
will remain subject to several qualifications: All allusions might
have been grasped by very acute spectators, by spectators who
had been forewarned, or by spectators who had already guessed
from past experience that Marlowe's ironic catastrophes emphasise meanings latent in his plays through allusions. Some of his
devices for obscuring allusions were probably familiar both to
more and to less well learned spectators. For example, when
Faustus quotes selectively from Romans [vi 23] and 1 John [i 18],
Marlowe may have expected most of his audience to supply the
missing verses. Not only were the texts themselves likely to have
been well known. Many in the audience were probably also
accustomed to the trick of quoting or alluding to part of a saying.
In order to characterise the sycophancy of courtiers, the Folly of

Erasmus recites a few words of Homer, then interrupts herself and challenges her learned reader: 'You know the rest of the verse, which Echo can give you better than I.'[9] 'Echo' was often relied upon to provide parts of less esoteric material, like proverbs. Shakespeare assumed an acquaintance with proverbs when he had Lady Macbeth ask her husband:

> Wouldst thou have that
> Which thou esteem'st the ornament of life,
> And live a coward in thine own esteem,
> Letting 'I dare not' wait upon 'I would,'
> Like the poor cat i' the adage?   [I vii 41-5]

Shakespeare probably thought that his popular audiences would know all about the poor cat.[10]

Clear allusions easily recognised create an effect of strong irony. They provide an instance of what Cole terms Marlowe's 'characteristic tendency to employ his formal knowledge with particular precision'.[11] So relevant are their original contexts as commentary on Marlowe's action that we cannot view them as either casual or decorative. A play which contains any number of obvious allusions can stand, in reference to the norms they provide, as a gigantic inversion, a world upside down. *Doctor Faustus* and *The Jew of Malta* both embody such worlds. But Marlowe does not always emphasise his allusions. Few are as conspicuous as the two half-texts read aloud by Faustus. Commonly, Marlowe alters the wording of his Biblical allusions; he works them unobtrusively into his swelling periods and exciting conflicts. We might consider, for a moment, the effect of that rhetorical question thrust at us by Faustus before he signs away his soul: 'When Mephistophilis shall stand by me, / What God can hurt thee, Faustus?' [II i 24-5]. Surely it will boggle the minds of those who fail to compare it with St Paul's affirmation of divine mercy, 'If God be on our side, who can be against us?' [Romans, viii 31]. In this particular case the memorable rhythms of the two questions might prompt a recognition strong enough to break through our absorption in events. But in other cases Marlowe may provide no more than a word or two which imports to the discourse a vaguely allusive quality. This quality might cause an audience to feel uneasy about Marlowe's characters; it would hardly encourage stronger judgements of the sort induced by the more obvious allusions.

The other ironic methods on which Marlowe relies are tendentiously direct forms of address to the audience, dramatic structures contrived through puzzling analogies, and spectacles or shows. All three will require careful distinctions in describing their nature and use. Knowledge of a convention like the soliloquy prepares us to recognise that Marlowe's direct addresses give speakers special claims on the attention of an audience, and that they articulate key attitudes and ideas. It does not warn us that the will of the speaker seems to come between Marlowe's meanings and our ready apprehension of them. It is as if the speaker seizes upon the advantages of soliloquy to commend himself and his desires. Once our ears are attuned to the persuasive, moving speech of a Tamburlaine or a Faustus we are less inclined to heed allusions which suggest illogic or self-deception.

One reason why Marlowe's soliloquies discourage an immediate critical response is their energetic pace. Another is their timing; we are less likely to question the implied self-praise of a Barabas or Faustus when it comes very early in the action of a play. A third cause of their persuasiveness is the fact that Marlowe's speakers resemble Sidney's 'Poet-haters', their soliloquies include many figures of speech particularly suited to stirring the spleen and staying the brain. In judging the effect which these figures can have upon a spectator, it will be helpful to remember that figures, as Puttenham pointed out, are not just 'instruments of ornament'; they are:

Also in a sorte abuses or rather trespasses in speach, because they passe the ordinary limits of common vtterance, and be occupied of purpose to deceiue the eare and also the minde, drawing it from plainnesse and simplicitie to a certain doublenesse, whereby our talke is the more guilefull & abusing.[12]

Significantly, in Marlowe's soliloquies which praise folly we often encounter those figures which, Puttenham concluded, may 'inucigle and appassionate the mind': metaphor ('an inuersion of sence by transport'), allegory ('duplicitie of meaning'), aenigma (riddles), paremia (adages), irony ('merry skoffe'), sarcasm

('bitter tawnt'), periphrase or circumlocution, and hyperbole
('incredible comparison').

Marlowe's dramatic structures sometimes invite the audience
to make its own 'incredible comparisons'. Like his predecessor,
John Lyly, Marlowe often appears to think dramatically in terms
of analogies.[13] The analogy may emerge between types of
assertion and attitude in a play. For example, we eventually
notice how very similar are all the speeches given by rulers in the
Tamburlaine plays. Some analogies broaden to include the
arrangement of incidents through which the characters move.
We can find such parallel plot lines running through all of the
plays except *Edward II*. This analogical method, although
potentially repetitious, implies a disciplined concentration on a
set of problems or issues. Such concentration is what shapes the
catastrophes so firmly. But Marlowe creates a compensatory
relationship between his own discipline and the freedom of his
audience; his handling of structure reveals a decided willingness
to let the reader or spectator interpret connections for himself.

When its analogies are fairly strong, the play is probably one
which generates a more satiric kind of irony. Such connections
are all the more gratifying if the reader or spectator must bring
them out from behind a facade of differences. He plays the poet,
in Bacon's sense, when he finds that the Turks, Jews and
Christians of Malta or the popes and vintners of Rome are
similar. Such a process of discovery seems to confirm Bacon's
belief that poetry 'raises the mind and carries it aloft, accommodating the shows of things to the desires of the mind'.[14] In
contrast, the *Tamburlaine* plays and *Edward II* frustrate these
desires by giving 'things' greater substance and duration. They
offer revealing identities which develop into profound differences.

By considering some of the analogies in Marlowe's earliest
play, *Dido Queen of Carthage*, we may begin to see why this ironic
technique can have a provocative effect. *Dido* begins with an
induction which shows Jupiter, the most powerful of the gods,
playing amorously with Ganymede, his cup-bearer and lover of
the moment. Venus interrupts this hyperbolic frivolity when she
bursts in to report that her son, Aeneas, is endangered because of
a storm which Juno has stirred up at sea. Jupiter reassures her
that Aeneas's 'wandering fate is firm' (1 i 83) and prophesies the

future greatness of both Aeneas and Rome. Jupiter's own dalliance with Ganymede may anticipate the mutual dalliance of Aeneas and Dido, although it is curious that Jove does not bother to mention Dido or Carthage. Jupiter's power, the power to 'control proud fate', eventually forces Aeneas to desert Dido, just as he has already deserted three Trojan women. One begins to surmise that for Virgil's grand conflict between heroic duty and love, *Pietas* and *Amor*, Marlowe has substituted a mere juggling contest between selfish power and equally selfish lust. The surmise could be reinforced when, at the end of the play, two blind and foolish lovers imitate Dido by committing suicide. Marlowe appears to have turned Virgil's historical motives into psychological, subjective ones. His strategy debunks both gods and men by intimating that passion can make puppets of us all.

We might confidently reach such reductive decisions about the meaning of *Dido*, if it weren't for the inconvenient fact that Marlowe's structural analogies are almost too firm for his play. They communicate attitudes towards the main characters inconsistent with the dramatic behaviour of these characters. Critics have been unable to agree on the exact connection between Dido and Aeneas, and either the narrative induction or the subordinate lovers whose passions Marlowe emphasises. Should we simply explain away this situation by agreeing that Marlowe was inexperienced or that he was collaborating with Nashe? These explanations cannot account for the similar lack of consensus about how we should respond to the relationships between Tamburlaine and other rulers, Edward II and his barons, Faustus and the clowns. . . . [My] hypothesis is that Marlowe must have wished his audience to sense a disproportion between the strong forms and forces which control his characters and the natures of those characters. He has prevented us from taking the justice of his plots for granted.

By looking briefly at Marlowe's presentation of Dido and Aeneas, we may see why an audience might not be guided by Jupiter's initial promise that 'Aeneas' wandering fate is firm'. Jupiter's own proud, wilful power finds more of an echo in the cruelty of the Greek soldiers, whom Aeneas describes as twirling Hecuba by her heels, than it does in Aeneas himself. This plain-spun soldier would have been much more at ease in the worlds of *The Wars of Cyrus* or *Alexander and Campaspe* than he is at Dido's exotic court. How reluctantly he puts on Dido's robes and participates in her ceremonies! Virgil's Aeneas had suddenly disclosed himself to Dido, shedding his miraculous invisibility and dazzling her with his shining, goddess-born splendour. Beggared by misfortune, Marlowe's Aeneas doubts that Dido will see him at all. 'Well may I view her; but she sees not me' (II i 73). This Aeneas is confused by shipwreck, haunted by the nightmare of Troy's defeat, thoroughly dependent upon his mother Venus and his loyal, protective retainers. How can a figure so sentimentally complicated and humble have become involved with the imperial destinies of Rome? Never does he tell Dido, as Virgil's Aeneas does, that he has been promised a home and kingdom of his own in Italy. Perhaps Marlowe would have agreed with Sidney's view of Aeneas, because he presents him as, 'Obeying the Gods commandement to leaue *Dido*, though not onely all passionate kindenes, but euen the humane consideration of vertuous gratefulnes, would haue craued other of him.'[15] Against Dido's ceremonious and fanciful enchantments Marlowe sets the ungarnished fact that Aeneas must necessarily obey the inscrutably wilful behest of Jove. Courtly bliss yields to an obligation for which Marlowe has provided decidedly inadequate motives.

Dido, too, is a more complex, attractive figure than the gods who manipulate her or the lovers who mirror her. Therefore her destiny does not shadow her, as it does in the *Aeneid*, where she is 'infelix' Dido, doomed from the moment she is poisoned by love. Towards the end of the play, Aeneas learns from Hermes that Venus has substituted Cupid for his son Ascanius, and he observes:

> This was my mother that beguil'd the queen
> And made me take my brother for my son.
> No marvel, Dido, though thou be in love,
> That daily dandlest Cupid in thine arms.   [v i 42–5]

No marvel, not much of Virgil's Bacchic frenzy, and little blame for Dido herself. To a great extent, Marlowe's development of subordinate lovers – Iarbas who loves Dido, and Anna who loves Iarbas – accentuates Dido's almost amoral freedom. By suggesting that until scratched by Cupid's dart, Dido had favoured

Iarbas over many rivals, Marlowe makes her resemble not her
Virgilian prototype but the Dido of the seventh Epistle in Ovid's
Heroides. As she baits Iarbas and enchants Aeneas, Dido seems to
exist in an intensely emotional space – a world of great power, but
little purpose or consequence. Instead of worrying about her
honour or her enemies, she attempts to rival the Sirens
[III i 129 & iv 39], alludes to Circe (IV iv 11), longs for a 'charm
to keep the winds / Within the closure of a golden ball' [IV iv 99–
100], and finally sends her sister after Aeneas to 'look upon him
with a mermaid's eye' [v i 201].

Dido refuses to believe that the gods are responsible for calling
Aeneas away from her:

> Wherein have I offended Jupiter,
> That he should take Aeneas from mine arms?
> O, no! the gods weigh not what lovers do:
> It is Aeneas calls Aeneas hence.   [v i 129 32]

And, until the catastrophe, analogies between her character and
those of the two other lovers seem tenuous. All three characters
are fanciful. But Dido, who struggles against her passion and
celebrates it in cosmic terms, will not seem as fatuous as Iarbas or
as weak as Anna. The soliloquy she speaks as she commits her
love tokens and finally herself to the fire is eloquent and
compelling. Marlowe forces one of his more incredible comparisons upon us when he abruptly follows Dido's attempt to
'cure my mind that melts for unkind love' [v i 287] with two anti-
climactic suicides, and when he gives Anna, the least and most
hopeless lover, the last words in his play. To create a tragedy,
rather than an Ovidian epyllion, a playwright must possess what
Ovid lacked – a strongly ethical apprehension of natural or
providential law. *Dido Queen of Carthage* leaves us with an
unpleasant contradiction between the magnitude of Aeneas and
Dido and the triviality of their universe. Later plays present
contradictions which at first may seem similar to this one, but
prove to be thoroughly different. The trivial worlds of Marlowe's
other heroes are worlds which they themselves have helped to
construct.

The last convention which Marlowe uses ironically is
spectacle. By spectacle I do not mean all representation. In that

sense most plays of the period are highly spectacular, for as
Theodore Spencer once pointed out, 'the medieval tradition of
play-writing made the Elizabethan spectators expect to see
everything acted out before them'.[16] I am concerned primarily
with representation as emphasis – the use of what is visible to
focus attention on behaviour or situations seemingly significant
in the play as a whole. I see little point in continuing to regard
Marlowe's spectacular technique as a pioneering attempt to
harmonise speech and action by substituting words for deeds.[17]
Marlowe's achievement may have been gravely underestimated
when judged in an evolutionary and pre-Shakespearean context.
A clearer understanding of how his 'spectacles' function can
bring us closer to an understanding of his basic subjects and style.

Again, because of its contradictory quality, *Dido Queen of
Carthage* may help us to define the extremes towards which
Marlowe's spectacular ironies tend. On the one hand, Marlowe
organises his characters into shows of which they are unaware so
as to sharpen the audience's awareness of external forces or fates.
The conspicuous dandlings of Ganymede by Jupiter and of
Cupid by Dido constitute such shows. By the time we see Dido's
old nurse dandle Cupid too, the universal power of passion will
be clear. Like the use of obvious allusions, such a technique
produces strong and relatively simple ironic effects. On the other
hand Marlowe uses spectacle to develop character. Surely it is no
accident that 'sight' and 'see' are among Marlowe's favourite
terms. His heroes and heroines share a predilection for spectacular display, whether it be expressed through the pageants
and ceremonies of the monarchs, the extravagant revenges of the
Machiavels, or the magic demonstrations of Faustus. The love-
struck characters of *Dido Queen of Carthage* refer repeatedly to
ceremonies, processions, costumes and costume changes,
portraits and other visible properties. Throughout the play he
associates spectacularly ceremonious types of behaviour with
fanciful, conceited attitudes. Later plays will work out a pattern
seemingly truncated in *Dido*; they will thoroughly involve these
attitudes with the choices and destinies of the protagonists.

It is Marlowe's characters, then, but not Marlowe, who fail to
criticise their visions when they attempt to turn them into
actions. As students of Marlowe's spectacles we can approach the
show through the character. We need not depend too far on

unreliable stage directions for information about appearances and gestures, because these are matters of central importance which Marlowe commonly emphasises in dramatic statement and conversation. His method encourages the spectators to compare what they see with what the characters see. The more satiric the spirit of the play is, the more confidently the audience may make the kind of discrimination Achates makes when his master Aeneas confuses a stone Priam with the real one:

> Thy mind, Aeneas, that would have it so,
> Deludes thy eyesight; Priamus is dead.   [II i 31-2]

Such discriminations grow more difficult when the characters themselves disagree about their visions. In the *Tamburlaine* plays and in *Edward II*, sight becomes a problem for the audience as well as for the characters.

The spectacular element in Marlowe's plays has always helped them to succeed on stage. My argument that spectacle is part of Marlowe's obliquely ironic style may seem suspiciously pedantic. Why should a playwright have needed that astounding collection of thrones, chariots, cauldrons and costumes if, like Aeneas, he doubted the value of display? The question is related to a more general question about this dark ironist. Why would he have lavished so much art on characters whom he considered merely foolish and self-deceived? Any answers to these questions must grow from detailed studies of the plays themselves. I believe they will grow more naturally if we begin with a play which seems to have been written in a pedantic, negative temper. The spectacles and shows of *The Jew of Malta* were created by a playwright who might have assented to this observation from *The Praise of Folly*: 'The mind of man is so constructed that it is taken far more with disguises than with realities.'[18] By letting his characters embody their pretensions in spectacle, he makes these pretensions far more accessible to the judgement of his spectators. An emblem, to use Bacon's terms, 'reduceth conceits intellectuall to Images sensible'.[19] Marlowe's spectacles often associate the minds of his characters with their 'sensible' eyesight. As a measure of wisdom, spectacles may be more reliable than plausible speeches and riddling plots.

Renaissance writers or artists who designed pageants sought to interest a variety of spectators. Some would be more pleased than instructed by the fine show. Others would judge the pageant much as they would judge an emblem, considering the designer's use of visual symbols which had established meanings.[20] Marlowe's way with icons resembles his way with allusions; he often makes even a commonplace image difficult to identify. In this respect his shows differ both from the ready intelligibility of the street pageant and the deliberate obscurity of the printed emblem. His most emphatic spectacles provide focal summaries of a character's past behaviour, and therefore derive much of their force from their dramatic contexts. In his more tragic plays Marlowe's stage imagery may actually reveal a basic schism between his attitude and that of some emblem-makers. In *A Choice of Emblemes and Other Devices* (1586), Geffrey Whitney describes emblems as 'Hauinge some wittie deuise expressed with cunning woorkemanship, somethinge obscure to be perceiued at the first, whereby, when with further consideration it is vnderstood, it maie the greater delighte the behoulder.'[21] Marlowe is not obscure because he is entertaining clever initiates. He is obscure because he wants his audience to discover that a delight in 'some wittie deuise' can be a self-destroying virtue. For Marlowe, human imagination lies at the centre of tragic experience.

Marlowe allows his dark art to imitate the disappointments endured by his heroes. Even the imaginations of Faustus and Tamburlaine can fail to carry more sceptical readers and spectators over plateaux of trivia or mountains of dead. To a surprising extent, Marlowe's muse follows, as do his heroes, the path of Icarus, with this essential difference. His 'intollerable poetry', which confounds Heaven in earth, can eventually create vision in his audiences. Like a prophetic mirror, Marlowe's ironic art gives us more awareness of our own minds and values, but only if we continue to examine the mirror as well as the artist who holds it up. His willingness to be misunderstood can then be viewed as an aspect of his skill in provoking an active, persistent kind of attention to his plays.

One might compare this attention to the way we respond when we study a puzzling Renaissance picture. Because it uses similar commonplace motifs, Brueghel's 'Landscape, with the Fall of Icarus' provides a helpful analogy. Is this painting an allegory? Is it a riddle? The incongruity between the drowning hero and the bright, busy landscape stimulates us to draw upon our knowledge – about Icarus, about the symbolism of sailing ships, even about the proverbial occupations of peasants. One of these peasants, ignoring Icarus, seems to be driving his plough towards some over-painted bones of the dead. Brueghel also invites us to exercise our ingenuity on the problem of our own perspective; he presents another peasant who apparently stares up at an invisible Daedalus flying into the darkness where we, the innocent onlookers, watch. Like Marlowe's, Brueghel's is a highly speculative art; it may lead us to reason very curiously. But that, I believe, is part of its excuse for being. One day, looking at Brueghel's 'Landscape', we begin to wonder how Icarus can have lost his wings when the warm sun, the simple focus of the entire design, lies barely above the horizon.

SOURCE: chapter 2, *Christopher Marlowe: Merlin's Prophet* (Cambridge, 1977), pp. 7–21.

NOTES

[Abbreviated and renumbered from the original – Ed.]

1. Douglas Cole, *Suffering and Evil in the Plays of Christopher Marlowe* (Princeton, N.J., 1962), p. 254.
2. Ibid., pp. 257, 259.
3. Sir Philip Sidney, *An Apologie for Poetrie* (1580–1): in G. Gregory Smith (ed.), *Elizabethan Critical Essays* (2 vols, Oxford, 1904), I, p. 181.
4. Ibid., pp. 181–2.
5. An extended discussion of Renaissance wisdom tradition may be found in Eugene F. Rice Jnr, *The Renaissance Idea of Wisdom* (Cambridge, Mass., 1958).
6. Sebastian Brant, *The Ship of Fools*, trans. William Gillis (London, 1971), p. 3.
7. Cornelius Agrippa, *Of . . . Artes and Sciences*, trans. James Sanford (London, 1575), sig. Ai^u.
8. Brant, op. cit., p. 4.
9. Erasmus, *The Praise of Folly*, trans. H. H. Hudson (New York, 1941), p. 96.
10. F. P. Wilson cites this passage as 'The most famous reference to a

proverb in the whole of Shakespeare', and suggests that 'in his day the saying that "the cat would eat fish yet dare not wet its feet" was in such common use that he could refer to it thus obliquely': *The Proverbial Wisdom of Shakespeare* (Cambridge, 1961), p. 3.

11. Cole, op. cit., p. 92.

12. George Puttenham, *The Arte of English Poesie* (1589); in G. Gregory Smith, op. cit., II, pp. 159–60.

13. 'It is the method of Lyly's art to accumulate parallels', writes G. K. Hunter in *John Lyly: The Humanist as Courtier* (London, 1962), p. 172. Cf. Cole's remark on the construction of *Tamburlaine, Part Two*: 'Marlowe, in putting together his play from diverse sources, has again fallen back on the principle of analogy as a unifying structural force, a tendency also evident in *Dido* and *Doctor Faustus*, and firmly implanted in the English dramatic tradition of his time' (p. 116).

14. Bacon, *Of the Dignity and Advancement of Learning* (1605): in James Spedding, Robert L. Ellis and Douglas D. Heath (eds), *The Works of Sir Francis Bacon* (7 vols, London, 1858–74); reprinted (14 vols, Stuttgart, 1963), IV, p. 316.

15. Sidney, in G. Gregory Smith, op. cit., I, p. 180.

16. Th. Spencer, *Death and Elizabethan Tragedy* (Cambridge, Mass., 1936), p. 219.

17. This is H. Levin's attitude in *The Overreacher* (New York, 1952; London, 1954), p. 66. [Ch. 3 of this study is reproduced in section 4 below –Ed.] His biographical approach to spectacle has in effect been controverted by studies like Jocelyn Powell's which rely on iconography and pageantry to argue that Marlowe's spectacle is consistently allegorical, like that in the morality plays: see 'Marlowe's Spectacle', *Tulane Drama Review*, VIII, 4 (1964), pp. 195–210.

18. *The Praise of Folly*, op. cit., p. 63.

19. Bacon's definition of 'emblem' is cited from *The Advancement of Learning* (1605) by the *OED*.

20. See G. Pellegrini, 'Symbols and Significances', *Shakespeare Survey*, XVII (1964), p. 181.

21. Geffrey Whitney, *A Choice of Emblemes and Other Devices* (Leyden, 1586): see his address 'To the Reader'.

2. *TAMBURLAINE THE GREAT, PARTS ONE AND TWO*

Eugene M. Waith 'Marlowe's Herculean Hero' (1962)

Hercules, as he appears in Sophocles, Euripides, and above all Seneca, is revitalised in Tamburlaine. No one of the older plays was used as a model, but Hercules was often in Marlowe's mind as he wrote. Several allusions in the play make this fact indisputable and, as Mario Praz pointed out many years ago, there are striking resemblances between Tamburlaine and Hercules Oetaeus.[1] However, it is finally less important to decide whether Marlowe was deliberately fashioning a Herculean hero than to remember that the traditional depictions of Hercules, especially those from Rome and Renaissance Italy, were thoroughly familiar to him. It is not surprising that Tamburlaine, who had already been used by Louis Le Roy and others as a symbol of the physical and intellectual vigour of the Renaissance,[2] should suggest the Greek hero to him. . . . The images created by Seneca and Pollaiuolo can be of great assistance to the spectator of the twentieth century, partially cut off from the tradition in which Marlowe wrote; for they prepare the eye to discern the outlines of Marlowe's heroic figure.

The figure is vast. The very structure of the play conveys this impression, for the succession of scenes – some of them might almost be called tableaux – stretching over great expanses of time and space, presents the man in terms of the places he makes his and of the time which at the last he fails to conquer. It is no accident that we always remember the effect of Marlowe's resounding geography, for earthly kingdoms are the emblems of Tamburlaine's aspirations. At the end of his life he calls for a map, on which he traces with infinite nostalgia his entire career and points to all the remaining riches which death will keep him from:[3]

And shall I die, and this unconquered?   [2: v iii 151]

To be a world conqueror in the various senses which the play gives to the term is the essence of Tamburlaine's character. That this insight is conveyed in part by the sprawling structure of the play is an important advantage to weigh against some of the obvious disadvantages of such a structure in the theatre. Although complication and even conflict in its fullest sense are almost missing, each successive episode contributes something to the dominant idea – the definition of a hero. There is a forward movement of the play in unfolding not only the narrative but the full picture of the hero. When the play is well acted and directed it has ample theatrical life, no matter how much the form is indebted to epic.

The first view we have of Tamburlaine is a kind of transformation scene. It is preceded by the brief, and basically snobbish descriptions given at the court of Mycetes, the ludicrously incompetent king of Persia, to whom Tamburlaine is a marauding fox,[4] a 'sturdy Scythian thief', and the leader of a 'Tartarian rout' [1: 1 i 31, 36, 71]. The Tamburlaine who walks on the stage dressed as a shepherd and leading Zenocrate captive has some of the outward appearance suggested by these descriptions, and the earlier impression of social inferiority is conveyed in the words of Zenocrate, who at first takes him for the shepherd he seems to be [1 ii 8]. However, his words and actions reveal a strikingly different man: he boasts like a genuine hero if not a gentleman, and exchanges his shepherd's weeds for complete armour and curtle-axe. Before our eyes he assumes the outward appearance which matches his warrior's spirit.

Tamburlaine is a proud and noble king at heart, yet his Scythian-shepherd origins give a clue to the absolute difference between him and the world's other kings. His is the intrinsic kingliness of the hero, associated with the ideal of freedom, whereas other kings are presented as oppressors, the products of a corrupt system. The garb of the Scythian shepherd, even though he discards it, relates Tamburlaine to the simpler world of an earlier, mythical time. The king he becomes carries with him into a decadent world something of this primitive simplicity. Like his successors, Chapman's Bussy and Dryden's Almanzor, he is an early edition of the 'noble savage'.

Thus far Tamburlaine appears as a hero in the classic mode, but when he tells Zenocrate that her person 'is more worth to Tamburlaine / Than the possession of the Persian crown' [90–1], the influence of the romance tradition is apparent. In fact, for the moment it seems that the 'concupiscible power' of his soul dominates the 'irascible power', though the subsequent action shows that this is not true. Tamburlaine's love, expressed in the poetry of the famous speech beginning 'Disdains Zenocrate to live with me?' [82–105], further distinguishes him from his rival warriors. Their pride and their ambition are not accompanied by the imagination which informs his promises to Zenocrate.

> With milk-white harts upon an ivory sled
> Thou shalt be drawn amidst the frozen pools,
> And scale the icy mountains' lofty tops,
> Which with thy beauty will be soon resolv'd.
>
> [*I*: 1 ii 98–101]

The cold fire of this speech is the first testimony of Tamburlaine's imaginative scope and of the paradoxes of his nature; the icy mountain tops are the first memorable image of his aspiration.

The arrival of Theridamas with the Persian forces provides for another surprising revelation of the hero. We have just seen him in the guise of a lover: we now see him as an orator, overcoming Theridamas with words. Marlowe insists on the unexpectedness of these aspects of the hero. 'What now! in love?' says Techelles [106], and, when Tamburlaine asks whether he should 'play the orator', replies disdainfully that 'cowards and faint-hearted runaways / Look for orations' [130–1]. In defiance of this advice, Tamburlaine delivers his brilliantly successful oration, winning from Theridamas the tribute that even Hermes could not use 'persuasions more pathetical' [211]. Yet, surprising as this eloquence is to Tamburlaine's followers, it is not alien to the Renaissance concept of the Herculean hero. Cartari specifically reminds his readers that Hercules, like Mercury, whom he has just discussed, has been called a patron of eloquence. It is, so to speak, perfectly proper to present a Herculean hero as orator.

Tamburlaine begins his oration with a complimentary picture of Theridamas, but soon turns to himself with the famous boast 'I hold the Fates bound fast in iron chains', and the comparisons of himself to Jove. The effect of the speech is double, for though it displays the hero as orator, it also presents, by means of eloquence, his self-portrait as conqueror of the world and even as demigod. Such self-praise might be taken as Marlowe's way of portrying a man who will say anything to get ahead or of pointing to the ironical contrast between a man's pride and his accomplishment, but one of the puzzling features of *Tamburlaine* is that the hero's actions also show him in the guise of a demigod, and only his death proves that he does not control the fates. Even death is not presented unequivocally as defeat. Tamburlaine's extravagant boasts, like those of Hercules, are largely made good, so that he and his followers become the amazement of the world. In Usumcasane's words, 'These are the men that all the world admires'.

Before Tamburlaine unleashes his persuasive forces Theridamas comments on his appearance in words which emphasize the importance of visual impressions in this play:

> Tamburlaine!
> A Scythian shepherd so embellished
> With nature's pride and richest furniture!
> His looks do menace heaven and dare the gods;
> His fiery eyes are fix'd upon the earth,
> As if he now devis'd some stratagem,
> Or meant to pierce Avernus' darksome vaults
> To pull the triple-headed dog from hell.

> [*1*: 1 ii 154–61]

Again we have the transformation of the Scythian shepherd into a noble warrior, but here even the armour appears as part of nature's endowment of the hero. The eyes fixed on the earth are the symbolic equivalent of one of Tamburlaine's best-known speeches, in which he makes an earthly crown the ultimate felicity, but this fixation on the earth is accompanied by looks which menace heaven and also suggest a Herculean conquest of hell. The description is perfect, though to use it when the character described stands before the audience is to risk a

ludicrous incongruity. Marlowe depends on unhesitating acceptance of the verbal picture.

Marlowe's heavy dependence on description is again illustrated in the next scene, when Menaphon gives Cosroe an
even fuller account of Tamburlaine's looks than we have had
from Theridamas. In this speech the hero's body is made
symbolic of his character. He is tall like his desire; his shoulders
might bear up the sky like Atlas; his complexion reveals his thirst
for sovereignty; he has curls like Achilles; and his arms and hands
betoken 'valour and excess of strength' [II i 7–30].

One of Tamburlaine's most important traits, his infinite
aspiration, receives its first major treatment in a much discussed
speech in the second act about the 'thirst of reign and sweetness of
a crown' [II vii 12–29]. Menaphon's encomium of Tamburlaine's physical beauty provides a clue to the understanding of
this passage. Just as his body seems beautiful not simply in itself
but in that it expresses his character, so Tamburlaine extols the
'sweet fruition of an earthly crown' not because anything the
earth has to offer has final value for him, but because domination
of the earth represents the fulfilment of his mission – the fulfilment of himself. The speech is about the infinite aspiration
taught us by nature and the never-ending activity to which the
soul goads us. 'The sweet fruition of an earthly crown' is indeed
bathos, as it has often been called, unless the earthly crown means
something rather special in this play.

There is a good deal of evidence that it does. In an earlier scene
Usumcasane says, 'To be a king, is half to be a god', and
Theridamas replies, 'A god is not so glorious as a king' [II v 56–7].
Tamburlaine never puts it quite thus, for it is clear that like
Hercules he already considers himself partly divine, yet kingship
is obviously glorious to him. The 'course of crowns' which he and
his followers eat in Act IV, scene iv of *Part One*, is the visual
equivalent of the constant references to sovereignty. The earth
itself is despicable – inert – the negation of heroic energy, as
appears in the speech of Theridamas immediately following the
lines about the earthly crown:

> For he is gross and like the massy earth
> That moves not upwards, nor by princely deeds
> Doth mean to soar above the highest sort.
>
> [*1*: II vii 31–3]

but ruling the earth is not an end in itself. It is a manifestation of the will to 'soar above the highest sort'. When Tamburlaine seizes his first crown, the crown of Persia, he makes the act symbolic of his will:

> Though Mars himself, the angry god of arms,
> And all the earthly potentates conspire
> To dispossess me of this diadem,
> Yet will I wear it in despite of them,   . . . [58–61]

His contempt for earthly potentates and the assertion of his will combine in his conception of himself as the scourge of God, a conception which he shares with Hercules [III iii 41–54].[5] He is the avenger, nemesis to the mighty of the world, contemptuous demonstrator of the absurdity of their claims, liberator of captives. He is not so much the instrument as the embodiment of a divine purpose. His serene confidence that his will is seconded by destiny gives him the magnificence of the hero who transcends the merely human. The activities of such a hero are always confined to the earth, though always pointing, in some sense, to a goal beyond. Thus Seneca's Hercules Oetaeus, while rejoicing in his earthly deeds, never forgets that he is destined to become a star. Toward the end of Part Two Tamburlaine begins to speak of an otherworldly goal,[6] but even before this time the thrones and crowns of the world stand for something which though in the earth is yet not of it. Their importance to Tamburlaine lies in taking them away from tyrants like Bajazeth, for whom they have intrinsic value. Tamburlaine's last instructions to his son are to sway the throne in such a way as to curb the haughty spirits of the captive kings [2: v iii 235–42]. An earthly crown represents the sweet fruition of his purpose in being.

Tamburlaine's moving description of the aspiration for sovereignty has the utmost value in the play in presenting his double attitude towards the earth. And as he both seeks and despises earthly glory, he both claims and defies the power of the gods. 'Jove himself' will protect him [1: i ii 179]; not even Mars will force him to give up the crown of Persia [II vii 58–61]. He does not belong entirely to either earth or heaven. Though he has distinctly human characteristics, both good and bad, he has something of the magnificence and the incomprehensibility of a deity.

Tamburlaine speaks of Mars as 'the angry god of war', and the words might serve as self-description, for when he is angry the awe that his looks inspire is almost that of a mortal for a god. Agydas, when Tamburlaine has passed, *'looking wrathfully'* at him, expresses a typical reaction:

> Betray'd by fortune and suspicious love,
> Threaten'd with frowning wrath and jealousy,
> Surpris'd with fear of hideous revenge,
> I stand aghast; but most astonied
> To see his choler shut in secret thoughts,
> And wrapt in silence of his angry soul.
> Upon his brows was pourtray'd ugly death,
> And in his eyes the fury of his heart,
> That shine as comets, menacing revenge,
> And casts a pale complexion on his cheeks.
>
> [*1*: iii ii 66–75]

Later a messenger speaks of 'The frowning looks of fiery Tamburlaine, / That with his terror and imperious eyes / Commands the hearts of his associates' [iv i 13–15], and the Governor of Damascus calls him 'this man, or rather god of war' [v i 1]. Anger is the passion most frequently displayed in his looks, his words, and the red or black colours of his tents.

Not only is he a man of wrath, as the Herculean hero characteristically is; he is also fiercely cruel. This trait of character receives a continually increasing emphasis; it is strikingly demonstrated in Tamburlaine's treatment of Bajazeth. In Scene ii of Act iv of *Part One* the defeated emperor is brought on in his cage, from which he is removed to serve as Tamburlaine's footstool. But Scene iv is even more spectacular. Tamburlaine, dressed in scarlet to signify his wrath towards the besieged city of Damascus, banquets with his followers while the starving Bajazeth in his cage is insulted and given scraps of food on the point of his conqueror's sword. In the midst of these proceedings Tamburlaine refuses Zenocrate's plea that he raise the siege and make a truce with her father, the Soldan of Egypt. In the last act of *Part One* we see Tamburlaine order the death of the virgins of Damascus, who have been sent to beg for mercy after the black colours have already indicated Tamburlaine's decision to destroy the obstinate city. With inhuman logic he points out that it is now too late and that they 'know my customs are as peremptory / As wrathful planets, death, or destiny' [v ii 64–5]. At the end he says that his honour – that personal honour which is the basis of the hero's *areté* – 'consists in shedding blood / When men presume to manage arms with him' [v ii 416–17]. Tamburlaine's is a cosmic extension of the cruelty Achilles shows to Hector or Hercules to the innocent Lichas. Though it is a repellent trait, it is entirely consistent with the rest of the character. Instead of passing over it, Marlowe insists on it. One need not assume, however, that Marlowe himself loved cruelty nor, on the other hand, that he is depicting here a tragic flaw. It is an important part of the picture, a manifestation of Tamburlaine's 'ireful Virtue', to use Tasso's phrase, and one of the chief occasions for wonder. One may disapprove and yet, in that special sense, admire.

Marlowe's method of constructing his dramatic portrait is essentially dialectical. Not only is love balanced against hate, cruelty against honour, but these and other traits are constantly brought out against a background of parallels or contrasts. Tamburlaine is contrasted with other monarchs and with Zenocrate. In the last act an entire city is his antagonist. Throughout the play his followers are like variations on the Tamburlaine theme, imitating his ferocity and zest for conquest, but incapable of his grandeur. The first three monarchs with whom the hero is contrasted are the foolish Mycetes, his brother, Cosroe, and the emperor Bajazeth. Mycetes is a grossly comic foil in his inability to act or speak well, to control others or himself. In the opening speech of the play he deplores his own insufficiency to express his rage, 'For it requires a great and thundering speech' [i i 1–3], a thing Tamburlaine can always provide.

In a low-comedy scene in the first act Mycetes comes alone on to the battlefield, the picture of cowardice, looking for a place to hide his crown. This action in itself takes on great significance when we come, three scenes later, to Tamburlaine's praise of crowns. Mycetes curses the inventor of war and congratulates himself on the wisdom that permits him to escape its ill effects by hiding the crown which makes him a target. To put the censure of war and the praise of scheming wisdom in the mouth of such a character inclines the audience to see virtue in the hero's pursuit of war and in a kind of wisdom more closely allied to action.

The contrast with Cosroe is another matter. Patently superior to his brother Mycetes, Cosroe appears to be an ordinarily competent warrior and ruler. In fact, his one crippling deficiency is his inability to recognise the extraordinary when he sees it in the person of Tamburlaine. His attempt to pat Tamburlaine on the head and reward him for a job well done by giving him an important post in the kingdom, as any normal king might do, is as inept, given the nature of Tamburlaine, as the feckless gesturing of Mycetes. Cosroe is perfectly familiar with the rules of the game as it is generally played in the world, where the betrayal of a Mycetes is venial and competence has at least its modest reward. His cry of pain when Tamburlaine turns against him, 'Barbarous and bloody Tamburlaine' [II vii 1], expresses the outrage of one who finds that the rules he has learned do not apply. Tamburlaine's strategy is so much more daring and his treachery so much more preposterous that they are beyond the imagination of Cosroe.

Bajazeth, Tamburlaine's third antagonist, is no mere moderately successful king. A proud and cruel tyrant, he rejoices in the sway of a vast empire. With his first words a new perspective opens up: 'Great kings of Barbary, and my portly bassoes' [III i 1]. Here is a ruler served by kings. 'We hear the Tartars and the eastern thieves, / Under the conduct of one Tamburlaine, / Presume a bickering with your emperor.' The tone is superb. One notes the condescension of 'one Tamburlaine' and the hauteur of 'Presume a bickering'. He is assured ('You know our army is invincible'); he is used to command ('Hie thee, my basso . . . Tell him thy lord . . . Wills and commands, (for say not I entreat)'); and he is obeyed by thousands ('As many circumcised Turks we have, / And warlike bands of Christians renied, / As hath the ocean or the Terrene sea / Small drops of water').

If Cosroe is a little more like Tamburlaine than is his foolish brother, Bajazeth is decidedly more so. He speaks of 'the fury of my wrath' [III i 30], and shows his cruelty by threatening to castrate Tamburlaine and confine him to the seraglio while his captains are made to draw the chariot of the empress. The famous (and to a modern reader ludicrous) exchange of insults between Zabina and Zenocrate reinforces the parallel. Yet Marlowe emphasises the ease with which this mighty potentate is toppled from his throne. The stage directions tell the story: 'BAJAZETH *flies and he pursues him. The battle short and they enter.* BAJAZETH *is overcome*' [III iii 211ff.]. This contrast brings out what was suggested by the contrast with Cosroe, the truly extraordinary nature of Tamburlaine. For Bajazeth is what Mycetes would like to be but cannot be for lack of natural aptitude. He is what Cosroe might become in time with a little luck. As a sort of final term in a mathematical progression, he presents the ultimate in monarchs, and in himself sums up the others. That even he should fall so easily defines the limitations of the species and sets Tamburlaine in a world apart. He is not merely more angry, more cruel, more proud, more powerful. Though sharing certain characteristics with his victims, he embodies a force of a different order.

Zenocrate, by representing a scale of values far removed from those of the warrior or the monarch, provides further insights into Tamburlaine's character. Something has already been said of his courtship of her in the first Act, when, to the surprise of Techelles, he shows that he is moved by love. The inclusion in his nature of the capacity to love is a characteristic Renaissance addition to the classical model of the Herculean hero. One recalls that Tasso's Rinaldo, though chiefly representing the 'ireful Virtue,' is susceptible to the charms of Armida. Yet Zenocrate is not an enchantress like Armida nor is Tamburlaine's love for her presented as a weakness.[7] Love, as opposed to pure concupiscence, is a more important part of Tamburlaine than of Rinaldo. As G. I. Duthie has pointed out, it modifies considerably his warrior ideal,[8] leading him to spare the life of the Soldan and 'take truce with all the world' [v ii 468].

Marlowe leaves no doubt that the commitment to Zenocrate is basic and lasting, but it is not allowed to dominate. Tamburlaine refuses Zenocrate's plea for Damascus, and when he also refuses the Virgins of Damascus he says:

> I will not spare these proud Egyptians,
> Nor change my martial observations
> For all the wealth of Gihon's golden waves,
> Or for the love of Venus, would she leave
> The angry god of arms and lie with me.
>
> [*1*: v ii 58–62]

This clear evaluation of the claims of Venus as opposed to those of Mars precedes by only a few lines the long soliloquy in which he extols the beauty of Zenocrate. Here he admits that he is tempted to give in to Zenocrate, who has more power to move him than any of his enemies. By implication it is clear that this power is due to her beauty, which is so great that if the greatest poets attempted to capture it,

> Yet should there hover in their restless heads
> One thought, one grace, one wonder, at the least,
> Which into words no virtue can digest. [108–10]

But on the verge, as it might seem, of capitulating to this softer side of his nature, he first reproves himself for these 'thoughts effeminate and faint', and then presents beauty as the handmaid of valour. This passage is a textual crux, and its syntax is so treacherous that a close analysis of the meaning is nearly impossible, but I think it is fair to say that Tamburlaine's convictions about the role of beauty are given in the lines:

> And every warrior that is rapt with love
> Of fame, of valour, and of victory,
> Must needs have beauty beat on his conceits:
> . . . [117–19]

The conclusion of the speech looks forward to what beauty may inspire Tamburlaine to do, and it is as important a part of his mission as the scourging of tyrants. This is to show the world 'for all my birth, / That virtue solely is the sum of glory, / And fashions men with true nobility' [125–7]; that is, that the hero's goal is to be attained by an innate power which has nothing to do with the accidents of birth. To Theridamas, Techelles and Usumcasane he has said much the same thing, assuring them that they deserve their titles

> By valour and by magnanimity.
> Your births shall be no blemish to your fame;
> For virtue is the fount whence honour springs.
> [*1*: IV iv 135–7]

In several ways the power of love and beauty is subordinated to

Tamburlaine's primary concerns. The encomium of Zenocrate leads to the statement of beauty's function in the warrior's life and then to Tamburlaine's intention of demonstrating true nobility. Furthermore the entire soliloquy is carefully framed. Before it begins, he orders a slaughter, and after his lines about true nobility he calls in a servant to ask whether Bajazeth has been fed. Tamburlaine's love for Zenocrate, extravagant as it is, is part of a rather delicately adjusted balance of forces.

Zenocrate is a pale character beside the best heroines of Shakespeare and Webster, but her attitude towards Tamburlaine is an important part of the meaning of the play. After her initial mistake – not wholly a mistake – of thinking he is just the Scythian shepherd he seems to be, her feelings towards him change rapidly. When she next appears she defends him to her companion, Agydas, who still sees Tamburlaine as a rough soldier. He asks:

> How can you fancy one that looks so fierce,
> Only disposed to martial stratagems?   [*I*:III ii 40–1]

Zenocrate replies by comparing his looks to the sun and his conversation to the Muses' song. When Tamburlaine enters he rewards each of them with behaviour suited to their conception of him: 'TAMBURLAINE *goes to her, and takes her away lovingly by the hand, looking wrathfully on* AGYDAS, *and says nothing*' [65ff.].

Zenocrate enters enthusiastically into the exchange of insults with Bajazeth and Zabina, but it is her speeches after the sack of Damascus and the suicides of Bajazeth and Zabina which truly reveal her attitude towards Tamburlaine. Sorrowing for the cruel deaths of the Virgins of Damascus, she asks:

> Ah, Tamburlaine, wert thou the cause of this,
> That term'st Zenocrate thy dearest love?
> Whose lives were dearer to Zenocrate
> Than her own life, or aught save thine own love.
>
> [*I*: v ii 274–7]

His cruelty is recognised for what it is without its impairing her love. Similarly, when she laments over the bodies of the emperor and empress, she acknowledges Tamburlaine's pride, but prays

Jove and Mahomet to pardon him. This lament is a highly effective set-piece, whose formality gives it a special emphasis. Its theme, the vanity of earthly power, is resoundingly stated in the refrain, 'Behold the Turk and his great emperess!' which occurs four times, varied the last time to 'In this great Turk and hapless emperess!' [293, 296, 301, 307]. But within the statement of theme there is a movement of thought as Zenocrate turns from the most general aspect of the fall of the mighty to what concerns her more nearly, its bearing on Tamburlaine. The orthodoxy of the moral she draws from this spectacle of death is conspicuous, and nowhere more so than in the central section:

> Ah, Tamburlaine my love, sweet Tamburlaine,
> That fights for sceptres and for slippery crowns,
> Behold the Turk and his great emperess!
> Thou that, in conduct of thy happy stars,
> Sleep'st every night with conquest on thy brows,
> And yet wouldst shun the wavering turns of war,
> In fear and feeling of the like distress,
> Behold the Turk and his great emperess!

The culmination of the speech is its prayer that Tamburlaine may be spared the consequences of 'his contempt / Of earthly fortune and respect of pity' [303-4].

When Tamburlaine's enemies inveigh against his pride and presumption, their protests have a hollow ring, and Marlowe may seem to be laughing at the point of view they express. He is certainly not doing so when he puts criticism of the same faults in the mouth of Zenocrate. Through her an awareness of the standard judgement of Tamburlaine's 'overreaching' is made without irony and made forcefully. Through her it is also made clear that such an awareness may be included in an unwavering devotion, just as Deianira's devotion can digest even the grave personal slight she suffers from Hercules. Zenocrate both presents the conventional view of hubris more convincingly than any other character, and shows the inadequacy of this view in judging Tamburlaine.

A contrast on a larger scale forms the final episode of *Part I*: Tamburlaine is pitted against the great city of Damascus. Since Zenocrate pleads for the city, this is an extension of the contrast between the hero and heroine. Since the city is ruled by

Tamburlaine's enemies, it is the climax in the series of contrasts
between him and the representatives of corrupt worldly power.
His first three enemies are individuals of increasing stature, but
the Governor of Damascus and his allies, the Soldan and Arabia,
are none of them imposing figures. Instead, the city of Damascus
becomes the collective antagonist, to which Tamburlaine opposes his personal will. Much more than the individual monarchs
of the first acts, the city seems to represent the point of view of
society, which Zenocrate also adopts when she becomes the
spokesman for conventional morality. When the delegation of
virgins asks the conqueror for mercy, the appeal is in the name of
the whole community:

> Pity our plights! O, pity poor Damascus!
> Pity old age, . . .
> . . .
> Pity the marriage-bed, . . .
> . . .
> O, then, for these, and such as we ourselves,
> For us, for infants, and for all our bloods,
> That never nourish'd thought against thy rule,
> Pity, O pity, sacred emperor,
> The prostrate service of this wretched town;
> . . .   [*1*: v ii 17–37]

Tamburlaine's refusal is based on the absolute primacy of his
will – of the execution of whatever he has vowed. He is as self-
absorbed as Hercules, whose devotion to his *areté* obliterates any
consideration for Deianira or Hyllus, in *The Women of Trachis*.
Homer portrays the hero's uncompromising adherence to his
own standard of conduct in the refusal of Achilles to fight. In
Book ix of the *Iliad*, when he is waited on by the delegation of
warriors, including his old tutor, Phoenix, heroic integrity
directly opposes obligation to others – to friends and allies in war.
The 'conflict between personal integrity and social obligation'
was inherent in the story of the Wrath of Achilles, according to
Cedric Whitman, but Homer gave it special importance, seeing
it 'as an insolubly tragic situation, the tragic situation *par
excellence*'.[9] In the Renaissance it is not surprising to find 'social
obligation' represented by the city, but in this case it is an enemy
city. Instead of being urged to fight for friends Tamburlaine is

urged to spare citizens whose only fault is the acceptance of the rule of their foolish, and finally weak, governor. Hence the social obligation denied by Tamburlaine is not that of supporting his friends' cause but of conforming to an ideal of behaviour which places mercy above justice. The code of Tamburlaine is a more primitive affair. His word once given is as inflexible as destiny, and the imposition of his will upon Damascus is also the carrying out of a cosmic plan. To the demands of a segment of society he opposes a larger obligation to free the world from tyrants. Marlowe's setting him against Damascus reaffirms both his colossal individuality and his god-like superiority. The siege of this city is used to present the core of the problem of *virtus heroica*.

Marlowe puts far less emphasis upon the benefactions of his hero's career than was put upon the benefactions of Hercules; the punishment of the wicked is what Tamburlaine himself constantly reiterates. Nevertheless, the punishment of Damascus is balanced by the hero's generosity in sparing the Soldan. This is not a matter of just deserts. It is Tamburlaine's god-like caprice to spare Zenocrate's father. Because he does so the end of *Part One* suggests a positive achievement. Zenocrate's greeting of her 'conquering love' is a mixture of wonder and gratitude, and even the vanquished Soldan joins in the general thanksgiving.

Whether *Part Two* was planned from the first, as some have thought, or written in response to the 'general welcomes Tamburlaine receiv'd', as the Prologue says, its general conception is strikingly similar to that of *Part One*. Its structure is again episodic, though the episodes are somewhat more tightly knit. The pattern is again a series of encounters between Tamburlaine and his enemies, leading at last to the one unsuccessful encounter – with death. To Mycetes, Cosroe and Bajazeth correspond the vaster alliance of Bajazeth's son Callapine and his allies. To the conflict between the factions in Persia corresponds the fight between Orcanes and Sigismund after a truce has been concluded. Here again, but even more circumstantially, we have the jealous struggles, the hypocrisies and the betrayals of conventional kings. Sigismund is a despicable figure, Orcanes a rather sympathetic one – even more so than his structural counterpart, Cosroe. He is portrayed as a religious man, is given some fine lines on the deity, '. . . he that sits on high and never sleeps, / Nor in one place is circumscriptible' [2: II ii 49–50], and,

though born a pagan, acknowledges the power of Christ. That
religion spares him none of the humiliations accorded to the
enemies of Tamburlaine suggests that his religion, like his
statecraft, is conventional. He is far from being the worst of men
or the worst of rulers, yet, like the kings in *Part One*, he is given to
boasting of his power and position and making snobbish remarks
about Tamburlaine's lowly origin. It may be significant that he
offers his partial allegiance to Christ as a means of obtaining the
victory over Sigismund, who is a perjured Christian. This
bargaining religion is the foil to Tamburlaine's impious self-
confidence.

Other elements of the pattern of *Part One* are also imitated
here. The siege of Damascus is matched by the siege of Babylon;
Bajazeth in his cage is matched by the conquered kings in
harness, to whom Tamburlaine shouts the famous 'Holla, ye
pampered jades of Asia!' [IV iii 1], so often parodied. Tamburlaine in his chariot, actually whipping the half-naked kings who
draw him, is a powerful theatrical image. Preposterous as the
scene may be, it is satisfyingly right as a visual symbol of one of
the principal themes of the play. *Part Two* develops the theme
more fully than *Part One*, giving it a prominent place in the dying
hero's instructions to his eldest son:

> So, reign, my son; scourge and control those slaves,
> Guiding thy chariot with thy father's hand.
> . . .
> For, if thy body thrive not full of thoughts
> As pure and fiery as Phyteus' beams,
> The nature of these proud rebelling jades
> Will take occasion by the slenderest hair,
> And draw thee piecemeal, like Hippolytus,
> . . .   [*2*: v iii 229–41]

Another theme developed in *Part Two* is the cruelty of
Tamburlaine. It is so prominent here that it may seem to mark a
loss of sympathy for the hero. Certainly the brutality to the
conquered kings and to the Governor of Babylon, and above all
Tamburlaine's murder of his son, constitute more vivid and more
shocking examples than even the treatment of Bajazeth. Yet one
need not conclude that Marlowe has changed his mind about his
hero. All of these scenes may be understood as part of a rhetorical

amplification of a theme which is, after all, unmistakable in *Part One*. Furthermore these scenes serve to emphasize other aspects of Tamburlaine's character indicated in *Part One*. The portrait is not changed: its lines are more deeply incised.

The scenes presenting Calyphas, the cowardly son, are perhaps the most shocking of all, and may be used as examples of the amplified theme of cruelty in *Part Two*. In the first of them [I iv] Celebinus and Amyras, the two brave sons, win paternal approval by vying with each other in promises to scourge the world, while Calyphas is furiously rebuked for asking permission to stay with his mother while the rest are out conquering. As in all the scenes with the three sons, the patterning is obvious to the point of being crude, and the humour in the depiction of the girlish little boy not much to our taste. Nevertheless, the scene does more than show how hard-hearted Tamburlaine can be. For members of the audience who have not seen *Part One* it presents Tamburlaine's relationship to Zenocrate, and for the rest it restates that relationship in different terms. The scene opens with a loving speech to Zenocrate, who replies by asking Tamburlaine when he will give up war and live safe. It is this question which the scene answers by asserting the primacy of the irascible powers in Tamburlaine's nature. In spite of his love he identifies himself with 'wrathful war', and as he looks at her, surrounded by their sons, suddenly thinks that his boys appear more 'amorous' than 'martial', and hence unworthy of him. Zenocrate defends them as having 'their mother's looks' but 'their conquering father's heart' [I iv 35–6], and it is then that they proclaim their intentions. Tamburlaine's rebuke to Calyphas is a statement of his creed, glorifying the 'mind courageous and invincible' [73], and drawing a portrait of himself comparable to several in *Part One*:

> For he shall wear the crown of Persia
> Whose head hath deepest scars, whose breast most wounds,
> Which, being wroth, sends lighning from his eyes,
> And in the furrows of his frowning brows
> Harbours revenge, war, death and cruelty;
> . . .
> $\lfloor 2$: I iv 74–8]

The furrowed brows belong to the angry demigod of *Part One*, and if the picture is somewhat grimmer, it is partly because of the hint that the demigod must suffer in the accomplishment of his mission.

The next scene with Calyphas [III ii] takes place after the death of Zenocrate, and like the former one, makes its contribution to the development of Tamburlaine's character. As the earlier scene began with the praise of Zenocrate, so this one begins with her funeral against the background of a conflagration betokening Tamburlaine's wrath. Again Calyphas is responsible for an unexpected note of levity when he makes an inane comment on the dangerousness of war just after his father has concluded stern instructions to his sons how to be 'soldiers, / And worthy sons of Tamburlaine the Great' [91–2]. The consequence is not only a rebuke but a demonstration. Never having been wounded in all his wars, Tamburlaine cuts his own arm to show his sons how 'to bear courageous minds' [143]. Here his cruelty and anger are turned against himself, as perhaps they always are in some sense in the scenes with Calyphas.

The last of these scenes [IV i] is the most terrible and by far the most important, for Calyphas here prompts Tamburlaine to reveal himself more completely than ever before. In the first part of the scene the boy has played cards with an attendant while his brothers fought with their father to overcome the Turkish kings. He has scoffed at honour and, like Mycetes, praised the wisdom which keeps him safe [49–50]. When the victors return, Tamburlaine drags Calyphas out of the tent and, ignoring the pleas of his followers and of Amyras, stabs him to death. It is almost a ritual killing – the extirpation of an unworthy part of himself, as the accompanying speech makes clear:

> Here, Jove, receive his fainting soul again;
> A form not meet to give that subject essence
> Whose matter is the flesh of Tamburlaine,
> Wherein an incorporeal spirit moves,
> Made of the mould whereof thyself consists,
> Which makes me valiant, proud, ambitious,
> Ready to levy power against thy throne,
> That I might move the turning spheres of heaven;
> For earth and all this airy region
> Cannot contain the state of Tamburlaine.   [2: IV i 113–22]

To interpret this murder as merely one further example of

barbarous cruelty is to accept the judgement of Tamburlaine's enemies. The cruelty is balanced against one of the most powerful statements of the spirituality of Tamburlaine. It is the 'incorporeal spirit' which makes him what he is, a hero akin to the gods, and which, because it cannot bear to be other than itself, pushes him to the execution of his cowardly son. As the great aspiring speech of *Part One* obliges us to see an earthly crown as the goal to which Tamburlaine's nature forces him, so this speech and its accompanying action oblige us to accept cruelty along with valour, pride and ambition as part of the spirit which makes this man great. The soul of Calyphas, by contrast, is associated with the 'massy dregs of earth' [125], lacking both courage and wit, just as Theridamas described the unaspiring mind as 'gross and like the massy earth' [*1*: II vii 31].

So far does Tamburlaine go in asserting his affinity to heaven and contempt for earth, that for the first time he hints that sovereignty of the earth may not be enough for him. It is an idea which has an increasing appeal for him in the remainder of the play. He makes another extreme statement in this scene when his enemies protest the barbarity of his deed. 'These terrors and these tyrannies', he says, are part of his divine mission,

> Nor am I made arch-monarch of the world,
> Crown'd and invested by the hand of Jove,
> For deeds of bounty or nobility;
> . . . [*2*: IV i 152–4]

To be the terror of the world is his exclusive concern.

The emphasis on terror is consistent with the entire depiction of his character. The denial of nobility is not. It is an extreme statement which the emotions of the moment and dialectical necessity push him to. Allowing for an element of exaggeration in this speech, however, the scene as a whole, like the other scenes with Calyphas, presents a Tamburlaine essentially like the Tamburlaine of *Part One*, and not seen from any very different point of view. As he grows older, as he encounters a little more resistance, his character sets a little more firmly in its mould. It remains what it has always been.

The death of Zenocrate is, as every critic has recognised, the first real setback to Tamburlaine. In view of her association with

the city in *Part One* it is appropriate that Tamburlaine makes a
city suffer for her death by setting fire to it. His devotion to her
and to the beauty she represents appears in the speech he makes
at her deathbed [II iv 1–37], in his raging at her death, in the
placing of her picture on his tent to inspire valour [III ii 36–42],
and in his dying address to her coffin [v iii 224–7]. As G. I. Duthie
says, death is the great enemy in *Part Two*, and his conquest of
Zenocrate is in effect his first victory over Tamburlaine.[10] As he
had to make some concessions to Zenocrate in *Part One*, so in *Part
Two* he has to come to terms with the necessity of death. The
process begins with the death of Zenocrate, to which his first
reaction is the desire for revenge. Not only does he burn the town
where she died; he also orders Techelles to draw his sword and
wound the earth [II iv 97]. This prepares us somewhat for his later
order, when death has laid siege to him, to 'set black streamers in
the firmament, / To signify the slaughter of the gods' [v iii 49–
50]. By keeping always with him the hearse containing her dead
body he refuses wholly to accept her death as he now defies his
own.

Only in the last scene of Act v does cosmic defiance give way to
acceptance, and when this happens Tamburlaine's defeat by
death is partially transformed into a desired fulfilment. I have
already mentioned his hint that the earth cannot contain him. It
is followed by a suggestion that Jove, esteeming him 'too good for
earth' [IV iii 60], might make a star of him. Now he says:

> In vain I strive and rail against those powers
> That mean t'invest me in a higher throne,
> As much too high for this disdainful earth. [*2*: v iii 121–3]

and finally:

> But, sons, this subject, not of force enough
> To hold the fiery spirit it contains,
> Must part, . . .   [169–71]

Like Hercules Oetaeus, he feels that his immortal part, that
'incorporeal spirit' of which he spoke earlier, is now going to a
realm more worthy of him, though imparting something of its
power to the spirits of his two remaining sons, in whom he will

continue to live. In these final moments we have what may be hinted at earlier in his self-wounding – a collaboration with death and fate in the destruction of his physical being. For the psychologist the drive towards self-destruction is latent in all heroic risks; it is the other side of the coin of self-assertion. Though Marlowe could never have put it this way, his insight may be essentially similar.

From the quotations already given it will be apparent that Tamburlaine's attitude toward the gods changes continually. He boasts of their favour or defies them to take away his conquests; likens himself to them, executes their will, waits for them to receive him into their domain, or threatens to conquer it. Tamburlaine's religious pronouncements, especially his blasphemies, have attracted a great deal of critical comment from his day to ours. Since Marlowe himself was accused of atheism, the key question has been whether or not Tamburlaine is a mouthpiece for his author. Some critics emphasise Tamburlaine's defiance of Mahomet and the burning of the Koran, but these episodes are surely no more significant than his 'wounding' of the earth. As Kocher has pointed out, his line, 'The God that sits in heaven, if any god' [*2*: v i 199] contains in its parenthetical comment more blasphemy for a Christian than does the whole incident of the Koran.[11] Yet even this questioning of God's existence is only one of the changes of attitude just cited. To try to deduce Marlowe's religious position from these speeches is a hopeless undertaking, and to try to decide on the basis of the biographical evidence which of them Marlowe might endorse is risky and finally inconclusive. Somehow the relationship of these opinions to the rest of the play must be worked out. Either their inconsistency is due to carelessness (in this case carelessness of heroic proportions) or it has some bearing on the heroic character. Seneca's Hercules displays a similar variety of attitudes. In the earlier play he thanks the gods for their aid in his victory over the tyrant, Lycus, and offers to kill any further tyrants or monsters the earth may bring forth. Moments later, as his madness comes upon him, he says:

To the lofty regions of the universe on high let me make my way, let me seek the skies; the stars are my father's promise. And what if he should not keep his word? Earth has not room for Hercules, and at length restores him unto heaven. See, the whole company of the gods of their own will summons me, and opens wide the door of heaven, with one alone forbidding. And wilt thou unbar the sky and take me in? Or shall I carry off the doors of stubborn heaven? Dost even doubt my power?

[*Hercules Furens*, 958–65]

In the first lines of *Hercules Oetaeus* he again boasts of his activities as a scourge of tyrants and complains that Jove still denies him access to the heavens, hinting that the god may be afraid of him. Later [1302–3] he almost condescends to Jove, remarking that he might have stormed the heavens, but refrained because Jove, after all, was his father. Greene could quite properly have inveighed against 'daring God out of heaven with that atheist Hercules'. At the end of *Hercules Oetaeus* the hero accepts his fate with calm fortitude and even helps to destroy himself amidst the flames. These changes in attitude are perhaps more easy to understand in Hercules, since his relationship to the gods was in effect a family affair. Tamburlaine is not the son of a god, but his facile references to the gods, sometimes friendly, sometimes hostile, may be interpreted as part of the heroic character of which Hercules is the prototype. He has the assurance of a demigod rather than the piety of a good man.

Such assurance, rather than repentance, breathes in the lines in which Tamburlaine advises his son Amyras:

> Let not thy love exceed thine honour, son,
> Nor bar thy mind that magnanimity
> That nobly must admit necessity.
> Sit up, my boy, and with those silken reins
> Bridle the steeled stomachs of those jades. [*2*: v iii 200–4]

The advice to admit necessity[12] may reflect Tamburlaine's own acceptance of his death, but in context it refers primarily to the necessity for Amyras to take over Tamburlaine's throne. The whole speech shows Tamburlaine's conviction of the rightness of what he has done. The place of love is again made subordinate to honour, the hero's chief concern. Magnanimity is stressed as it is in Tamburlaine's advice to his followers to deserve their crowns 'By valour and magnanimity' [*1*: iv iv 135]. Even the bowing to fate is to be done nobly, as Tamburlaine himself is now doing. Finally, the heroic enterprise of controlling tyrants is to be

continued. There is no retraction here, no change in the basic
character. He has come to terms with death, but this is more a
recovery than a reversal. He has spoken earlier in the play of his
old age and death, but, very humanly, has rebelled when death
struck at Zenocrate and then at himself. Now he has regained
calm with self-mastery.

Though the suffering of Tamburlaine is so prominent from the
death of Zenocrate to the end, retribution is not what is stressed.
The last scene of the play presents a glorification of the hero
approaching apotheosis. It opens with a formally patterned
lament, spoken by Theridamas, Techelles and Usumcasane, the
last section of which expresses the theme of the scene, Tamburlaine as benefactor:

> Blush, heaven, to lose the honour of thy name,
> To see thy footstool set upon thy head;
> And let no baseness in thy haughty breast
> Sustain a shame of such inexcellence,
> To see the devils mount in angels' thrones,
> And angels dive into the pools of hell!
> And, though they think their painful date is out,
> And that their power is puissant as Jove's,
> Which makes them manage arms against thy state,
> Yet make them feel the strength of Tamburlaine,
> Thy instrument and note of majesty,
> Is greater far than they can thus subdue;
> For if he die, thy glory is disgrac'd,
> Earth droops, and says that hell in heaven in plac'd.
>
> [2: v iii 28–41]

His sons live only in his life, and it is with the greatest reluctance
that Amyras mounts the throne at Tamburlaine's command.
When he speaks in doing so of his father's 'anguish and his
burning agony' [210], he seems to imply that Tamburlaine's
sufferings are the inevitable concomitants of his greatness and
his service to humanity. It is he who pronounces the final
words:

> Meet heaven and earth, and here let all things end,
> For earth hath spent the pride of all her fruit,
> And heaven consum'd his choicest living fire!
> Let earth and heaven his timeless death deplore,
> For both their worths will equal him no more.   [250–4]

Full of Herculean echoes, the lines form a perfect epitaph for the hero, the product of earth and heaven.

Three times in this scene Tamburlaine adjures his son to control the captive kings and thus maintain order. He compares the task with Phaëton's:

> So reign, my son; scourge and control those slaves,
> Guiding thy chariot with thy father's hand.
> As precious is the charge thou undertak'st
> As that which Clymene's brain-sick son did guide
> When wandering Phoebe's ivory cheeks were scorched,
> And all the earth, like Ætna, breathing fire.
> Be warned by him, then; learn with awful eye
> To sway a throne as dangerous as his;
> . . .
>   [229–36]

Despite his ambition and pride, Tamburlaine is no Macbeth to seek power 'though the treasure / Of nature's germens tumble all together, / Even till destruction sicken . . .' [*Mac.*, IV i 58–60].[12] Rather, he identifies himself with universal order, as does Seneca's Hercules. The very chariot which is a symbol of his cruel scourging is also the symbol of control and hence of order. Compared to the chariot of the sun, it is also the bringer of light.

In the depiction of the Herculean hero there is no relaxation of the tensions between his egotism and altruism, his cruelties and benefactions, his human limitations and his divine potentialities. Marlowe never lets his audience forget these antitheses. In the first scene of Act V this great benefactor orders the Governor of Babylon to be hung in chains on the wall of the town. He rises from his deathbed to go out and conquer one more army. It is Marlowe's triumph that, after revealing with such clarity his hero's pride and cruelty, he can give infinite pathos to the line, 'For Tamburlaine, the scourge of God, must die' [v iii 249].

In obtaining a favourable reception for his hero among the more thoughtful members of his audience Marlowe could no doubt count on not only some familiarity with the heroic tradition in which he was working, but also on the often-voiced regard for the active life. Gabriel Harvey, it will be recalled, asks who would not rather be one of the nine worthies than one of the

seven wise masters. He also expresses another attitude on which
Marlowe could count, the Stoic regard for integrity – truth to
oneself. Harvey prefers Caesar to Pompey because Pompey
deserts himself, while Caesar remains true to himself. He notes
that it was Aretine's glory to be himself.[13]

The last moments of the play appeal to the spectator's pity by
insisting on the tragic limitation of Tamburlaine as a human
being. 'For Tamburlaine, the scourge of God, must die' is
comparable to Achilles's lines: 'For not even the strength of
Herakles fled away from destruction, / although he was dearest of
all to lord Zeus . . .' But the play's dominant appeal is to the
wonder aroused by vast heroic potential. The very paradoxes of
Tamburlaine's nature excite wonder, and this was supposed in
Marlowe's time to be the effect of paradox. Puttenham, in his
familiar *Arte of English Poesie*, calls paradox 'the wondrer'.
Tamburlaine's 'high astounding terms', for which the Prologue
prepares us, clearly aim at the same effect. Many years later, Sir
William Alexander, the author of several Senecan tragedies,
wrote that the three stylistic devices which pleased him most
were: 'A grave sentence, by which the Judgement may be
bettered; a witty Conceit, which doth harmoniously delight the
Spirits; and a generous Rapture expressing Magnanimity,
whereby the Mind may be inflamed for great Things.' The last of
these three he found in Lucan, in whose 'Heroical Conceptions'
he saw an 'innate Generosity'; he remarked the power of 'the
unmatchable Height of his Ravishing Conceits to provoke
Magnanimity'.[14] Marlowe was undoubtedly influenced by the
style of the *Pharsalia*, the first book of which he had translated,
and in any case Alexander's words might justly be applied to
Tamburlaine. The epic grandeur of the style, with its resounding
catalogues of exotic names, its hyperboles and its heroic boasts
and tirades, 'expresses magnanimity', that largeness of spirit so
consistently ascribed to the great hero. Alexander testifies that
such a style may inflame the mind 'for great things', and general
as this description is, it serves well for the feeling aroused by the
play. Another name for it was admiration.

SOURCE: extract from *The Herculean Hero in Marlowe, Chapman,
Shakespeare and Dryden* (New York, 1962; London, 1962), pp.
63–87.

NOTES

[Abbreviated and renumbered from the original –Ed.]

1. Mario Praz, 'Machiavelli and the Elizabethans', *Proceedings of the British Academy*, xiv (1928), 71ff. See also Roy W. Battenhouse, *Marlowe's Tamburlaine* (Nashville, Tenn., 1941), pp. 196ff., where the parallel with Seneca's Hercules is used to show that Marlowe depicts Tamburlaine as the type of insatiable conqueror who falls victim to his own covetousness. Since my interpretation of Seneca is totally different from Battenhouse's, the parallel does not seem to show anything of the sort.

2. See Hallett Smith, 'Tamburlaine and the Renaissance', *Elizabethan Studies – University of Colorado Studies*, series B, ii, 4 (Boulder, Col., 1945); and Erich Voegelin, 'Das Timurbild der Humanisten', *Zeitschrift für öffentliches Recht*, xvii (1937), pp. 545–82.

3. In the performance of Tamburlaine directed by Tyrone Guthrie in New York in 1956, a very large map was spread on the floor of the stage, making possible an extraordinarily effective theatrical image. Tamburlaine walked on the map as he pointed to his conquests, and at the end fell down on it, almost covering the world with his prone body.

4. Battenhouse has pointed to the Machiavellian combination of the fox image in this scene with that of the lion in the following scene (op. cit., p. 209). See also Harry Levin, *The Overreacher* . . . (Cambridge, Mass, 1952), pp. 37–8; (London, 1954), p. 56.

5. On the importance of this idea in *Tamburlaine*, see Battenhouse, op. cit., pp. 99–113.

6. Early in *Part One*, he promises Theridamas friendship 'Until our bodies turn to elements, / And both our souls aspire celestial thrones' [i ii 235–6], but here the reference seems more conventional.

7. I cannot agree with Battenhouse (op. cit., pp. 165ff.), who believes that the comparison of her to Helen of Troy in Tamburlaine's lament for her death shows her to be a 'pattern of pagan, earthly beauty' and 'devoid of religion or conscience'. Her attitude towards her father and towards the deaths of Bajazeth and Zabina leads to an opposite conclusion.

8. G. I. Duthie, 'The Dramatic Structure of Marlowe's *Tamburlaine the Great, Parts One and Two*', *English Studies (Essays and Studies*, New Series), i (1948), pp. 101–26. I do not wholly agree as to the extent of the modification Duthie sees. I am not so sure as he is that the marriage of Tamburlaine and Zenocrate symbolises the establishment of an ideal relationship between beauty and the warrior.

9. Cedric Whitman, *Homer and the Heroic Tradition* (Cambridge, Mass., and London, 1958), p. 182.

10. Duthie, op. cit., pp. 118, 124.

11. P. H. Kocher, *Christopher Marlowe: A Study of His Thought, Learning and Character* (Chapel Hill, N.C., 1946), p. 89.

12. Helen L. Gardner has written about the importance of the theme of necessity in *Part Two* in 'The Second Part of *Tamburlaine the Great*', *Modern Language Review*, xxxvii (1942), pp. 18–24. I cannot agree with her that Marlowe's sympathies are much changed, however, nor that the moral of *Part Two* is 'the simple medieval one of the inevitability of death'.

13. *Gabriel Harvey's Marginalia*, pp. 134, 156.

14. Sir William Alexander, *Anacrasis* (1634?), in J. E. Spingarn (ed.), *Critical Essays of the Seventeenth Century* (Bloomington, Ind., and London, 1957), I, pp. 182, 183.

Johnstone Parr Tamburlaine's Malady (1944)

. . . Tamburlaine's catastrophe remains one of the unsatisfactorily explained enigmas of the play. The unwary reader doubtless assumes that at the end of *Part Two* the Scythian conqueror simply – though somewhat vitriolically – dies, and that Marlowe should be called to account for marring his play with a badly-motivated catastrophe. The careful reader of Marlowe's text doubtless perceives (or at least suspects) that Tamburlaine's 'distemper' at the end of the play is linked definitely with Renaissance medical, physiological, psychological and astrological concepts. Yet no satisfactory analysis of how these concepts are involved in Tamburlaine's death has been made. Carroll Camden hazards the suggestion that Tamburlaine's death is immediately resultant upon his choleric humour.[1] . . . Don Cameron Allen, believing that 'Marlowe conceived of his hero as a typical representative of the *fortunati*', a Renaissance type of fortunate man upon whom Fortune never failed to smile, contends that Tamburlaine comes to no catastrophe at all but triumphantly 'dies of old age'.[2] Roy W. Battenhouse has . . . considered Tamburlaine as an instrument

by means of which God, in His providential justice, scourges the
world, and then, when the mundane chastisement is completed,
strikes down His tyrannical instrument. Although in that article
Professor Battenhouse does not explain, or even consider, the
express bodily workings of Tamburlaine's malady, in his
[subsequent] book he assumes (following Camden) that Tamburlaine is – among other things – a typical choleric man, and affirms
that the physician's diagnosis indicates that Tamburlaine dies in
a mad frenzy brought on by that disastrous affliction of the
'humours' which Elizabethans termed *choler adjust*.[3]

Professor Allen's interpretation ignores the physician's
diagnosis, and Professors Camden and Battenhouse's interpretation . . . is based upon a complete misunderstanding of some
pertinent words in Marlowe's text. For the physician's diagnosis
says nothing whatever about the choleric humour. I do not wish to
detract from the general idea in these enlightening interpretations. It may well be that Marlowe had both of them in mind.
But I do wish to point out a third possible interpretation,
and to correct these commentators on the physician's diagnosis of
Tamburlaine's malady. The purpose of this article, therefore, is
(1) to suggest that Tamburlaine's inordinate and innate passions
(and incidentally his stars) precipitate his death, and (2) to
explain fully the medical, psycho-physiological, and astrological
concepts mentioned by Tamburlaine's physician and, therefore,
specifically involved in the conqueror's decease.

I

Marlowe presents Tamburlaine as a gigantic and energetic man
lusting for military dominion, believing in his own destiny, and
withal being particularly cruel, proud, and wrathful; and he
definitely links Tamburlaine's reiterated invincibility with the
impelling power of the stars.[4] All of these physical qualities,
mental characteristics and cosmological concepts Marlowe
found in his sources.[5] But he did not get specifically from his
source material the cause and the manner of Tamburlaine's
death; for the acknowledged sources of the play state that in the
full vigor of his life the great Scythian died a peaceful and natural
death in Samarcand.[6] Undoubtedly not wanting to foist on his
audience a unique catastrophe incompatible with the histories,

Marlowe had to fabricate adroitly a reasonable manner in which to dispatch his hero and at the same time stay within the bounds of historical expediency. Having allowed his hero in *Part One* to become gloriously invincible and heavenly-guarded in military affairs, Marlowe doubtless decided that the only appropriate conqueror of Tamburlaine should be Tamburlaine himself. Accordingly he allowed his wrathful Scythian to die from a malignant 'distemper' which might be brought on as a result of his fiery temperament.

From various medieval and Renaissance treatises we may gather that violent passions can cause malignant distempers of the body. Virtually all the classical and medieval physicians stated that abnormal emotion (anger, for example) can produce fevers.[7] The *De occulta philosophia* of Henry Cornelius Agrippa, who drew immeasurably upon the physicians and other wise men of the early Renaissance, contains several chapters under such captions as 'The Passions of the Mind and the Soul Can Change the Proper Body'. Agrippa writes, for instance:

The passions of the soul are the chiefest cause of the temperament of its proper body. So the soul, being strongly elevated, and inflamed with a strong imagination, sends forth health or sickness in its proper body. . . . To these things Avicen, Aristotle, Algazel and Gallen assent.

The passions . . . change the proper body with a sensible transmutation, by changing the accidents of the body, and by moving the spirits upward or downward, inward or outward, and by producing divers qualities in the members. So in joy, the spirits are driven outward; in fear, drawn back; in bashfulness, are moved to the brain. . . . After the same manner in anger or fear, but suddenly. Again, anger, or desire for revenge, produceth heat, redness, a bitter taste and a looseness. Fear induceth cold, trembling of the heart, speechlessness and paleness. Sadness causeth sweat and a bluish whiteness. Pity, which is a kind of sadness, doth often ill affect the body. . . . Anxiety induceth dryness and blackness. And how great heats love stirs up in the liver and pulse, physicians know. . . . It is also manifest that such like passions, when they are most vehement, may cause death. And this is manifest to all men that with too much joy, sadness, love or hatred, men many times die. And so we read that Sophocles and Dionysius, the Sicilian tyrant, did both suddenly die at the news of a tragical victory. So a certain woman, also, seeing her son returning from the Canensian battle, died suddenly. . . . Sometimes, also, by reason of these like passions, long diseases follow. . . . And how much vehement anger, joined with great audacity, can do, Alexander the Great shows, who, being circumvented with a battle in India, was seen to send forth from himself lightning and fire; the father of Theodoricus is said to have sent forth out of his body sparks of fire, so that sparkling flames did leap out with a noise.[8]

Numerous other sixteenth-century treatises give evidence that Elizabethans were well aware that passions produce physiological changes in the body and its working organisms. Pierre Charron writes:

Anger makes the Blood boil in our hearts, and raises wild and furious Vapours in our Mind. . . . The signs and Symptoms of this Passion make a mighty difference in the Person, alter the whole Temper and Frame both of Body and Mind, transform and turn him into quite another man. Some of these changes and Symptoms are outward and apparent: Redness and Distortions of the Face, Fieryness of the Eyes, a wild and enraged look, . . . quickness and unevenness of the Pulse, Swelling and bursting of the Veins, . . . and in short, the whole Body is set on Fire, and in a perfect Fever. Some have been transported to such a degree . . . that their very Veins have broke, their Urine stopt, and they have dropt down dead, being stifled and strangled with excess of Passion.[9]

. . . It was common knowledge, therefore, among sixteenth-century intellectuals that passions could initiate all sorts of bodily distempers and bring one ultimately to ruin.[10] Keeping in mind this tenet of Elizabethan psycho-physiology, let us examine Tamburlaine's catastrophe.

Toward the end of *Part Two* the Scythian conqueror's enemies deliver themselves of several uncomplimentary epithets regarding Tamburlaine's violent and unmerciful onslaughts. The King of Jerusalem, affording us a premonition that Tamburlaine shall be punished by the heavens, cries out:

> Thy victories are grown so violent,
> That shortly heaven, fill'd with meteors
> Of blood and fire thy tyrannies have made,
> Will pour down blood and fire on thy head,
> Whose scalding drops will pierce thy seething brains,
> And, with our bloods, revenge our bloods on thee.
>
> [*2*: IV i 142-7]

And the King of Soria gives us a hint as to what shall happen to
Tamburlaine when the former exclaims:

> May never spirit, vein or artier feed
> The cursed substance of that cruel heart;
> But, wanting moisture and remorseful blood,
> Dry up with anger, and consume with heat!   [180–3]

These men have ample reason to regard Tamburlaine thus, for
his inordinate lust for conquest and his fiery temperament have
indeed led the seemingly invincible Scythian to ravage, pillage
and devastate. Particularly after the death of Zenocrate [II iv], his
raging anger attains a noticeable crescendo. He consumes with
fire the town Zenocrate died in simply because he believes that
the place itself bereft him of his love. He burns continually
thereafter with an increasing ardor for conquest; he devises
harrowing punishments for his enemies; his 'wrathful looks' and
his eyes 'composed of fury and of fire' presage death to those who
stand in his way. Eventually his violent wrath and anger –
specifically mentioned innumerable times – become so unbridled
that he murders his own son merely because the boy fails to
participate in battle. After hanging the Babylonian governor and
unmercifully riddling this official's body with bullets, Tamburlaine orders his soldiers to sack the city and drown in Asphaltis
Lake 'every man, woman, and child' who lives in Babylon. This
his soldiers do until the fishes are well-nigh choked.

Suddenly, amid these frenzied outbursts in which Tamburlaine considers himself the 'wrathful messenger of mighty Jove'
[v i 92], the raging conqueror is 'distempered' – from what, he
knows not [216–20]. But shortly thereafter we find in the remarks
of Theridamas a hint as to the nature of Tamburlaine's illness:

> Weep, heavens, and vanish into liquid tears!
> Fall, stars that govern his nativity,
> And summon all the shining lamps of heaven
> To cast their bootless fires to the earth,
> And shed their feeble influence in the air;
> Muffle your beauties with eternal clouds,
> For Hell and Darkness pitch their pitchy tents,
> And Death, with armies of Cimmerian spirits,
> Gives battle 'gainst the heart of Tamburlaine.
> Now, in defiance of that wonted love

Your sacred virtues pour'd upon his throne,
And made his state an honour to the heavens,
These cowards invisibly assail his soul,
And threaten conquest on our sovereign;
But if he die, your glories are disgrac'd,
Earth droops, and says that hell in heaven is plac'd.
[2: v iii 1–16]

Theridamas, we notice, specifically asks the fortunate stars of
Tamburlaine's natal horoscope to assert their power and overcome the 'armies of Cimmerian spirits' as they 'battle' against the
conqueror's heart. But in spite of this and other pleas by
Tamburlaine's henchmen, the torments of the conqueror
increase. He knows that he shall die. Perhaps he knows that the
'Cimmerian spirits', the 'invisible cowards', are causing all the
trouble. But apparently he does not know that his passion is the
root of the evil; or if he does, he cannot check himself, for he
resumes unhesitatingly his attempts to be 'the terror of the
world'. He continues to rave of war and revenge:

Come, let us march against the powers of Heaven,
And set black streamers in the firmament,
To signify the slaughter of the gods.
Ah, friends, what shall I do? I cannot stand.
Come, carry me to war against the gods,
That thus envy the health of Tamburlaine.
[2: v iii 48–53]

Theridamas, perhaps understanding that Tamburlaine's passion
is probably the source of his illness, admonishes:

Ah, good my lord, leave these impatient words,
Which add much danger to your malady!   [54–5]

But Tamburlaine, as fiery as ever, replies that 'in revenge of this
[his pain]' he will forestall 'the ugly monster death' [57, 67] by
getting immediately to the battlefield, where

I and mine army come to load thy bark
With souls of thousand mangled carcasses.
. . .
            Techelles, let us march,
And weary Death with bearing souls to hell.   [74–5, 77–8]

Tamburlaine's physician then attempts to calm him. He administers medicine and pronounces (in what has now become an almost 'obscure' passage) that Tamburlaine's state of health is perilous indeed:

> Pleaseth your majesty to drink this potion,
> Which will abate the fury of your fit,
> And cause some milder spirits govern you.
> . . .
> I view'd your urine, and the hypostasis,
> Thick and obscure, doth make your danger great.
> Your veins are full of accidental heat,
> Whereby the moisture of your blood is dried:
> The humidum and calor, which some hold
> Is not a parcel of the elements,
> But of a substance more divine and pure,
> Is almost clean extinguished and spent;
> Which, being the cause of life, imports your death.
> Besides, my lord, this day is critical,
> Dangerous to those whose crisis is as yours:
> Your artiers, which alongst the veins convey
> The lively spirits which the heart engenders,
> Are parch'd and void of spirit, that the soul,
> Wanting those organons by which it moves,
> Cannot endure, by argument of art.
> Yet, if your majesty may escape this day,
> No doubt but you shall soon recover all.
>
> [*2*: v iii 78 80, 82 99]

But Tamburlaine does not recover. A messenger enters to announce that Callapine's freshly-gathered army is ready to set upon them. Rising in agony from his couch, Tamburlaine rejoices that he may again vent his anger and (so he thinks) stave off death:

> See, my physicians, now, how Jove hath sent
> A present medicine to recure my pain!
> My looks shall make them fly;
> . . .   Draw, you slaves!
> In spite of death, I will go show my face.
>
> [106–9, 114–15]

In such a rage he does indeed put his opponents to flight, but he then perceives that all his martial strength is spent:

> In vain I strive and rail against those powers
> That mean t'invest me in a higher throne,   . . . [121-2]

But he cannot check his passion for conquest even after this admission. He calls for a map, that he may see how much of the world is left for him to overwhelm. And with his last breath he urges his son to be one like him, a wrathful, uncompromising conqueror of the world, a 'scourge of God'. Thus the vitriolic conqueror's violent outbursts have precipitated and perpetuated such a malignant malady that even his hitherto auspicious stars are powerless to mitigate the illness which rapidly overwhelms him.

Tamburlaine's end is, therefore, quite adequately motivated if we consider that his dominant characteristic is his inordinate passion – the passion of ambition, hatred, wrath and revenge – from which the Elizabethan readily perceived that devastating results may be wrought upon the body. In thus allowing his gigantic and powerful character to die suddenly from some peculiar 'distemper', Marlowe has not (as Horace might say) 'brought on the gods'. The catastrophe of Tamburlaine is not at all out of joint with his character; for his peculiar distemper has been occasioned by his innate passions, and in the light of sixteenth-century psycho-physiology it was perfectly obvious to an intelligent Elizabethan that the wrathful Scythian should have been dispatched in such a manner.

I have previously stated that I do not quarrel with the principal idea in Professor Battenshouse's interpretation (that Tamburlaine was an instrument of Providence ultimately struck down by God), or with that of Professor Allen (that Tamburlaine was a typical Pontanian *fortunatus*). I simply maintain that my interpretation is an equally plausible one. It could be, moreover, that in bodying forth his character of the Scythian tyrant Marlowe purposedly fused all three of these conceptions, for it is a truism that unusually striking personalities in Elizabethan drama are not anything if not complex.

II

. . . Tamburlaine's malady is undoubtedly of a febrile nature. The King of Soria remarks significantly – if his words may be taken as premonitory – that Tamburlaine's heart shall 'dry up with anger and consume with heat'. The physician mentions that the 'heat' in Tamburlaine's veins had dried up the moisture of his blood. Tamburlaine's son Amyras, ascending his father's throne while Tamburlaine is in the very jaws of death, refers to his father's 'burning agony' [2: v iii 209]. And, as we have seen . . . , classical and Elizabethan physicians were agreed that fevers could result from such violent passions as those with which Tamburlaine seems to be possessed. Undoubtedly we may conclude that Tamburlaine has contracted a fever, or at least some distemper of a febrile nature.

The physician has reported first that the 'hypostasis' of Tamburlaine's water is 'thick and obscure'. All the classical medical authorities discuss in detail the different appearances and substances of the sick man's urinal discharges, and the indications which may be gleaned therefrom.[11] Besides the watery portion, there were three variegated substances to be distinguished in the urine: the *hypostasis* (or the sediment), the *enaeorema* (or substances which float in the watery part), and the *nubeculae* (or scum which floats on the surface). All of the learned doctors are agreed that the *hypostasis* is of the most importance in determining the diagnosis. And Hippocrates, perhaps the supreme authority, records in his *De prognosticis*:

The urine is best when the sediment is white, smooth, and consistent during the whole time, until the disease comes to a crisis, for it indicates freedom from danger, and an illness of short duration. . . . But if the urine be reddish, and the sediment consistent and smooth, the affection in this case will be protracted but still not fatal. But farinaceous sediments in the urine are bad, and still worse are the leafy; and white and thin are very bad, but the furfurcaceous are still worse than these. Clouds carried about in the urine are good when white, but bad when black. When the urine is yellow and thin, it indicates that the disease is unconcocted. . . . But the most deadly of all kinds of urine are the fetid, watery, *black* and *thick*; . . .[12]

Though the cordial administered by the physician seems in

Tamburlaine's case to be of no avail, Tamburlaine's physician knows his business at least in prognosticating that an *hypothesis* 'thick and obscure, doth make your danger great', and indeed has due cause to be alarmed.

Tamburlaine's physician hopes that the medicinal potion will 'cause some milder spirits' to 'govern' his patient . . . . Innumerable Elizabethan treatises explain in detail the manner in which the *soul* and the *spirits* function in the human body.[13] The soul, they maintain, is provided with three distinct faculties: vegetative, sensible, and rational. It gives to the body its life, motion and sense through its association with the three principal organs of the body: the liver, the heart and the brain. The vegetative faculty, provided by the liver, promotes nutrition, growth, and reproduction; the sensible faculty, provided by the heart, promotes the body's motions and desires; the rational faculty, provided by the brain, promotes the intellectual appetites and reason. But in order to make possible these operations, the body is provided with certain fumes or vapors or substances known as *spirits*. Bartholomaeus Anglicus's treatment of these is lengthy and explicit:

A spirit is called a certain substance, subtle and airy, that stirreth and exciteth the virtues of the body to their doings and works. . . . The same spirit piercing and passing forth to the dens of the brain, is there more directed and made subtle, and is changed into the *animal* spirit, which is more subtle than the other. And so this animal spirit is gendered in the foremost den of the brain, and is spread into the limbs of feeling. But yet nevertheless some part thereof abideth in the aforesaid dens, that common sense, the common wit, the virtue imaginative, the intellect and understanding, and the memory may be made perfect. From the hindermost parts of the brain he (the spirit) passeth by the marrow of the ridge bone, and cometh to the sinews of moving, so that wilful moving may be engendered, in all parts of the nether body. Then one and the same spirit is named by divers names. For by working in the liver it is called the natural spirit, in the heart the vital spirit, and in the head, the animal spirit. We may not believe that this spirit is man's reasonable soul, but more smoothly, as saith Austin, the car therof and proper instrument. For by means of such a spirit the soul is joined to the body: and without the service of such a spirit, no act the soul may perfectly exercise in the body. And therefore if these spirits be impaired, or let of their working in any work, the accord of the body and soul is resolved, the reasonable spirit is let of all its works in the body. As it is

seen in them that be amazed, and mad men and frantic, and in others
that oft lose use of reason. . . .[14]

. . . As a result of his intense passion (and, as I shall show anon, as
a result of the position of his stars), Tamburlaine has occasioned
in his body an excess of febrile heat. This 'accidental heat'
parches his arteries and dries up in his blood the radical moisture
(*humidum*) which is necessary for the preservation of his natural
heat (*calor*). The depletion of his *humidum* and *calor* (whose
admixture in the blood gives rise to the *spirits*) prevents his soul's
functions, stops his bodily activities, and thereby causes his death.
Although Tamburlaine does not realise it, the more his passion is
enraged the more malignant his bodily condition becomes, and
the result is of course disastrous. Blindly . . . , because of this
'tragic flaw' in his character, Tamburlaine hurls himself onward
to his death. The play is, from the Elizabethan point of view,
therefore a tragedy of inordinate passions based somewhat
painstakingly on sound Elizabethan psychological and physiological principles.

We have not completed our diagnosis of Tamburlaine's
malady, however, until we ascertain what the stars have been
doing while Tamburlaine suffered the throes of his agony. In
more than half a dozen passages Marlowe calls attention to the
fact that Tamburlaine's stars have ordained that he succeed. At
the time of Tamburlaine's illness, three of his soldiers plead with
the stars to shed benevolent influences and overcome the malady
which assails their leader. They plead in vain, for apparently the
stellar powers forsake Tamburlaine at the very time when he
needs them most. . . . Possibly the same celestial force which
made Tamburlaine's career heaven-ordained at last deals to him
a kind of retributive justice in that the celestial bodily ingredients
refuse to function properly. At any rate, to understand clearly
what has happened in the heavens, we must proceed to the last
item of the physician's diagnosis – the critical days.

The physician has remarked significantly:

> Besides, my lord, this day is critical,
> Dangerous to those whose crisis is as yours:
> . . .
> [2: v iii 91–2]

Critical days, the history of which goes back to Hippocrates and
Galen, were in general medical practice the days when the
malignancy of a disease was suddenly and swiftly altered for
better or for worse – usually the seventh, fourteenth, twentieth
and twenty-seventh day after decumbiture. Since 'Galen and
most of the ancient authorities believed that critical days were
influenced by the moon',[15] the medieval astrologers erected
elaborate systems by which a disease could be diagnosed,
attended and healed according to the positions and influences of
the planets during these critical days. Wise medieval physicians
believed implicity that any alteration of the qualities of a man's
body was dependent upon the stars;[16] Renaissance treatises on
this subject give abundant evidence that the tradition carried
over into Elizabethan times, and that many sixteenth-century
doctors, living in the shadow of medievalism, tempered their
somewhat more orthodox medical practices with astrological
tenets.

Arriving at the sick man's bedside, the physician who accepted
these iatromathematical doctrines would set about immediately
to cast a horoscope for the patient according to the hour or
moment when the poor man first experienced his distemper – just
as Tamburlaine's physician seems to have done. The position of
the moon would indicate the time of the crisis, and principally
the nature of her aspects with the other planets would indicate
whether things would go well or no. Thus an astrologer-physician
who was well acquainted with the technicalities of his business
could tell as soon as he got his patient's horoscope cast just what
positions the planets were in at decumbiture and would be in at
any given time in the near future, and he could judge accordingly
as to the sick man's chances for recovery. He might observe, for
example, that at the decumbiture the moon was in opposition to
Mars and squared with Saturn. Such a malefic configuration
would bring about a dreadful illness indeed. But he might notice
that when the critical day arrives the moon will have progressed
to a point in the horoscope where she will be in conjunction with
Jupiter and in trine aspect with Venus. This would be a favorable
configuration, and the patient would doubtless recover. If,
moreover, the physician should discover that a malignant
configuration would exist on the critical day, but should notice
that two days before that time the planetary aspects and positions

will be favorable, he could bleed the patient (in the hour proper for phlebotomy), or administer the proper drugs, purgatives, cooling or hot drinks, and 'comforters' of all sorts, by which he might be able to 'break' the malady before the direful critical day arrives. Such was the method by which the astrologer-physician presaged as to his patient's illness and administered remedies accordingly; and such is the method that Tamburlaine's physician apparently pursued. . . .

. . . Undoubtedly an Elizabethan audience understood by what means these speculations were ascertainable. Possibly the very mention of 'critical day' would suffice to convey the playwright's meaning – as would, say, 'appendectomy' for us today. At any rate, Marlowe – possibly to avoid being obvious – left entirely to his audience's imagination the specific planets which were woefully aspected when the accidental febrile heat dried up Tamburlaine's blood, parched his veins, and so debilitated his *humidum* and *calor* that he was speedily dispatched.

We have, therefore, a direct and an indirect cause for Tamburlaine's decease: his passion and his stars. His malady, involving a portion of his body comparable to and influenced by the essence of the celestial bodies, is initiated by his innate passion, but his illness occurs at a time when the stars, previously favorable to his fortunes, are in some way conspiring against his state. His catastrophe is, therefore, precipitated not only by the 'tragic flaw' in his character but also by his astral destiny.

SOURCE: extracts from essay in *PMLA*, LIX (1944), pp. 696–9, 700–6, 710, 711–12, 713–14.

NOTES

[Abbreviated, with some reorganisation, and renumbered from the original –Ed.]

1. Carroll Camden's articles – 'Marlowe and Elizabethan Psychology', *Philological Quarterly*, VIII (1929), pp. 69–78, and 'Tamburlaine: The Choleric Man', *Modern Language Notes*, XLIV (1929), pp. 430–5 – do not satisfactorily explain Tamburlaine's malady.
2. Don Cameron Allen, 'Renaissance Remedies for Fortune: Mar-

lowe and the *Fortunati'*, *Studies in Philology*, XXXVII (1941), pp. 195–7.
   3. Roy W. Battenhouse: 'Tamburlaine, The "Scourge of God"',
PMLA, LVI (1941), pp. 337–48; and *Marlowe's Tamburlaine: A Study in
Renaissance Moral Philosophy* (Nashville, Tenn., 1941), pp. 174ff., 217ff.
   4. Throughout both Parts not only Tamburlaine but also his friends
and some of his enemies exclaim knowingly that the great Scythian is
fated by the stars to succeed in his conquests. See: *1*: I ii 91–2; II i 33–4; III
iii 41–3; IV ii 33–4; V ii 167–71 & 297–8; and *2*: III v 79–89.
   5. For Marlowe's sources, see: *Tamburlaine the Great*, ed. Una Ellis-
Fermor (London, 1930), pp. 17ff.; H. C. Hart, 'Tamburlaine and
Primaudaye', *Notes and Queries*, 10th Series, V (January–June, 1906),
pp. 484–7, 504–6; Ethel Seaton, 'Fresh Sources for Marlowe', *Review of
English Studies*, V (1929), pp. 385–401; Leslie Spence, 'The Influence of
Marlowe's Sources on Tamburlaine I', *Modern Philology*, XXIV (1926),
pp. 181–99, and 'Tamburlaine and Marlowe', *PMLA*, XLII (1927), pp.
604–22.
   6. Miss Seaton (op. cit., p. 398) points out that in André Thevet's
Cosmographie Universelle (1575) three portents – a man with a spear, a
comet and the ghost of Bajazeth – manifest themselves at
Tamburlaine's death. The last portent in Thevet's account supposedly
terrified Tamburlaine to death.
   7. Cf. Francis Adams, *The Seven Books of Paulus Aegineta*, trans. from
the Greek, 3 vols (London, 1844), I, pp. 229ff.
   8. Henry Cornelius Agrippa von Nettesheim, *Three Books of Occult
Philosophy or Magic*, trans. by J.F. (London, 1651), Bk. I, ch. lxv, and ch.
lxiii. I cite from Willis F. Whitehead's reproduction of J.F.'s translation
(New York, 1897), pp. 200–1, 195–7.
   9. Pierre Charron, *De La Sagesse* (Bordeaux, 1601); trans. by George
Stanhope, D.D., as *Of Wisdom, Three Books, Written Originally in French by
the Sieur de Charron* (London, 1697), pp. 205–8. There existed a
contemporary English translation by Samson Lennard.
   10. For further information on the action of the passions, see
particularly Ruth Leila Anderson, *Elizabethan Psychology and
Shakespeare's Plays* (Iowa City, 1927), Lily B. Campbell, *Shakespeare's
Tragic Heroes, Slaves of Passion* (Cambridge, 1930), and the array of
bibliographical items which they cite.
   11. Cf. Francis Adams, . . . *Paulus Aegineta*, op. cit., I, pp. 225ff.
Adams has annexed to each section of his translation voluminous
commentary which reports on similar medical judgements by all the
authorities from Hippocrates to the late medieval physicians.
   12. *The Genuine Works of Hippocrates*, trans. from the Greek by Francis
Adams (New York, n.d.), I, pp. 202–3.
   13. Cf. Anderson, op. cit., chs III and VII; Campbell, op. cit., chs VI
and VIII; and the authorities which they cite.

14. Robert Steele, *Mediaeval Lore from Bartholomaeus Anglicus* (London, 1924), pp. 28–31. Steele has produced selections from the Berthelet edition of Bartholomaeus's *De Proprietatibus Rerum* (London, 1535).

15. Francis Adams, . . . *Paulus Aegineta*, op. cit., 1, p. 198. Cf. Galen, *De Crisibus*.

16. W. C. Curry, *Chaucer and the Mediaeval Sciences* (New York, 1926), ch. 1.

J. S. Cunningham and Roger Warren
Tamburlaine the Great Rediscovered (1978)

JSC. The integrity of *Tamburlaine*, in virtually a full text, as a two-part play; its diversity and forcefulness as theatre; its resourcefulness as drama – Peter Hall's production at the National Theatre has put such claims as these beyond reasonable doubt. Admirers of the play need no longer suspect that they may be wishfully imposing their cherished views on a primitive original.

RW. To those who (like myself) admired its poetic power but had fears about possible monotony, it provided a shatteringly convincing answer: virtually *everything*, virtually every single scene worked. Everything in this production came straight out of the text, though executed with quite exceptional flair and imagination. Peter Hall seized, for instance, on Marlowe's visual symbolism of the white, red and black tents, and made such symbolism a basic principle of the whole production. In the first two scenes alone, the entire colour-scheme of the stage changed three times – pink for the court of the effeminate Mycetes, blue for the crowning of Cosroe, and gold for the arrival of Zenocrate and Tamburlaine. The production strikingly established how bold colour changes can reflect changes of situation, long before Tamburlaine's tents appeared, themselves vividly and uncompromisingly realised: everything (including costumes, props and furniture) would move from white to scarlet to black, achieving Marlowe's effect with a thoroughness that his own theatre can scarcely have managed. And so with the appearance of each new dramatic group: blazing red and gold for the Turks, whether under Bajazeth or Orcanes; Crusaders' white with black crosses for Sigismund and the Christian troops; cool mauve and silver grey for the Soldan and the Men of Memphis.

jsc. Bold, but essentially simple – even, chastened – contrasts in style: echoing and enforcing the verse, not sensationally distracting from it or fussily refining upon it. In black at the sack of Babylon, as the text implicity requires, Tamburlaine's three main followers were, consequently, in black when they uttered the three-part threnody over the onset of his fatal illness:

> For Hell and Darkness pitch their pitchy tents.

One felicitous extension of the colour-coding marked the ceremonious reuniting of Theridamas, Techelles and Usumcasane with Tamburlaine early in *Part Two*, each of them fully blazoned by one of his three symbolic colours (white, for instance, being particularly right for the cool, restrained Theridamas). And the three followers, dressed in these three colours, formed one of three groups of three during the death-scene of Zenocrate, with Tamburlaine (now white-haired) in white to speak the line

> Black is the beauty of the brightest day.

Essentially true to the text, such effects might have been expected. For me, the real surprise was the lively diversity of the human interplay among the characters between and within the bold groupings, and between them and the audience. Not that simple motives and bold impressions were capriciously embroidered: complications were themselves kept well-defined and simple. Drawn into the web of response and judgement promptly, laughing at the seemly ineptitudes of Mycetes, we were soon involved with the human material – the experience, convincingly grasped, of Cosroe, Zenocrate, Theridamas, each of them creatively conceived. Tamburlaine himself excited an expectant delight from the outset, admiration of his temerity and verve ever ready to broaden into partisan laughter. And this human involvement (as distinct from exploiting the text for mannerisms and jokes) meant that the audience was all the more painfully confronted with the cruelty, wilfulness, even 'madness' of Tamburlaine and the world he creates (or de-creates). We were partisan, to our amusement, and invigorated – to our cost.

RW. All this was acted out on a bare but strikingly designed stage. An enormous golden circular lighting grid was suspended over the whole stage, pouring down light on to another matching circle painted on the floor. On to this floor was projected, before the play began, a map of Tamburlaine's conquests. The whole stage design was perhaps a Renaissance symbol of heaven and earth; more immediately, it provided a focal point for the action of each scene without cramping it. At the back and sides, panels either reflected the current colour-scheme or slid back to reveal huge golden friezes of soldiers or horsemen to suggest armies, notably Bajazeth's two thousand horse, or Theridamas's thousand, whose

> . . . plumed helms are wrought with beaten gold,
> Their swords enamell'd, and about their necks
> Hangs massy chains of gold down to the waist;
> In every part exceeding brave and rich.
>
> [*I*: 1 ii 124–7]

Within so boldly uncompromising a design scheme, the action had to be equally bold and formal, and so it was, utterly symmetrical. But this symmetry again and again reinforced the point of a scene, especially in the first encounter between Tamburlaine and Bajazeth, for me the highlight of the first play, where the staging mirrored every shift and contrast of personality and emphasis.

Marlowe's structure here is strictly symmetrical: Bajazeth is accompanied by his queen Zabina, her maid, and his three contributory kings, Tamburlaine by Zenocrate, her maid, and his three lieutenants; after the antithetical 'And dar'st bluntly call me Bajazeth?' . . . 'And dar'st thou bluntly call me Tamburlaine?', the three contributory kings have speeches which are then exactly paralleled by the three lieutenants'; Bajazeth seats Zabina and gives her his crown to wear; Tamburlaine echoes the process with Zenocrate; the rivals fight off-stage, while Zabina and Zenocrate engage in balanced mutual recrimination onstage. These symmetrical antitheses were not only scrupulously observed, but *used* to sharpen the dramatic impact. Marlowe's requirement of the two thrones, for instance, suggested a nice point: Bajazeth was carried on by attendants, sitting in the elaborate throne in which he had first appeared, 'the greatest potentate of Africa'; as he was lowered to the ground, Tamburlaine hastily adjusted the positioning of his own throne so that it exactly balanced Bajazeth's, in order to lose no advantage in his 'encounter with that Bajazeth'. The others were grouped round them with severest symmetry: Zabina marking Zenocrate, the two maids behind them, the three contributory kings on one side of the stage marking the three lieutenants on the other.

JSC. This scene was a momentous and richly entertaining climax in the absorbing process of Tamburlaine's discovery of his own powers, the evolving of his own style, assisted by the observant, half-parodic mimicry of imperial style, above all the style of Bajazeth. The process blended wit, opportunism, a strutting confidence, and engagingly mischievous provocations to mirth. Tamburlaine had basked in homage from his supporters after the defeat of Cosroe, defiantly front of stage, palms open, drawing audience applause – childlike partisanship on our part, surprised by sheer high spirits and risky verve. He registered a fleeting fear of being overshadowed and out-spoken by Bajazeth, but recovered to match him, his own impromptu stage-director, setting up Zenocrate's throne to counterbalance Zabina's, and evolving a verbal style more than adequate to the challenge. This sense that the early Tamburlaine is inventing his own style, trying out formal poses and gestures, learning to out-Herod Herod, can lie dormant on the page. Awaking it, Albert Finney's interpretation was totally convincing, rich in mirth, playing fluency off against formality: the reader's possible impression of monotonous and ready-made verbosity was contradicted (except, of course, for the powerful adverse criticisms that emerge, to Tamburlaine's own cost, when he, too, hardens into a ranting automaton).

RW. The effect of the Bajazeth / Tamburlaine confrontation was repeated in *Part Two* when Tamburlaine encounters Bajazeth's son; again symmetry emphasised, rather than freezing, point and

humour, as in Almeda's desperate plea to Tamburlaine on being
offered a crown by Callapine: 'Good my lord, let me take it!'
[*2*: III v 134]. But obviously the greatest effect of the symmetry
was to reinforce the large-scale issues of the play, especially
Tamburlaine's facing death or challenging heaven. The placing
of the *three* sons, *three* lieutenants, *three* doctors in the scene of
Zenocrate's death was equally emphatic; and so was the entire
stage picture whenever Tamburlaine appeared in his chariot,
especially during the burning of the Koran.

JSC. Stage area, lighting, tableaux groupings – these all carried a
powerful symbolic charge without hardening into a code which
would unduly limit the play's implications. The stage circle
shaded off beyond the rim of lights, which brightened sugges-
tively from time to time, into *terra incognita.* A stain of blood at
each horrific moment of conquest obliterated the circle of the
known world – which is itself, as Tamburlaine declares, mapped
by those who tread over it and conquer it. These visual
hyperboles matched those of the text, and had a simple validity,
in experience: each atrocity, each imaginative probing of the
unknown, transforms the known.

RW. The lighting from the overhead grid caught and highlit
characters at crucial moments: Zenocrate in her first scene; the
dead Zenocrate and Theridamas to reinforce 'for she is dead'; the
three lieutenants as they emphasised, in extremely formal
repetitions, both Tamburlaine's approaching death and his still
surviving greatness:

> Earth droops, and says that hell in heaven is plac'd.
>   [*2*: v iii 16]

The more detailed effects derived equally from the text: the
panels at the back provided walls to be scaled; the lieutenants
exchanged their scimitars of *Part One* for huge muskets in *Part
Two,* mounted on elaborate stands to shoot down the Governor of
Babylon, who was suspended in mid-air between the back panels;
a trap in the centre of the floor lowered to form a pit either to
dispose of bodies or to provide the repeatedly required flames to
burn Larissa, Olympia's family, and above all the Koran, ten

great bundles of it. Here, especially, none of the stage-directions were shirked, and their implications were developed. Usumcasane's grinning relish of the book-burning had viciously barbaric Hitlerian overtones. The scene posed, in the most striking way possible, the central dilemma of the play: how far is Tamburlaine actually defeated in *Part Two*, how far does he in fact decline? He was placed in his chariot above Usumcasane, who sat by the smoking pit; in contrast to Usumcasane's sadistic grinning, Tamburlaine grimly challenged Mahomet to react. A pause followed, as they all looked up to heaven, waiting; then Tamburlaine quietly concluded, 'Mahomet remains in hell'. But as the chariot was swung round and moved off, Tamburlaine was 'distemper'd suddenly'; the movement after the challenging stillness raised the possibility of Mahomet's revenge, reinforced by the subsequent build-up of Callapine – only to shatter that possibility by Tamburlaine's triumphant routing of him. *Maybe* Mahomet could hear, maybe not – this exactly catches Marlowe's equivocal tone.

JSC. Tamburlaine glanced up, when struck ill, as if to acknowledge Mahomet's intervention – and yet, I agree, the production kept faith with Marlowe's own refusal to allow us the solace of such a simple allegorising of the event. What is equivocal, in this play, is borne in upon us as the collision of powerful contraries – contrary values, colours, styles – with a Titanic figure at the centre who dares to attempt, and in part contrives to sustain within his own enterprise, the stress of these oppositions. The trap at the centre of the stage circle (the round earth's imagined centre) served a range of purposes whose very diversity concentrated our awareness of these contraries that mark the extreme limits of experience. Forming a raised plinth for Zenocrate in grief, it disposed of the dead Agydas, driven to suicide by a stare of displeasure; Zenocrate's death-bed was brought on to the trap straight after the descent of the dead King of Hungary; as the chariot backed off-stage at the end, Tamburlaine went down into the pit that had seen so many of his atrocities, dead but undefeated across her coffin – futile and magnificent. The collisions and transitions were at once extravagant and rudimentary: triumph and atrocity, crownings and dyings, sharpened in the one lens. The pressure this put us under cannot be adequately represented in terms of morality's approvals and disapprovals.

RW. Marlowe's ambiguity was reinforced by pervasive humour, from the very start. When the posturing Mycetes claimed that he might command his brother to be slain for telling him home truths, 'Meander, might I not?', Meander wryly answered 'Not for so small a fault, my sovereign lord', at once making the point and, by releasing the audience's laughter, allowing them to unwind for much of the first play, before making such demands on them later on. Again, Tamburlaine's radiant 'milk-white harts' speech to Zenocrate *appeared* to be sent up by an off-hand 'women must be flattered'; but the joke was used to emphasise the contrasted conviction of the next line, 'But this is she with whom I am in love'. [*1*: 1 ii 108]. The magnificent golden carpet laden with blindingly glaring jewels was both a marvellously concrete embodiment of

> See how [Jove] rains down heaps of gold in showers
> As if he meant to give my soldiers pay!
>
> [1 ii 182–3]

yet the lightly humorous delivery was also part of Tamburlaine's winning over of Theridamas by his magnetic personality. Humour also helped to make clear points of Marlowe's which one can miss in reading. After the killing of Bajazeth's contributory kings, Tamburlaine's three lieutenants romped onstage with their crowns, obviously thinking they were now theirs for the wearing, only to be deflated by Tamburlaine's

> Why, kingly fought, i'faith!
> Deliver them into my treasury.   [111 iii 216–17]

so that he could bestow them at the subsequent banquet, dropping a crown on to each head as the captains squatted on enormous red cushions, all part of the resplendent red-and-gold-covered stage at that point.

Humour was especially used to round the characterisation of the Turks, notably well done by Marlowe himself, and also by Hall and his Bajazeth (Denis Quilley) and Orcanes (Robert

Eddison). The treatment of both strongly recalled how Peter Hall in his Stratford days would mine a Shakespeare text for humorous potential, not in order to cheapen character but on the contrary to emphasise its roundness and humanity. At his first grand entry, enthroned on high, with the world at his feet, Bajazeth didn't need over-emphasis: 'You know our army is invincible' was genially urbane; he was hard put to remember the name at 'one Tamburlaine'; he offered a truce, condescendingly, 'because I hear he bears a valiant mind'; to his contributory kings' effusive praise, he could only conclude, 'All this is true', again genially. All this served to make his fall the greater, both humorous ('O Mahomet! O *sleepy* Mahomet!') and grim also, when Tamburlaine trod on him to ascend his throne.

JSC. With 'Ah fair Zabina, we have lost the field', we experienced yet another switch of sympathy – achieved, like much else, by a quite natural call on our resources of human feeling.

RW. Orcanes was given an even more rounded, expansive portrayal by Robert Eddison, again seconded by humour throughout his dealings with the Christians, a rumpled collection with rouged cheeks, the only characters *overtly* sent up, but that matches Marlowe's own emphasis, as Sigismund breaks the truce in order to 'take the victory our God hath given'. This extended Clifford Williams's treatment of Christian duplicity in his RSC *Jew of Malta*, which culminated in Ferneze's outrageous

> let due praise be given
> Neither to fate nor fortune, but to heaven.
>   [*Jew*, v v 130–1]

– so similar to Sigismund's view. Against the caricature Christians was Eddison's endlessly varied delivery, infinite distaste packed into the word 'Christian', and a hovering defiance (almost like Tamburlaine to Mahomet) in his emphatic 'Thou [*pause, then challengingly emphatic*] – Christ – that art esteemed omnipotent'. His mocking reminder to Sigismund that he wasn't always King of Hungary ('thyself, then County Palatine') was angrily picked up by Sigismund, doubly provoked by the rapid, ironic smile Orcanes suddenly switched on after his speech of defiance. Orcanes and the Turks found Sigismund's 'issue of a maid' extremely amusing; similarly the Christians reacted with embarrassed distaste to Orcanes's obeisance to Mahomet. This clash of political and cultural interests in a less than central scene was exactly the kind of point which Peter Hall used to bring out so superbly in his Stratford days; but the strength of the technique is that it is vastly entertaining and at the same time brings out meaning: Orcanes's superb hedging of his bets after victory ('Christ *or Mahomet* hath been my friend' or 'Yet in my thoughts shall Christ be honoured, / Not doing Mahomet an injury') absolutely reflects Marlowe's ambivalent attitude to heavenly influences in this play.

Elsewhere, too, the bold, uncompromising style of the production encouraged strong performances, often revaluing apparently unimpressive characters. Brian Cox's Theridamas, for instance, was consistently developed as a voice of reason counteracting Tamburlaine's sweeping dismissal of the reasonable. Though echoing Tamburlaine's praise of kingship, he could add wryly, 'Nay, though I praise it, I can live without it'; though impressed by Tamburlaine, he could be daunted by his sheer nerve. 'A jest to charge on twenty thousand men!' At the 'feeding' of Bajazeth, he could voice the doubts of an ordinary man (thus helping the production underline the barbarous cruelty here). 'Dost thou think that Mahomet will suffer this?' and 'If his highness would let them be fed it would do them more good'. Marlowe, of course, is inconsistent on such matters, for soon Theridamas is enjoying the spectacle with the rest. Still, the strength of the portrayal gave Theridamas added authority as he quietly and directly brought home to Tamburlaine the unpalatable truth of Zenocrate's death:

> Ah good my lord, be patient. She is dead
> And all this raging cannot make her live.
> . . .
> Nothing prevails, for she is dead, my lord.
>
> [2: II iv 119–24]

So interesting had Theridamas become that the death of Olympia *almost* came off; but not quite, for here Marlowe's overingenuity and the pale echo (?parody) of Tamburlaine/

Zenocrate seem irretrievably contrived. Calyphas, a powerful, bearded figure, was no stereotype of weakness. 'My wisdom shall excuse my cowardice' was taken seriously, the policy of a rational being opposed to pointless, showy slaughter:

> I know sir what it is to kill a man:
> It works remorse of conscience in me.   [IV i 27–8]

Perhaps the anger he expressed here conflicts somewhat with the jokes about fighting a naked lady in a net of gold but it hung together surprisingly well, and there was no attempt to underplay Tamburlaine's bestiality in his savage cutting of Calyphas's throat.

This brings us to the production's view of Tamburlaine himself. Just before the opening, Peter Hall said in an interview in *The Times* (20 September 1976):

> *Tamburlaine* uses a morality play structure to be totally immoral. Indeed it's the most immoral play before Genet. It sets out to prove that there is no God, no Jove, no Mohammed, no Nirvana. Man, for all his aspirations, ends up with Hitlers, Mussolinis, Tamburlaines.

And yet the production itself suggested something less clearcut, more varied and interesting, and in the process made Marlowe's ambivalence seem genuine ambivalence, not mere fumbling or confusion. Certainly the dare-devil gaiety of *Part One* darkened decisively in the savage scenes of Tamburlaine's feast with Bajazeth's torment and death, and Zabina's madness. Nothing was shirked here: terrifying percussion underscored the braining against the cage; Barbara Jefford's superlative Zabina went mad with harrowing, effortless conviction; 'Is there left no Mahomet, no God?' certainly rang out on this darkened, empty stage; Susan Fleetwood's Zenocrate developed the mood with 'another bloody spectacle' at her entry.

JSC. This entry itself enforced silently the awareness that Zenocrate is herself one of the victims of Tamburlaine's career: the production was punctuated by horrific entries of the maimed after battle, from the deep recesses of centre-stage, like travesties of triumphal arrivals. We were spared none of the consequences

of our impulse to admire the conqueror. Zenocrate's betrothed
staggered on with one arm lopped off to say of himself:

> And let Zenocrate's fair eyes behold,
> That, as for her thou bear'st these wretched arms,
> Even so for her thou diest in these arms,
> Leaving thy blood for witness of thy love.
>
> [*1*: v ii 347–50]

Zenocrate witnesses this; and the stage bears the brained corpses
of Zabina and Bajazeth and a bloody dress from the murder of the
Virgins: 'such are objects fit for Tamburlaine', as he triumphantly boasted, in a climactic moment of stress on our
comprehension. We speak habitually of ambiguity, sometimes
almost as a point of doctrine: it was a truly painful feature of the
play for us to reflect on as we applauded Tamburlaine – not just
the play, but, embarrassingly, the hero – as he left this obscene
stage in triumph at the end of *Part One*.

RW. Zenocrate's repetitions and variations of 'the Turk and his
great emperess' showed how apparent artifice can in fact reveal
intense emotion when delivered with such raw, committed
power; and the whole sequence demonstrated the flexibility of
the production, the bare stage, and ultimately of the play itself.
The stage was at its barest as Albert Finney sat on the floor in the
centre, thinking his way through the 'What is beauty' speech
[*1*: v ii 97ff.]. Far from jumping arbitrarily from one excess
(killing the virgins) to another (feeding Bajazeth), as it can seem
to do when merely read, the speech seemed to lead logically to the
conclusion of sparing the Soldan for the sake of 'sweet Zenocrate'
('That will we chiefly see unto, Theridamas') – to the marked
amazement of the captains. Their reactions (and those of
Tamburlaine's sons) were constantly used to mark developments
in Tamburlaine, as when he ordered them to attack the heavens
at Zenocrate's death, and when, in a shrewd piece of psychological interpretation, Tamburlaine's long lesson in fortification to
his sons was interpreted as a desperate attempt to keep his mind
off Zenocrate after her death. They were amazed too, when he
first hit on the idea of the kings drawing the chariot; this follows
the savage killing of Calyphas, and the whole sequence – the
astounding treatment of the kings, the shooting of the Governor

of Babylon, the burning of the Koran, the daring Mahomet out of heaven – these certainly built up the maniac element with full brute force.

JSC. Albert Finney's delivery of the speech about military techniques – 'his fourme of exhortation and discipline to his three sons' – was an astounding feat of dramatic *invention*. I had thought of it as a diversion, awkwardly stitched in from Marlowe's recent reading of a (known) military text-book. It was spoken rapidly, as if learnt by heart, up to a moment of breathlessness, as a diversion of Tamburlaine's own attention from the fact of Zenocrate's death – and to the incredulous shock of his sons and followers. This incredulity ranked with other moments in the play, giving stage embodiment for the audience's feelings. Cosroe, dying horribly on a full description of the process of dying, was kneeling as he heard, astounded, the bragging celebration of 'the thirst of reign and sweetness of a crown'. And here again, one effect opens the way to another, adjusting our feelings and complicating our efforts to judge: Cosroe's killers knelt in their turn to witness his death, in formal recognition of a momentous human event, for all their outlandishness ('the strangest men that ever nature made'), with Cosroe's curse leading directly into Tamburlaine's seizure of the crown.

RW. But all the time the grandeur of Tamburlaine remained; he never seemed *totally* a Hitler; at one point the chariot moved off, drawn by the kings, stressing the horror; but then it stopped with them in unemphatic sideways positions and Tamburlaine head on to the audience to make the most of the splendid speech about riding in golden armour like the sun. Callapine was set up for a Malcolm-like victory, only to be utterly routed (on-stage) *despite* his prayer to Mahomet and *despite* the possibility that Mahomet appeared to be taking revenge on Tamburlaine by afflicting him with illness in the previous scene. To the end, the ambiguous quality remained: Tamburlaine looks forward to a 'higher throne' and to living 'in all your seeds *immortally*'. Albert Finney's tremendous achievement was his sheer staying power; he not only had the vital animal vigour for the part, but the ability to *keep us interested* to the end, and especially to keep Marlowe's, and Tamburlaine's, options open. He did nothing the easy way,

skimped nothing in the part, and kept to the end that essential
balance between aspiration –

> Come let us march against the powers of heaven
> And set black streamers in the firmament,
> . . .
>   [*2*: v iii 48–9]

– and mortality:

> Ah friends, what shall I do? I cannot stand.   [51]

So whatever the intention, the final impression given by
Tamburlaine was of something subtler, more enigmatic, than a
mere Hitler or Mussolini, making clear once and for all that the
double nature of Marlowe's vision is deliberate and effective, not,
as might have been feared, merely contradictory.

jsc. I can't recall a single arbitrary or capricious effect. Even the
most direct raids on audience response were wholly in tune with
the way in which the production set itself to redeem from
grandiloquent oblivion the diverse and pressing human sense of
the play. An engaging air of teasing connivance – 'look you I
should play the orator', 'shall I prove a traitor' – landed *us* with
the answering of the questions, in our comfortable seats. Praised
by his mother, Celebinus raised a prizefighter's arm to the
audience, to coerce hero-worshipping applause. The cast continuously registered the surprises and the scope of the play they
were in. A comic variant of this was (brilliantly) Mycetes
declaring 'I am the king', only to be suddenly aware of the
meaning of that assertion. And all of this was framed, at the
National, by a kind of 'scholarly' introduction to each *Part* – the
title-page descriptions from the octavos declaring for us the play's
gist, and the Prologue giving his words a corresponding decorum
of utterance. . . .

SOURCE: *Shakespeare Survey*, 31 (Cambridge, 1978), pp. 155–62

3. EDWARD THE SECOND

Irving Ribner '*Edward II* as a
Historical Tragedy' (1957)

. . . In Marlowe's *Edward II* we have the beginning of a type of
historical tragedy not based upon the Senecan formula, although
the play displays a horror more moving than the Senecan clichés
ever could, because it is more realistic. We have in *Edward II*,
perhaps for the first time in Elizabethan drama, a tragedy of
character in which a potentially good man comes to destruction
because of inherent weaknesses which make him incapable of
coping with a crisis which he himself has helped to create. And in
his downfall he carries with him the sympathies of the audience.
Like the traditional tragic hero he is a king, and his downfall is
thus intimately involved with the life of the state, but in this
instance Marlowe gives us a king drawn from the English
chronicles, and in effecting his tragedy he accomplishes also the
purposes of the Elizabethan historian. He interprets an earlier political situation which was of particular interest to
Elizabethans, as we can tell from the many treatments of it in
prose and verse, for it mirrored the type of civil war which they
most dreaded. In *Edward II* tragedy and history are perfectly
combined. Edward's sins are sins of government; the crisis he
faces is a political one, and his disaster is ruin to his kingdom in
the form of civil war.

Marlowe's play covers a long and involved period of history,
from the accession of Edward II in 1307 to the execution of Roger
Mortimer in 1330. For almost all of his material he went to
Holinshed, but he went also to Stow, from whom he took the
episode of the shaving of Edward in puddle water, and to
Fabyan, from whom he took the jig quoted by the Earl of
Lancaster on England's disgrace at Bannockburn. It further has
been suggested that Marlowe's first interest in the subject may

have been aroused by the tragedy of 'The Two Mortimers' in the 1578 *Mirror for Magistrates*.[1] Marlowe approached his sources with a sure awareness of his purposes and perhaps a keener dramatic skill than had ever before been exercised in the dramatising of English history. For out of the great mass of material in Holinshed he carefully selected only what he needed for a well integrated tragedy. He omitted most of Edward's long and involved relations with the barons, his wars in France and Scotland, with the disastrous defeat at Bannockburn. He condensed the events of almost thirty years into what appears to be about one year, although the play gives us little real indication of the passage of time. The resulting inconsistencies and errors in chronology are too numerous to list, but all of Marlowe's manipulation of his sources serves the functions of his play, and there is very little invented matter. By this compression and rearrangement of his sources, Marlowe achieved an economy and effectiveness which had not before been seen in the history play.

In every respect Marlowe prepared the way for Shakespeare's great historical tragedy of *Richard II*, and not least in that he gave a new tragic significance to the *de casibus* theme of rise and fall which we have already noted in the *Henry VI* plays and in *Richard III*. As Edward falls, young Mortimer rises in his place, only to fall himself as the new King Edward III assumes his position. Edward and Mortimer are fashioned by Marlowe as protagonist and antagonist, two parallel characters, each serving as foil to the other. All of Edward's weaknesses are mirrored in Mortimer's strength; what private virtue Edward may have is set off by Mortimer's total lack of it. Those elements which cause Edward to fall cause Mortimer to rise. This use of two contrasting and complementary characters in tragedy Shakespeare was to learn from Marlowe in his *Richard II*, and he was to continue to use it in some of the greatest of his later plays.

We have already indicated that in his *Tamburlaine*, written some four or five years earlier, Marlowe had expressed a philosophy of history which was largely classical in origin. Marlowe, however, appears to have undergone some development between the two plays. The classical substantialism of *Tamburlaine*, with its resulting fixity of character, is now gone, and we find instead characters who change and develop under the pressure of events. This is as true of Mortimer and Isabella as it is of Edward; the adultress and the scheming traitor of the final scenes are hardly recognisable for the long suffering wife and the courageous patriot of the play's beginning. Edward changes and develops under the pressure of disaster, and his brother, Edmund, serves as a kind of chorus to guide the shifting sympathies of the audience. The tragedy of Edward would have been impossible within the substantialist framework of *Tamburlaine*, and only by abandoning it was Marlowe able to attain the stature of tragedy. We may attribute this change in large part to Marlowe's evident growth both in human understanding and in dramatic skill.

In its larger aspects, the humanism of *Tamburlaine*, however, persists in *Edward II*, although it is not so strongly emphasised, and it is tempered by a kind of medieval fatalism which is wholly absent from the earlier play. This is most evident in Mortimer's final speech:

> Base fortune, now I see, that in thy wheel
> There is a point, to which when men aspire,
> They tumble headlong down: that point I touch'd,
> And, seeing there was no place to mount up higher,
> Why should I grieve at my declining fall?
>   [v vi 59–63]

There is nothing here of the Christian attitude which would emphasise man's fall as divine retribution for his sins, merely a calm acceptance of the inevitable destruction at the hands of fate of all who aspire beyond a certain point. What we have is a stoical acceptance of fortune in the manner of the classical historians.

It is largely in this pessimism that the view of history to which Marlowe came in *Edward II* differs from that in *Tamburlaine*, where there are no limits to what the ever-triumphant superman may attain, where ruthless self-sufficiency may create empires, and where human attainments are limited only by the death which must inevitably come to all, and which to the hero like Tamburlaine will come at the very height of his achievement. The flamboyant optimism of the earlier play is now replaced by a more tragic view of life, perhaps most evident in the decline of Mortimer. For as he achieves success his character steadily degenerates. His initial concern for England soon becomes a concern only for his own aggrandisement, and there is no baseness to which he will not resort for his own advancement. When he is cut off by fortune, he has lost all sympathy the audience may have had for him at the play's beginning. Marlowe's abandonment of substantialist fixity of character and his tempering of his humanism with this fatalistic perspective account for much of the difference in tone between *Tamburlaine* and *Edward II*, and they make possible a kind of tragedy which was not possible before.

The tragedy of Mortimer, moreover, indicates some departure from the Machiavellian philosophy which Marlowe had embodied in *Tamburlaine*.[2] Mortimer is an embodiment of Machiavellian self-sufficiency, strength and aspiring will, but he degenerates and is destroyed, and it is because of his lack of private virtue that he does so. Marlowe fashioned Edward and Mortimer as parallel characters, each serving as foil to the other. Just as a lack of public virtue destroys Edward, a lack of the private destroys Mortimer. It is in this emphasis upon private virtue and the impossibility of its divorce from public virtue that Marlowe departs chiefly from the Machiavellianism he had espoused in *Tamburlaine*. In short, although Machiavelli's humanistic non-providential view of history is still in *Edward II*, Marlowe's enthusiasm for the Machiavellian superman is considerably diminished. He has come to see the moving spirits of history not as prototypes of an impossible ideal, but as men who are themselves moulded by the pressure of events, who develop and change. He has come to recognise that to rule well in the secular absolutist state, the Machiavellian brand of *virtù* alone will not suffice. Combined with it must be a private humanity.

Tillyard has commented that there is in *Edward II* 'no sense of any sweep or pattern of history' such as we find Shakespeare's history plays,[3] and F. P. Wilson has made essentially the same observation.[4] Marlowe sees no pattern in history simply because, unlike Shakespeare, he does not see in history the working out of a divine purpose, and therefore he cannot see in it any large scheme encompassing God's plans for men and extending over many decades. Marlowe sees history entirely as the actions of men who bring about their own success or failure entirely by their own ability to cope with events. This is the humanistic attitude of both the classical and the Italian Renaissance historians, and if it is not

proclaimed in *Edward II* as loudly and as flamboyantly as it is in
Tamburlaine, it is nevertheless present.

Tillyard has called the political doctrine in *Edward II* impec-
cably orthodox; but if this were so, it would be indeed strange to
note, as Alfred Hart has pointed out, that there is in *Edward II* not
a single reference to the divine right of kings.[5] Nor is there any
mention of the king's responsibility to God, a cornerstone of
orthodox Elizabethan doctrine. The truth is that the political
milieu of *Edward II* is the same as that of *Tamburlaine*, in which the
unquestioned absolutism of the king is based not upon divine
ordination, but upon human power, and in which the king is not
controlled by any responsibility to a God who will destroy him if
he neglects his duties to his people, but only by the limits of the
king's own ability to maintain his power in spite of any
opposition.[6] This calls for the Machiavellian superman like
Tamburlaine, and perhaps something more, as the fall of
Mortimer may indicate. The tragedy of Edward II is that he is
born into a position where he must be such a superman in order to
survive, and since he is not he is doomed to destruction. Michel
Poirier has summed up the play's content very neatly: 'It is the
story of a feudal monarch who attempts to govern as an absolute
monarch and fails.'[7] But we must note that it is not in the divinely
sanctioned absolute monarchy of Elizabeth that he attempts to
rule, but rather in the powerful secular autocracy of Italian
Renaissance political theory. In his failure to maintain his
position in such a state, Edward loses all of the appurtenances of
kingship, as he himself affirms:

> But what are kings, when regiment is gone,
> But perfect shadows in a sun-shine day?   [v i 26]

In the tragedy of Edward II Marlowe accomplishes the political
purposes of the Elizabethan historian, for in his downfall
Marlowe emphasises the qualities which a king must have in
order to rule successfully in the absolutist state. Some of Edward's
shortcomings in this respect had already been indicated by
Holinshed:

. . . he wanted iudgement and prudent discretion to make choise of
sage and discreet councellors, receiuing those into his fauour, that

abused the same to their priuate gaine and advauntage, not respecting the aduancement of the common-wealth.[8]

It was the 'couetous rapine, spoile and immoderate ambition' of these favorites which alienated the nobles and caused them to rise up against their king. Marlowe thus warns that a king must be prudent in his choice of counsellors. He must further be strong, able to control his nobles, cut off those who oppose him, which Edward manifestly cannot do. But a successful king does not alienate his nobles in the first place, for they are an important bulwark of his power. At Edward's brief reconciliation with the barons, Queen Isabella directs an important bit of didacticism to the audience:

> Now is the king of England rich and strong,
> Having the love of his renowned peers.   [1 iv 368 9]

This theme of a king's relation to his nobles is one of the chief political themes in *Edward II*.

Edward II would be an absolute ruler. He regards his kingdom as personal property which he is free to give to his parasitic Gaveston if he chooses:

> If for these dignities thou be envied,
> I'll give thee more; for, but to honour thee,
> Is Edward pleas'd with kingly regiment.
> Fear'st thou thy person? thou shalt have a guard:
> Wantest thou gold? go to my treasury,
> Wouldst thou be lov'd and fear'd? receive my seal.
> Save or condemn, and in our name command,
> What so thy mind affects or fancy likes.
>   [1 i 163–70]

He places his personal pleasures above the interests of his government, and perhaps worst of all, he has no real desire to rule. He will see England quartered and reduced to chaos rather than forgo his homosexual attachment to his minion:

> Make several kingdoms of this monarchy,
> And share it equally amongst you all,
> So I may have some nook or corner left,
> To frolic with my dearest Gaveston.   [1 iv 70–3]

If a Renaissance absolute monarch required anything to maintain himself in power, it was a paramount desire to rule and a
concern above all else with the maintenance of his power in spite
of all opposition.

Paul H. Kocher has found in *Edward II* two new political
considerations which are not in *Tamburlaine*: 'one is the fundamental principle of Renaissance political science that the
sovereign must observe justice. The second is the elementary
awareness that the nobles and commons are political forces of
prime importance.'[9] Edward's sins are violations of political
ethics which the Renaissance had come generally to accept. The
absolute ruler must rule justly, and this Edward does not. His
people, both noble and common, are a potent political force
which may make its pressure felt in a kingdom, no matter how
absolute the ruler may be. An absolute monarch must be aware
of this force, as Machiavelli's prince always is, for if he does not
learn to handle it properly it may overwhelm him. Marlowe thus
incorporates into *Edward II* some awareness of the parliamen-
tarianism which had been a part of his own English government
for several centuries. An absolute ruler may continue to be one
only so long as he knows how to rule: with strength, justice and an
awareness of both the power and the needs of his subjects.

There are further at least two minor political issues in
Edward II. In one important passage Marlowe disposes of the ever
present problem in Elizabethan England of the relation of king to
pope, and his statement is one to gladden the hearts of patriotic
Elizabethan Protestants:

> Proud Rome, that hatchest such imperial grooms,
> For these thy superstitious taper-lights,
> Wherewith thy antichristian churches blaze,
> I'll fire thy crazed buildings, and enforce
> The papal towers to kiss the lowly ground,
> With slaughter'd priests make Tiber's channel swell,
> And banks rais'd higher with their sepulchers!
> As for the peers, that back the clergy thus,
> If I be king, not one of them shall live.
>   [i iv 98–106]

A second minor issue is the relation of kingship to noble birth. In

Tamburlaine Marlowe had proclaimed that there was no relation between the two, that it was in the nature of every man to aspire to kingship, that only the man of merit could achieve it. In *Edward II* this notion has been greatly modified and tempered, but a slight note of it nevertheless persists. Although Marlowe probably shares the abhorrence of the barons for Piers Gaveston, he does not scorn Gaveston for his lowly birth, as Mortimer does [1 iv 29, 293]. We detect a note of sympathy in Edward's defense of the lowly born against the overbearing barons:

> Were he a peasant, being my minion,
> I'll make the proudest of you stoop to him. [1 iv 30–1]

One wonders why Marlowe insisted that Gaveston be of lowly birth, when the chronicles report no such thing, if it were not for the opportunity which this afforded him to repeat, although in a greatly subdued manner, the doctrine he had so loudly and defiantly proclaimed in *Tamburlaine*: that kingship and nobility have small relation to birth.

In dramatic structure *Edward II* marks a new departure in that for the first time in an English history play all of the elements are completely integrated. Every incident furthers the total effect of the play, which is concentrated in the downfall of Edward. To accomplish this Marlowe had to abandon the episodic survey treatment...found in earlier history plays, and notably in his own *Tamburlaine*. Of the morality influence there is little in *Edward II*, although it is possible to conceive of Edward as faced with a choice between his barons and his favorites and choosing his favorites to his own destruction. There is none of the awareness of error and consequent regeneration which is so much a part of the morality tradition; Edward never really learns the cause of his downfall, and although he undergoes a kind of regeneration through suffering, he is not penitent at the end. There is little thematic statement by means of ritual: the washing of Edward in puddle water, which might be interpreted to have some such significance, was merely rendered literally from his sources. The morality play, which appears to have influenced Marlowe strongly in *Doctor Faustus* had little effect upon *Edward II*.

SOURCE: excerpt from ch. 5, *The English History Play in the Age of Shakespeare* (Princeton, N.J., 1957; reissued, New York, 1979), pp. 127–36.

NOTES

[Abbreviated and renumbered from the original – Ed.]

1. Alwin Thaler, 'Churchyard and Marlowe', *Modern Language Notes*, xxxviii (1923), pp. 89–92.
2. See Irving Ribner, 'Marlowe and Machiavelli', *Comparative Literature*, vi (1954), pp. 349–56.
3. E. M. W. Tillyard, *Shakespeare's History Plays* (London, 1944), p. 108.
4. F. P. Wilson, *Marlowe and the Early Shakespeare* (Oxford, 1953), p. 125.
5. Tillyard, pp. 107–8; and Alfred Hart, *Shakespeare and the Homilies* (1934), p. 25.
6. See Paul H. Kocher, *Christopher Marlowe: A Study of His Thought, Learning and Character* (Chapel Hill, N.C., 1946), p. 189.
7. Michel Poirier, *Christopher Marlowe* (London, 1951), p. 173.
8. Raphael Holinshed, *Chronicles . . . The Historie of England* (1577; 2nd edn 1585–7), iii (1587), p. 327.
9. Kocher, p. 207.

Clifford Leech 'Power and Suffering' (1959)

The Marlowe Society production of *Edward II* at Cambridge, Stratford-upon-Avon and London, in the summer of 1958, has been widely acclaimed, and I wish to take it as the starting-point for a discussion of the play. For indeed it was a production with several features worth noting. First, it was well spoken, both audibly and with a proper feeling for Elizabethan blank verse. It used a simple permanent setting, with entrances at the back and on either side, roughly in the manner of the Elizabethan stage. The acting-area was a fairly steep ramp, which had the effect of bringing the actors closer to the audience. But, above all, this production was characterised by something that we may call 'neutrality'. This is a quality generally absent from twentieth-century productions of Shakespeare and his contemporaries. The director, like the scholarly critic, will commonly try to find something that he can see as the 'meaning' of the play, and he will aim at emphasising the things in the writing that will bring that 'meaning' into sharper focus. If certain passages run counter to the alleged 'meaning', he will often not scruple to omit them. In recent years Shakespeare's histories and dark comedies have notably suffered in this way, and audiences have for some time expected to see not Shakespeare's *Hamlet* but the *Hamlet* that a particular director or actor has decided to give them. But the neutral acting-area of the Elizabethan theatre should give us a clue to the nature of most of its drama. The stage can at one moment represent Rome, at another Alexandria, it can be the open country or a king's palace, a ship at sea or a battlefield. In the same way the play itself is hospitable to all sorts of feelings and ideas that may find expression in the dramatist's words. Sometimes, indeed, the Elizabethans and Jacobeans did approach the 'drama of ideas', and in *Troilus and Cressida* and in Chapman's tragedies we may feel that the action and characters are subordinate to the working out of an intellectual theme. But these are extreme and uncharacteristic instances. At the opposite extreme, and still on a notable level of dramatic achievement, we find Beaumont and Fletcher choosing a particular dramatic action because they are interested in the way in which it will develop towards its point of conclusion: ideas and attitudes will emerge from time to time, but intellectual argument will remain a side-issue. Between these two extremes we have, I believe, the bulk of Elizabethan and Jocobean drama. Initially the playwright is attracted to a story because he sees it as representing, in a particularly striking way, a recurrent and significant pattern in human life. The fact that he sees certain patterns as significant depends on his having a total attitude to the world, a cosmology or *Weltanschauung*, and the stories he chooses will therefore be such as have a general congruence with that total attitude. But it will be the story, the dramatic action, that is in the forefront of his mind during the time of composition. He will not consistently be anxious for it to demonstrate the validity of his thinking, and in

the course of the writing it will often happen that ideas and.
feelings will emerge that are altogether at odds with the initial
intellectual impulse. In this respect he is far from the allegorist or
the writer of a morality play, who is concerned throughout with
the demonstration of a thesis. When he was writing *Edward II*,
Marlowe was, I believe, much concerned with the ideas of power
and suffering and the relation between the two, and it was this
that led him to choose the subject. But during the actual process
of composition what concerned him more directly was part of the
spectacle of human life, the things that happened to Edward and
Mortimer and Isabella and Gaveston. At times the impetus of
their story led him indeed to ideas – like Fortune's wheel, the
power of the Roman church, the 'unnaturalness' of rebellion, and
the part played by Heaven in human affairs – that have little or
no connection with the play's primary intellectual concern.
Nevertheless, such ideas are there and clearly illustrate the
multiplicity of statement that is typical of the drama of the time.
In production, therefore, and in criticism, we should put our
immediate stress on the thing that was most fully and persistently
alive to the dramatist as he was writing, and that is the action and
the human beings involved in it. Each character must be allowed
to make his bid for our attention and our sympathetic response,
despite the obvious fact that we shall be more interested in some
than in others. The Marlowe Society, giving us a performance in
which we felt the diffused vitality of the human spectacle, seemed
to make the play more available to us as a whole than it had
previously been. On the stage, through the persons of the actors,
we could become more deeply aware of the mental pressures
exerted on Edward and Isabella and the rest. The play was their
story, not a demonstration of the Tudor myth or of any private
scheme thought out by Christopher Marlowe. Nearly all the best
plays of the time have indeed this quality of objectivity, of
belonging ultimately to their characters rather than to the
dramatist. And contradictions, or at least dissonances, of idea are
as much at home in this drama as in our everyday conduct and
thinking. When talking about the plays, we inevitably refer to the
ideas that they suggest to us; but we must never forget that a
dramatist, when writing, is normally concerned with such things
only in the second place.

Though we are uncertain about the dating of Marlowe's plays, we can be quite sure that *Tamburlaine* preceded *Edward II*. It is, therefore, worth looking back to *Tamburlaine* to see how even there we have no simple demonstration of a unitary idea. Formerly this play was seen as a highly subjective portrayal of Marlowe's own aspiring mind, with the dramatist exulting in his hero's victories, sharing his dreams of beauty and power, and experiencing something of Tamburlaine's own anguish in the recognition of time and death. Professor Roy W. Battenhouse, however, would have us take the play as a critical presentation of a great disturber of men's peace, at whose fall we should rejoice.[1] To say that both these views have an element of truth is easy enough, but we should also see that they are only two among the many ideas that jostle one another in the play. *Part One* traces Tamburlaine's rise from obscurity to the point where he can decide to make truce with all the world, content for a while with his great power and his possession of Zenocrate. There is no doubt that Marlowe can respond sympathetically to his hero: one has only to read some of the verse to feel how close to self-identification Marlowe can at moments come. Yet it is in this same First Part that we have the spectacle of Bajazeth in his cage, his raging and suicide, and then the madness and death of his wife Zabina. When Zenocrate enters to find the dead bodies of the Turk and his empress, she and her maid Anippe cry out against Tamburlaine's cruelty, and Zenocrate prays that retribution will not fall upon him. And she begs the pardon of Jove and Mahomet for her own earlier indifference to their sufferings. Now we can take Zenocrate as a point of reference here, and we are not reassured when Anippe tells her that Tamburlaine, master of Fortune's wheel, is safe. Earlier, indeed, Marlowe's presentation of the slaughter of the Virgins of Damascus is such as to put a shadow on Tamburlaine's glory. When the first Virgin begs for pity for the town, we cannot banish from ourselves the need to listen. At the end of *Part One*, with Tamburlaine making peace and with Zenocrate as his bride, the dead bodies of Bajazeth, Zabina and the King of Arabia (who loved Zenocrate) are still lying on the stage, a sign of the price of military triumph. If Marlowe had stopped there, we should still feel an ambivalence in the play, an exaltation of the aspiring mind along with a realisation of its destructiveness, a delight in power and a sense of human suffering: we should need to associate the caged and despairing Bajazeth with Edward in the foul stench of his cell, in the barbarity of his murder.

But Marlowe went on to write *Part Two* of *Tamburlaine*, and there the shadows on the hero's face grow darker. He is not outside our sympathy: his love for Zenocrate, his very powerlessness to keep her, his almost pathetic attempt to re-create himself in the persons of his sons, all make him close to us, and at the same time he remains the great conqueror, triumphant in battle even when his last sickness is on him. Yet he falls into self-caricature in his attempts to find a satisfactory objectification of his power. Bajazeth's cage was a small device compared with the chariot drawn by kings that he uses in *Part Two*. Here it is significant that 'Holla, ye pamper'd jades of Asia' became a comic catch-word in the years that immediately followed the first acting of the play. And Fortune's wheel, mentioned in *Part One*, is not now in Tamburlaine's control: the Prologue to *Part Two* briefly tells us that the deaths of Zenocrate and Tamburlaine will be the principal matters of the play, so that from the beginning we are reminded of his power's limits. In this Part, moreover, he can be made ridiculous. Calyphas is no admirable young man, but we see his point of view when he comments on the tedium of his father's victories, on his own uselessness on the battlefield, and on the absurdity of encountering danger merely for glory's sake. When Calyphas has played cards instead of fighting, Tamburlaine comes back and kills him. The dramatist here is careful not to let Calyphas say a word in Tamburlaine's presence: if he had defended himself, he might have produced an argument that would, for the rest of the play, have made us feel the absurdity of Tamburlaine's course of action. As it is, the lonely, rather squalid, but not unsensible rebellion of Calyphas is made to take its place in the dramatic pattern without completely changing the character of that pattern. Moreover, the notion of divine retribution, hinted at in Zenocrate's speech in *Part One* when she saw the dead bodies of Bajazeth and Zabina, becomes more evident in *Part Two*. We have the story of Sigismund, the Christian who swore by Christ to keep the truce and then disregarded his oath for the sake of military advantage: in his defeat the Turks find evidence that God has taken his revenge. And at the end of the play, Tamburlaine has just burned the Koran, has denied the Prophet, and has come near to denying

God, when he is stricken with his fatal sickness: 'I feel myself distemper'd suddenly', he says, sixteen lines after his speech of blasphemy. It should perhaps be emphasised that there is nothing specifically Christian in these passages: Sigismund has sworn by Christ, by what he holds most sacred, and the non-Christian Turks understand that he is punished for that; Tamburlaine blasphemes against Islam, the faith that he would still hold were it not for his boundless aspiration. Along with all this, there continues still from *Part One* the sense of what is entailed by suffering. Marlowe indeed is fascinated by the lengths a human being can go in the infliction of suffering, and also by the limits of human endurance. The kings who draw the chariot, and who are killed as soon as they can draw it no further, are very subordinate characters in the action, but what has happened to them is highly indicative of the playwright's trend of thinking. And Tamburlaine's mourning for Zenocrate and his attempts to compensate for her death, by threatening war against Heaven and by sacrificing men and cities to her memory, give formal expression to the idea of personal loss. What we find in *Part Two* is, in fact, a more overt manifestation of strains that are dimly heard in *Part One*. Marlowe, we can be sure, was originally attracted to the theme of *Tamburlaine* because he was fascinated by, and sympathetic with, the aspiring mind: as he began to dramatise tht story, he was gradually led to an awareness of suffering, in the hero and in his victims, and to a consideration of his inevitable fall. Fortune's wheel, divine retribution, the human inability to shore up the ruins of time – all these things came into his mind, all found their place in the two-part play. The different elements came together in such a way that the total work leaves no simple impression on us. And we should note, too, that the common judgement that Tamburlaine is a giant hero surrounded by pygmies is hardly justified: in *Part Two* Marlowe has gone out of his way to put temporary stress on other figures – notably on Sigismund, Calyphas and Olympia – and the human touch which is given to each of them modifies our attitude towards the hero. The diffusion of interest among the characters of *Edward II* is thus not without foreshadowing in Marlowe's first major play.

But behind *Edward II* there stands not only *Tamburlaine* and doubtless other of Marlowe's work: there is also, it is generally

believed, Shakespeare's *Part Two* and *Three* of *Henry VI*. We need
not consider *Part One* of *Henry VI*, for that is of more doubtful
authorship and largely concerned with material of a different
sort. But *Parts Two* and *Three*, which we might do well to think of
as a two-part play on the 'Contention' between the two houses of
York and Lancaster, have many points of similarity to *Edward II*.
The fact that a number of fairly close verbal parallels have been
noted reinforces the structural and thematic relationship which I
am concerned with here. In both cases we have an action
involving a king unfitted for rule, a rebellion which leads to the
king's murder, and fluctuating fortunes in the civil strife, with
characters on both sides gaining our sympathy in their moments
of death. At the centre there is a man born to a position of power,
but overshadowed by his father's renown, ready, indeed, if only it
were possible, to find peace in obscurity. During the battle of
Towton, Shakespeare's Henry is banished from the field by his
warlike Queen and meditates on the destruction and on the
quieter and more ordered life possible for the simple countryman.
Marlowe's Edward, threatened with Gaveston's exile, offers rich
bribes to his discontented nobles, and adds:

> If this content you not,
> Make several kingdoms of this monarchy,
> And share it equally amongst you all,
> So I may have some nook or corner left,
> To frolic with my dearest Gaveston.   [i iv 69–73]

And, when he is a fugitive and takes his last refuge in the Abbey of
Neath, he imagines the quiet joys of a life of contemplation:

> Father, this life contemplative is heaven:
> O, that I might this life in quiet lead!   [iv vi 20–1]

And in both Shakespeare and Marlowe we find a series of
characters who notably bid for our attention. Margaret the
Queen, without scruple or evidence of human kindness, becomes
an emblem of suffering when her son Edward is murdered after
the last battle; Richard of York, wholly given over to the pursuit
of kingship, has yet one of the most moving speeches in the play
when he is taken prisoner and his enemies gather round him to

mock before they kill; the Cliffords are strong and thoughtless
warriors, yet Young Clifford's lament for his father at the end of
Part Two has so much authority that Professor F. P. Wilson has
wondered if it is a later insertion in the play;[2] Edward of York, the
lucky careless son of an ambitious father, is sketched with
remarkable shrewdness, especially in the matter of his impolitic
wooing of the Lady Grey; his brother Richard of Gloucester,
more ruthless and cleverer than them all and increasingly
dominant as the play comes to its end, ominously tells us in his last
soliloquy of his dreams and his plans. The action, too, is spread
widely through England, with a brief passage in France.

Marlowe, I have suggested, came in the writing of *Tamburlaine*
to a fuller perception of the things that went along with the
possession of power – its fragility, and the suffering that its free
exercise involved. But in *Tamburlaine* he was telling the story of a
man wholly successful in his conflicts with other men: the
sufferings of the hero were merely the operations of time or of
Fortune's wheel or of cosmic justice. Now we can assume that
Parts Two and *Three* of *Henry VI* gave him a model for a play
differently centred. His main figure could still be a man of power,
but of power inherited not won, power insecurely held and ever
limited by the opposition of other men. This entailed his giving
greater prominence than in *Tamburlaine* to the subordinate
figures in the drama, and thus in *Edward II* he came closer to
Shakespeare's normal structural method than elsewhere in his
writing. As in *Henry VI*, the action was spread widely through the
country, from London to Tynemouth in the remote north and to
Neath in South Wales, and, as in *Part Three* of *Henry VI*, there was
a short excursion to France. The effect of this in Marlowe is,
however, different from what we find in Shakespeare. In *Henry VI*
it is justifiable to claim that the diffusion of the action brings more
fully into mind the sense of the nation, and Henry's lament for his
country's sufferings [*3*: II v] constitutes a key-passage for the play.
But in Marlowe the idea of the country and its war is very much
in the background. *Edward II* is a more personal play than *Henry
VI*, and the rapid movement of the action gives us the feeling of
Edward being driven by the course of events haphazardly
through his realm, until at the end he is confined to a small dark
cell in which he is secretly murdered. It is as if all the time that
cell were waiting for him, and his long journeyings were

circuitous routes to that last place of suffering and humiliation. Marlowe, we shall see, makes strong use of the passage in Holinshed which says that he was continually taken, on Mortimer's orders, from 'one strong place to another, . . . still remoouing with him in the night season';[3] these shorter journeys are the last stages of his wanderings, until in the end even that motion stops and he is still at last. This difference is related to the fact that Edward is a more important figure in Marlowe's play than Henry is in Shakespeare's. For Shakespeare, beyond Henry lie England and the doom she must suffer through civil strife. For Marlowe, the concept of England means little – he was, after all, a servant in Elizabeth's secret police – and he cared only for what happened to the individual human being. He was interested in Edward, not as embodying a suffering England, but as a man, a man who had and lost power.

Yet it can be said that, at the beginning of the play, no one in *Edward II* makes a good impression on us. First we meet Gaveston, delighted to be recalled to England on Edward I's death. He makes it plain that he has no love for the London to which he has returned:

> Not that I love the city or the men,
> But that it harbours him I hold so dear,
> The king, upon whose bosom let me die,
> And with the world be still at enmity.   [I i 12–15]

Then he encounters three 'Poor Men' who wish to enter his service: he behaves churlishly until he reminds himself that they may have their uses. Then in soliloquy he thinks of how he may 'draw the pliant king which way I please', and the devices he imagines show how he thinks to exploit Edward's homosexual leanings. When we meet the king and his nobles, we find Edward thinking only of Gaveston, whose worth we have already seen exposed, and the nobles pouring out their venom against him but with no indication that they have the country's good in mind. Then Edward and Gaveston meet, and we see Edward bestowing on him almost any office that comes into his mind:

> I here create thee Lord High Chamberlain,
> Chief Secretary to the state and me,
> Earl of Cornwall, King and Lord of Man.   [I i 154–6]

The king's brother, the Earl of Kent, though as yet wholly on Edward's side, protests:

> Brother, the least of these may well suffice
> For one of greater birth than Gaveston. [158–9]

Then we see Edward and Gaveston laying hands on the Bishop of Coventry, and the king sending him to prison and giving his see and revenues to Gaveston. Here we must recognise an ambivalence in Marlowe's attitude. The conduct of Edward and Gaveston is arbitrary and cruel, yet the references to the see of Rome and to the Bishop's wealth are in tune with the anti-Romish feeling which we find in *The Massacre at Paris* and which would awaken sympathetic echoes in many spectators of the time. As the first scene ended, the Elizabethan audience might well feel in two minds about the King and his favourite, being properly scandalised by their behaviour and yet taking in it a measure of delight.

In the second scene we meet Isabella, and her grief at Edward's desertion of her is likely to strengthen the audience's feeling against him. At once, however, we have a hint of a special relationship between the queen and Mortimer. Her last words here are:

> Farewell, sweet Mortimer; and, for my sake,
> Forbear to levy arms against the king. [I ii 81–2]

We see her kindness for him ('sweet Mortimer') and her belief in having some power over him ('for my sake'), and also her wish for peace. But Mortimer's reply is brusque and has little love in it:

> Ay, if words will serve; if not, I must.

When we see the king and the nobles together again, Edward is confronted with a demand for Gaveston's exile. This king has no concern for his country:

> Ere my sweet Gaveston shall part from me,
> This isle shall fleet upon the ocean,
> And wander to the unfrequented Inde. [I iv 48–50]

He yields only because the Archbishop of Canterbury, as papal legate, threatens to release the nobles from their allegiance. And almost at once, as if this hint of Rome's power turns the scales, Marlowe gives Edward a line of verse that carries our sympathy to him. When Mortimer asks:

Why should you love him whom the world hates so?   [76]

Edward's reply is simply:

Because he loves me more than all the world.

We know what Gaveston's love is worth, yet this naïve utterance of Edward is enough to put us, for the moment, on his side: he becomes an emblem of the human need for love, the very human joy when love seems offered.

No sooner is Gaveston banished than the queen persuades Mortimer, and through him the other lords, to consent to his recall. There is no hint yet of any infidelity on Isabella's part, yet she makes free use of her power over Mortimer, and Marlowe thus prepares us for a closer relationship between them. When the king learns that Gaveston may return, he entertains the kindest thoughts of the barons, and plans triumphs and revels. Then follows a significant conversation between Mortimer and his uncle. The older man counsels peace: 'The mightiest kings have had their minions,' he says, and quotes examples from history and mythology:

Then let his grace, whose youth is flexible,
And promiseth as much as we can wish,
Freely enjoy that vain, light-hearted earl,
For riper years will wean him from such toys.

[I iv 400–3,]

Mortimer replies that he has no objection to Edward's wantonness:

Uncle, his wanton humour grieves not me.

Rather, he will not tolerate Gaveston's enjoyment of riches idly bestowed on him and his mockery of those of more ancient lineage. It is true that Mortimer refers to 'the treasure of the realm' and to the fact that 'soldiers mutiny for want of pay' but in the speech as the whole there is little sense of the kingdom's good. The objection to Gaveston is the common objection to an upstart, and this comes out clearly in Mortimer's final words in this scene:

> But, whiles I have a sword, a hand, a heart,
> I will not yield to any such upstart.
> You know my mind; come, uncle, let's away.   [424–6]

There is no act-division in the early copies of *Edward II*, but modern editors usually end Act I at this point. It is therefore convenient to sum up here our initial responses to the four main characters: Gaveston we know for a rogue, though a lively one; Mortimer is rough and self-centred, responsive, however, at moments to the queen; Isabella is anxious for Edward's love, yet we can see she is playing dangerously with her power over Mortimer; Edward, we should know without history's warrant, is doomed: he can control neither his barons' unruliness nor his own blind passion.

We meet other associates of Gaveston at the beginning of the next scene. The younger Spencer and Baldock are servants in the household of the Earl of Gloucester, who has just died. The Earl's daughter, Edward's niece, is bethrothed to Gaveston: she is a rich heiress, another prize that the king will give to his favourite, and she has the misfortune to love Gaveston. Marlowe does not much develop this part of his story, possibly because to do so would over-dangerously emphasise the homosexual element. Yet we have seen enough of Edward's relations with Gaveston to find this marriage painful. But Marlowe does exhibit more fully the characters of Spencer and Baldock, and he lets us be under no illusion there. Spencer gives his fellow servant advice:

> You must be proud, bold, pleasant, resolute,
> And now and then stab, as occasion serves.   [II i 42–3]

And Baldock replies that he is

> inwardly licentious enough,
> And apt for any kind of villainy.

To find equally frank avowals we must go to Marlowe's Jew of
Malta or his Duke of Guise in *The Massacre at Paris* or to
Shakespeare's Richard of Gloucester. These men are about to
enter Gaveston's service and through him to serve the king, who
welcomes them in the next scene. In that scene we have
Gaveston's return and the immediate outbreak of fresh enmity: it
ends with the barons' declaration of revolt and with Kent's
abandoning his brother's cause. If we disregard act-division, for
which, as we have seen, the early copies give us no warrant, we
can regard this as the end of the play's first movement. From this
point we have civil war, the barons fighting first for the removal
of Gaveston and then for the removal of his successors in
Edward's favour.

And at once there is a crucial moment in the presentation of
Isabella. The king's forces are defeated, and Edward and
Gaveston fly different ways in order to divide the barons'
pursuing forces. Isabella is abandoned by her husband: she meets
Mortimer and the rest, and tells them the route that Gaveston has
taken. This is the first time she has acted against the king, and her
final soliloquy in this scene shows how she hesitates between a
new loyalty and an old hope to regain Edward's love:

> So well hast thou deserv'd, sweet Mortimer,
> As Isabel could live with thee for ever.
> In vain I look for love at Edward's hand,
> Whose eyes are fix'd on none but Gaveston,
> Yet once more I'll importune him with prayers:
> If he be strange and not regard my words,
> My son and I will over into France,
> And to the king my brother there complain,
> How Gaveston hath robb'd me of his love.
> But yet, I hope, my sorrows will have end,
> And Gaveston this blessed day be slain.
>
> [II iv 60–70]

The change of Isabella from the wronged but loving wife to the
woman acquiescent in her husband's murder has commonly been
regarded as a blemish on the play. We should rather think of it, I
suggest, as one of the most perceptive things in Marlowe's
writing – at least in the planning, for one must admit that the
words he gives her have not much life in them. Never before had
he attempted the probing of a woman's character, for the

presentation of Zenocrate, Olympia, Abigail, is for the most part emblematic. He knew a woman's frustrated love could turn rancid, as Dostoievsky shows in Katya's treachery to Mitya Karamazov, and Marlowe, like Dostoievsky, has not let the woman change without deep provocation. We have seen how she has long been conscious of Mortimer's feeling for her, how Mortimer for her is always 'gentle' or 'sweet' Mortimer, how Edward has taunted her with his love for Gaveston and accused her of infidelity. Now she finds herself deserted, with Edward's reproach still in her ears. This is the turning-point for her, though she does not know it yet. It is psychologically right that the moment of crisis should come without her realising it.

In the scenes that follow we have Gaveston's capture, Edward's attempt to see him before he dies, and Warwick's brutal despatching of the favourite. There is an echo of Tamburlaine's blasphemy here. Marlowe's early hero had urged his soldiers to worship only 'the God that sits in heaven, if any god'. Now, when Gaveston asks 'Shall I not see the king?' Warwick replies: 'The king of heaven perhaps, no other king.' The scepticism of the 'perhaps' may be Marlowe's own, but the conduct of Warwick is base. Gaveston is allowed no eloquent last words, yet Marlowe suggests that he has a genuine desire to see Edward once more. There is at least no final stress on his villainy, and it is his killers who shock us and thus prepare us for their later barbarity to Edward. When the king hears of Gaveston's death, he vows revenge and in the same speech adopts Spencer as his new favourite, making him Earl of Gloucester and Lord Chamberlain – 'Despite of times, despite of enemies'. There is *hubris* in this, and yet almost at once Edward wins his first success in the play: he defeats the barons and takes them captive. Warwick and Lancaster are executed, going to their death with brief and obstinate words. Kent is sent away in disgrace, Mortimer committed to the Tower. Here Marlowe was in a difficulty: from Holinshed he knew that Mortimer had taken no part in this battle, having submitted to the king before it took place, but it would not do for him to follow his source in this regard, for Mortimer must throughout be the dominant figure among the barons. So we have the near-absurdity that Lancaster and Warwick are executed, while Mortimer, the most outspoken of the king's enemies and the suspected lover of the queen, is given a further chance of life. This could have been avoided if Mortimer had been allowed to escape from the battlefield and to find his way at once to France. Probably, however, Marlowe wanted to suggest that Edward was a man incapable of profiting from Fortune's momentary favour. This temporary victory of the king brings the second movement of the play to an end. That Mortimer is alive and Isabella's loyalty now doubtful makes evident the continuing precariousness of Edward's position, and it is clear too that in replacing Gaveston by Spencer he has learned nothing.

Kent and Mortimer are soon in France, Mortimer having escaped from the Tower, and they meet Isabella and Prince Edward, who have been sent on an embassy to the French king. Together they plan new wars, nominally on behalf of the young prince. Quickly the scene returns to England, and Edward is defeated and a fugitive. With Spencer and Baldock he attempts flight to Ireland, but contrary winds drive him back to Wales. He takes refuge in the Abbey of Neath, but there he is quickly apprehended: Baldock and Spencer are taken to their deaths, the king to prison. Baldock, whom we first met as a villain in a puritan's disguise, is ready with rather hollow 'preachments', as his captor calls them, when he is led away to death. Marlowe has not much pity for these, though neither is he on their captors' side. In this scene, however, we have the beginning of the king's long journey to death. We have seen how he envies the monks their quiet life of contemplation, and when he hears the name of 'Mortimer' he shrinks and would hide his head:

> Mortimer! who talks of Mortimer?
> Who wounds me with the name of Mortimer,
> That bloody man? Good father, on thy lap
> Lay I this head, laden with mickle care.
> O, might I never open these eyes again,
> Never again lift up this drooping head,
> O, never more lift up this dying heart!   [IV vi 37–43]

When he takes his farewell of Spencer, he cannot believe that Heaven is punishing him:

K. EDW.   Spencer, ah, sweet Spencer, thus, then, must we part.
SPEN. J.   We must, my Lord; so will the angry heavens.
K. EDW.   Nay, so will hell and cruel Mortimer;
            The gentle heavens have not to do in this. [IV vi 72–5]

Yet this denial of divine intervention is also in line with the general trend of the play's thought. There are few references to cosmic powers here: the conflict is on a purely human level, between a king who cannot control his lords or his passions and his unruly subjects who overreach themselves. By the end of the play Isabella has been sent to the Tower and all the rest of the prominent characters are dead, but it is their folly, their mismanagement of the situation, that has destroyed them. The heavens, whether 'angry' or 'gentle', have it seems 'not to do in this'. But the scene of the king's capture is remarkable also for a piece of effective but unobtrusive symbolism. Before Mortimer's men arrive, Spencer has referred to a 'gloomy fellow in a mead below', who 'gave a long look after us', and it is this 'gloomy fellow' who betrays them. The stage-directions call him 'a Mower', and we must assume he comes carrying his scythe. At the end of the scene, when the king has been taken to prison and Baldock and Spencer are about to be put to death, the Mower asks for his reward. He has had only two lines to speak, but his presence on the stage makes it evident that the king is being cut down.

The abdication scene follows. There is no stress here on any sacredness in the idea of royalty, no suggestion of woe falling upon the land because of an act of deposition. But there is great poignancy in Edward's relinquishing of his crown. Like Faustus, shortly before or shortly after this play was written, he wishes time to stand still. 'Stay awhile. Let me be king till night', he says, and then would have the day not cease:

> Stand still you watches of the element;
> All times and seasons, rest you at a stay,
> That Edward may be still fair England's king!
>
>   [v i 66–8]

An ironic touch of legality is given to the affair in that it is the Bishop of Winchester who comes to demand the crown, and, when Edward proves obstinate, he is told that his son will 'lose his right'. He prays to be able to 'despise this transitory pomp / And sit for aye enthronized in heaven'. For a moment he admits his guilt, but at once retracts the admission:

> Commend me to my son, and bid him rule
> Better than I: yet how have I transgress'd,
> Unless it be with too much clemency?   [121–3]

Marlowe could enter fully into the mind of a man whose power
was slipping away from him. He had shown Tamburlaine in his
attempt to build his power on surer foundations than life allows
and in his final vain persuasion of himself that his sons would
reign and conquer in his behalf. Now he shows us a king bereft of
his crown, the symbol of the power already lost. Yet even that
symbol was some kind of protection. As soon as it is gone, Edward
is told of a change in his jailor and his place of imprisonment.
Further changes are to come, and each for the worse. From the
Earl of Leicester he is given to Sir Thomas Berkeley, and then to
Gurney and Matrevis, and finally to Marlowe's fictitious
executioner, Lightborn.

The remaining scenes alternate between the court, where
Mortimer, now Lord Protector and the queen's lover, is all-
powerful but intent, for safety's sake, on the king's death, and the
places where Edward and his jailors are. The barbarity of these
latter scenes makes them painful to read or to see or to speak of.
No other tragic figure in Elizabethan or Jacobean times is treated
in the degrading way that Mortimer permits for Edward. Henry
VI is suddenly stabbed, Richard II dies fighting and eloquent,
Richard III and Macbeth are killed in battle, the Duchess of
Malfi makes a brave and pious speech before she is strangled,
Marlowe's own Faustus dominates the scene in his hour of
despair. The Jacobean playwrights could think of strange ways of
torment and murder, but they never tear at our nerves as
Marlowe does in this play. First we have the brief scene in which
the king, on his journeying with Matrevis and Gurney, begs for
water to drink and to clean his body. Their response is to take
water from a ditch, pour it over the king's face and shave off his
beard. In the last scene in which he appeared, Edward had been
robbed of his crown: now he is further stripped, is nearer the
ultimate humiliation. This incident of the shaving is not in
Holinshed. Marlowe found it in Stow's *Annals*,[4] and it is
significant that he decided here to supplement his primary
source. The scene of the murder is dominated by the figure of
Lightborn, who comes with Mortimer's commission. This is the

professional murderer, devoid of pity but curiously intimate with
his victim. He pretends to sorrow for the king's wretched state,
and urges him to rest. Edward is half-ready to trust him, yet can
sleep only for a moment, his fears returning strongly upon him:

> Something still buzzeth in mine ears,
> And tells me, if I sleep, I never wake.
> This fear is that which makes me tremble thus;
> And therefore tell me, wherefore art thou come?
>
> [v v 105–8]

Then he has only two brief speeches more:

> I am too weak and feeble to resist:
> Assist me, sweet God, and receive my soul!   [110–11]

and:

> O, spare me, or despatch me in a trice!   [113]

And then the murder is done. The manner of its doing has been
softened by most editors, who have inserted a form of stage-
direction not in the early copies. There can, I think, be no doubt
that Marlowe intended the mode of killing to be that narrated in
Holinshed and clearly indicated by Lightborn in his talk with the
jailors at the beginning of the scene. That indeed is how it was
staged in the recent Marlowe Society production, and I think
rightly. The mode of killing may have been one of the reasons
why Marlowe chose this story for dramatisation. We have seen
how in *Tamburlaine* he could hint at something near the ultimate
in human suffering in referring to the fate of the kings who drew
their conqueror's chariot. In *Faustus* he imagined damnation.
Here in *Edward II* he stages the ultimate physical cruelty. He was
a man who speculated on, and brought alive to his mind, the
furthest reaches of human power and of human suffering and
humiliation. These things, he saw, men could do and had done,
could suffer and had suffered, and his wondering mind gave them
dramatic shape. And 'the gentle heavens have not to do in this'.
There is no justice which works in this way.

Not so long ago it was possible for readers of Marlowe, and of
the dramatists who followed him, to look on such scenes as relics

of a barbarous though brilliant age. We have not to-day that way out, for evidence is plentiful that in this twentieth century there are Lightborns enough. I do not think that, when he wrote the play, Marlowe had a moral purpose: he was intent only on the imagining of an ultimate in suffering. Such imaginings are dangerous, for a cruelty grown familiar is the greatest corrupter. Nevertheless, Marlowe has brought before us part of the truth about men, and we must learn to recognise and to control it.

In the last scene of the play Fortune's wheel turns for Mortimer and Isabella, and the young king mourns for his father. This is briefly and almost casually done. It was necessary that the story of Edward's reign should be rounded off, and that Mortimer's stratagems should entrap him. But Marlowe's interest in this was not profound. He had traced with some care the working of power's corruption in Mortimer and the slow hardening of Isabella's heart, but he could part with them as perfunctorily as with Gaveston or Spencer. There is indeed a rather empty rhetoric in Mortimer's acceptance of the turning wheel and his readiness for what may come:

> Farewell, fair queen. Weep not for Mortimer,
> That scorns the world, and, as a traveller,
> Goes to discover countries yet unknown.
>
> [v vi 64–6]

Certainly it would be difficult to find two other lovers in Elizabethan drama who parted with words so chill.

In this play the final impression is of Edward's suffering. It is bound up with power, the power that Edward loses, the power that Mortimer wins, the power he delegates to Lightborn. If a man had no power over other men, there could be no suffering such as Edward knew. There could be other forms of anguish, but not this. And Marlowe, in a story where there was much to interest him, comes into full command of his imagination when he considers the last stages of Edward's journey. The association of the king and Gaveston, the process of Isabella's inconstancy, the barons' resentment of the favourite of humble origin, the slow transformation of Mortimer from a quarrelsome noble to a ruthless autocrat, the changing loyalties of Kent, the lightly sketched relations of the royal and the papal power –all these are part of the play, and they help to give to it the solidity of the world we know. Nevertheless, these things form the setting for the individual Edward's solitary journey to his end. And for Edward Marlowe does not ask our liking: he is foolish, he is at his best pathetic in the belief that Gaveston loves him more than all the world, he is cruel to his wife and drives her to Mortimer, he knows himself so little that he thinks he erred only in too much clemency. There is barely a redeeming moment in the long presentation of his conduct. Yet what Marlowe has done is to make us deeply conscious of a humanity that we share with this man who happened to be also a king. If there were a touch of greatness or even much kindness in him, as there is in Shakespeare's Richard II, we could remember that along with his suffering and find some comfort in it. As it is, we know only that he has human folly and in his suffering makes contact with an ultimate.

There is no theory here which Marlowe illustrates, no warning or programme for reform, no affirmation even of a faith in man. The playwright merely focuses attention on certain aspects of the human scene. In *Tamburlaine* he had already contemplated power, and saw that the spectacle inevitably included suffering. Here the suffering, still consequential on the exercise and the dream of power, is the major fact.

Source: the Ann Elizabeth Sheble Lecture (Bryn Mawr College, Pennsylvania: 17 November 1958); printed in *Critical Quarterly*, I, i (1959), pp. 181–96.

NOTES

[Abbreviated and renumbered from the original – Ed.]

1. Roy W. Battenhouse, *Marlowe's Tamburlaine* (Nashville, Tenn., 1941).
2. F. P. Wilson, *Marlowe and the Early Shakespeare* (Oxford, 1953), pp. 117–18.
3. Raphael Holinshed, *Chronicles . . . The Historie of England* (1577; 2nd edn 1585–7), III (1587), p. 341.

4. Cf. John Stow, *The Annales of England* (1580 [entitled *Chronicles*]; 1592 edn), p. 342: here the incident is recorded with the marginal gloss 'King Edward shauen with colde water'.

David Hard Zucker   'Images of Royal Richness and Private Pleasure' (1972)

. . . Images of royal richness and private pleasure that Edward longs for are the first elements established in the play. Gaveston is himself an emblem of this richness and pleasure. His solitary presence, his rich costume (the splendid excess of which is described in Act I [iv 40ff.]), his realistically evaluated yet enthusiastic response to Edward's infatuation with him, combine to present a complex tempter and an embodiment of Edward himself. Gaveston's opening lines present the kingdom of *Edward's* dream – it is never the real England with its factions, its realities of governing – as a huge playground for king and minion. Edward is introduced through the device of having Gaveston begin his speech by reading aloud from Edward's letter: a device which has an ironic echo in Act v when the king reads the warrant of his own arrest. For Edward the physical kingdom is a place of pleasure:

> My father is deceas'd. Come, Gaveston,
> And share the kingdom with thy dearest friend.'
> Ah, words that make me surfeit with delight!   [I i 1–3]

Pervading the speech is the image of constant sunlight: an image which has a prominent place in Edward's language from the time shortly before his arrest until his death. To be without sun, as Edward is actually without it when he is imprisoned in Berkeley Castle, is to be isolated from the natural condition of kingship, one of the common emblems of which is the sun. For Gaveston, however, the sun is a kind of isolation from the political realities of the kingdom. The barons and the people have only his contempt:

> The sight of London to my exil'd eyes
> Is as Elysium to a new-come soul;
> Not that I love the city or the men,
> But that it harbours him I hold so dear, –
> The king, upon whose bosom let me die,
> And with the world be still at enmity.
> What need the arctic people love star-light,
> To whom the sun shines both by day and night?
> Farewell base stooping to the lordly peers!
> My knee shall bow to none but to the king.   [10–19]

It is profoundly ironic that the sunshine Gaveston associates with Edward changes to the total darkness of the dungeon where the king is imprisoned and where he imagines a sunshine-paradise, a child's world. Ironic also is the fact that Edward himself thinks in terms of the sun-image when he is forced to surrender his crown:

> But what are kings, when regiment is gone,
> But perfect shadows in a sunshine day?   [v i 26–7]

Gaveston's contempt for the harmony of the social order under a king who, unlike Edward, rules not for himself but for the common profit, expresses itself by a hedonism which makes the world over in the image of a dream-like and sensual pageant. The influence of Spenser's allegorical imagery in the manner of the Bower of Bliss [in *The Faerie Queene*] can be seen here. Further heightening the paradisal image is the brief conversation with the three poor men who interrupt Gaveston by asking for employment. They are the physical embodiments of the world he has contempt for. Yet aware of the ways of the world, knowing that 'it is no pain to speak men fair' [1 i 42], he dismisses them by keeping them in hope. The three men – one a soldier, one a traveller, one who simply says he can ride – contrast in their poverty with the splendidly dressed and arrogant Gaveston.

The speech which follows his dismissal of the poor men[1] then builds the contrasting fantasy-world of pleasure:

> I must have wanton poets, pleasant wits,
> Musicians, that with touching of a string
> May draw the pliant king which way I please.
> Music and poetry is his delight;

Therefore I'll have Italian masks by night,
Sweet speeches, comedies and pleasing shows;
And in the day, when he shall walk abroad,
Like sylvan nymphs my pages shall be clad;
My men, like satyres grazing on the lawns,
Shall with their goat-feet dance an antic hay;
Sometime a lovely boy in Dian's shape,
With hair that gilds the water as it glides,
Crownets of pearl about his naked arms,
And in his sportful hands an olive-tree,
To hide those parts which men delight to see,
Shall bathe him in a spring; and there, hard by,
One like Actaeon peeping through the grove,
Shall by the angry goddess be transform'd,
And running in the likeness of an hart,
By yelping hounds pull'd down, and seem to die; –
Such things as these best please his majesty.

[i i 51–71]

The speech projects an idealised sensuality and a paganised paradise mixed with a formalised homosexuality. It is interesting that the idea of *play* is conveyed by the word 'frolic' three times early in [the drama] to heighten the sense of frivolity.[2] The speech combines in an erotic unity the *tableaux vivants* and the royal shows accompanying Elizabethan progresses.[3] The symbolic core of the speech is the story of Actaeon, which has a retrospective relevance to the fate of Edward. The young noble torn to bits by hounds, after being changed into a stag for having seen Diana bathing naked, is emblematic of the king's excess. Edward indirectly applies the legend when, in his forced abdication scene, he compares himself to the royal stag: 'The forest deer, being struck, / Runs to an herb that closeth up the wounds' [v i 9–10]. In Gaveston's speech the legend lends itself to a moral application that would not escape the subtler interpreters in the Elizabethan audience. Whitney gives a moral interpretation to the story and cites Ovid,[4] the classical source on which Marlowe probably drew directly. Whitney draws the moral that obviously applies to Gaveston's sensual relishing of the scene in his mind's eye. After his describing the device – the stag-man is pictured being rent by hounds in a forest with a house in the background – the motto *voluptas aerumnosa*, 'calamitous pleasure', is developed:

> By which is ment, That those whoe do pursue
> Theire fancies fonde, and thinges unlawfull craue,
> Like brutish beastes appeare unto the viewe,
> And shall at lengthe, Actaeons guerdon haue;
>   And as his houndes, soe theire affections base,
>   Shall them deuore, and all their deedes deface.[5]

Gaveston shows here the dramatic outlines of the Vice, but not strictly as tempter. The temptation has taken place long before the play begins, when Edward and Gaveston spent their boyhood together in France. Gaveston is rather the embodiment of the weaknesses of the king. After Gaveston's death, his role is assumed by Spencer Junior and Baldock, who again illustrate Edward's inability to tell appearance from reality.

To emphasise Gaveston's role visually, Marlowe has him stand to the side and observe, unseen, the debate between the barons and the king. His isolated, splendidly dressed figure contrasts with the earnest debate as he broods over the scene – the Vice overseeing the performance of the king. The use of dramatic time contributes to the effect as well. Gaveston has not yet seen the king, but the dialogue implies that he has already made his influence well felt at court. Thus Gaveston's observation of the debate just after his speeches describing what he *will* do is a visual compression of a lapse in time. The dialogue develops strong contrasts. Mortimer (since Mortimer Senior and Spencer Senior are minor characters and seldom speak, I will use the names Mortimer and Spencer only in referring to the younger men) immediately establishes himself as a strong, wilful soldier. His first speech is full of images of war in contrast to Gaveston's images of pleasure. In further contrast, Marlowe presents Edward as both self-pitying and impulsive. The result of his stupid insistence on his right to 'have' Gaveston will be civil war, as Lancaster makes clear. Edward's response to this threat anticipates his behaviour for the rest of the play: he rages like a child that has had its toys taken from it. Ellis-Fermor points out how this childlike inability to think of his kingdom as something beyond a mere gift which commands unthinking respect marks the king from beginning to end.[6] Thus he complains to Kent after the barons leave:

> Am I a king, and must be over-rul'd?
> Brother, display my ensigns in the field:
> I'll bandy with the barons and the earls,
> And either die, or live with Gaveston.   [I i 135–8]

As a physical response to this rejection of all responsibility and to
the sound of his own name, Gaveston rushes forward and they
embrace. The visual grouping – the embrace of king and minion,
the barons gathered around them – makes the thematic contrast
clear: private pleasure and infantile wilfulness opposed to the
public demands and stern challenges of the barons. Both forces
represent a kind of selfishness, a claim for power which is lacking
in magnanimity. The inseparability of Gaveston and Edward is
emblematised by the embrace. The relationship might suggest
the ideal classical friendship, especially as Edward mentions the
love of Hylas and Hercules, and Mortimer Senior tries to excuse
Edward by listing the great minions of antiquity [I iv 393–9].[7]
Such a friendship, however, has already been shown to be
perverted by Gaveston's and Edward's obsessed vision of a
pleasure-kingdom. And now Edward places Gaveston ahead of
himself; the minion replaces the king:

> EDW. If for these dignities thou be envied,
>   I'll give thee more; for, but to honour thee,
>   Is Edward pleas'd with kingly regiment.
>   Fear'st thou thy person? thou shalt have a guard:
>   Wantest thou gold? go to my treasury:
>   Wouldst thou be lov'd and fear'd? receive my seal.
>   Save or condemn, and in our name command
>   Whatso thy mind affects, or fancy likes.
> GAV.   It shall suffice me to enjoy your love;
>   Which whiles I have, I think myself as great
>   As Caesar riding in the Roman street,
>   With captive kings at his triumphant car.
>   [I i 163–74]

The reversals of normal relations between king and subject are
given force by the minion's being *satisfied* with a love that is
compared with a triumph. The excess of Edward and Gaveston is
expressed in visual terms in this scene as they mishandle the

Bishop of Coventry, another sober figure like Edmund, duke of
Kent. Both the Bishop and Kent warn and are unheeded. The
height of Edward's folly is reached when he wishes to rechristen
the Bishop with channel water: an ironic visual foreshadowing of
his own terrible rechristening with puddle water by Matrevis and
Gurney [v iii].

To summarise thus far: This first scene presents Edward's
frivolous immaturity and its probable disastrous consequences
through the interplay of visual and verbal images. Gaveston is the
vivid character-emblem of Edward's irresponsibility. His speech
and his presence, both alone and in relation to the king and his
party, reveal his subtly pagan flavour and his function as a Vice.
The sensuous, erotic language of both Gaveston and Edward
contrasts sharply with the stern demands and warlike images of
Mortimer and Lancaster. Finally, this eroticism gives way to
cruelty in the mishandling of the Bishop, bringing to a climax the
reversal of the natural order. The fact that Mortimer himself
turns out to be a villain, and as such another enemy of the order of
the realm, does not alter his role here as manly opponent to the
king's senseless retention of Gaveston.

The formal accusation of Gaveston several scenes later [i iv]
applies to him the theme of aspiration and hubris in the form of
the Phaethon image. It is a paradoxical point of view in the play
to identify Gaveston by this image, for his aspiration is that of the
social climber, not of the heroic rebel. The animal image – 'Can
kingly lions fawn on creeping ants?' [i iv 15] – deepens the
paradox. Majesty and Love indeed do not consort well, as
Marlowe indicates by a passing allusion to Ovid. It is noteworthy
that the sun image, so prominent in Edward's abdication scene, is
used here to link Gaveston and Edward even more closely. Such
an imagistic linking corresponds to the play's structure, where
the climax – Gaveston's downfall – is the beginning of the end for
the king. The sun imagery, like the lion image, places the king at
the height of earthly rule, the 'body' of the king, in medieval
political theory, belonging to the realm; but his other nature, his
human frailty, belongs to Gaveston, who represents the downfall
of Edward's potential greatness as a ruler. As Warwick says of
Gaveston:

> that, like Phaeton,
> Aspir'st unto the guidance of the sun! [i iv 16–17]

Edward, in this scene as elsewhere before his final pitiful
illuminations of self-knowledge, speaks of Gaveston as the whole
world. His private life and his public duty have merged into the
passion for defending his minion:

> Ere my sweet Gaveston shall part from me,
> This isle shall fleet upon the ocean,
> And wander to the unfrequented Inde.
> . . .
> Thou, Lancaster, High Admiral of our fleet;
> Young Mortimer and his uncle shall be earls;
> And you, Lord Warwick, President of the North;
> And thou of Wales. If this content you not,
> Make several kingdoms of this monarchy,
> And share it equally amongst you all,
> So I may have some nook or corner left,
> To frolic with my dearest Gaveston.
>
> [48–50, 66–73]

The imagery *contracts* the world into Gaveston by making the
enlarging, Tamburlaine-like geographical images of conquest
mean the opposite of what Edward most wants: erotic isolation
from public cares. His passion notwithstanding, however, he still
consents reluctantly to sign the banishment decree. The visual
act of signing undercuts his pathetic attempts to enforce his will.
The scene is full of such irony; it is, in fact, structured on the
opposition between what Edward says and what he does, or is
forced to do. The king is not his own. 'But I will reign to be
reveng'd of them', he says impotently. Then, after his capitu-
lation to the barons, he joins Gaveston in an exchange of pictures:
a stage image which concentrates the erotic theme. Gaveston's
actual banishment is really a symbolic projection of Edward's
exile from power over his own kingdom, for nothing that he does
now can restore the barons' confidence in his capacity for rule.
Edward himself seems to realise this, and he gives expression to
his own uneasy sense of self-betrayal by a conventional but
powerful image of the heart: an image that is strikingly
developed . . . in the scene with Lightborn in Berkeley Castle:

> Rend not my heart with thy too-piercing words.
> Thou from this land, I from myself am banish'd.
>
> [1 iv 118–19]

When Edward enters later in this scene in 'mourning', as Gaveston later does in Act III [i], the parallel in their stage actions again suggests the intimacy of their natures. Douglas Cole comments that the stage image of mourning represents the psychological distance between Edward and his opponents.[8]

The passivity of his mourning figure is reinforced by the verbal images of passive acceptance expressed in the exaggerated passion of the hero in defeat. Typical of Marlovian technique, the speech both reinforces and subtly undercuts:

> My heart is as an anvil unto sorrow,
> Which beats upon it like the Cyclops' hammers,
> And with noise turns up my giddy brain.
> And makes me frantic for my Gaveston.
> Ah, had some bloodless Fury rose from hell,
> And with my kingly sceptre struck me dead,
> When I was forc'd to leave my Gaveston!   [314–20]

Lancaster's comment provides a distanced view of the unmanliness of the speech:

> *Diablo*, what passions call you these?   [321]

Edward's lugubrious solemnity is now converted into an imagined role as a responsible and grave ruler. Imagining the costume and triumphs of his new role as a kind of symbolic answer to the excesses of clothes and pageants of his life with Gaveston, he singles out Warwick as the visual model of the 'new' reign of sobriety and dignity:

> Warwick shall be my chiefest counsellor:
> These silver hairs [*gesturing to Warwick*]
>   will more adorn my court
> Than gaudy silks or rich imbroidery.
> . . .
> In solemn triumphs and in public shows
> Pembroke shall bear the sword before the king.
>   [I iv 347–53]

He calls for 'a general tilt and tournament' [379] as an outward proof of his new self. In contrast to this new image of an heroic

and solemn kingdom, however, is the reality of Gaveston's dress
and deportment (the reality which began as fantasy) which Mortimer describes to refute his father's defence of Edward's keeping
a minion. The foppishness and the exaggeration are the verbal
projections of the kind of dress that Gaveston very likely wore on
stage; but more importantly, the speech emphasises the fickleness
of the dress, thereby linking Gaveston with the excesses of
Edward's fantasies. It is also appropriate that the speech is
spoken by Mortimer, who has exemplified thus far a young, sober
nobleman:

> But this I scorn, that one so basely born
> Should by his sovereign's favour grow so pert,
> And riot it with the treasure of the realm,
> While soldiers mutiny for want of pay.
> He wears a lord's revenue on his back,
> And, Midas-like, he jets it in the court,
> With base outlandish cullions at his heels,
> Whose proud fantastic liveries make such show
> As if that Proteus, god of shapes, appear'd.
> I have not seen a dapper Jack so brisk.
> He wears a short Italian hooded cloak,
> Larded with pearl, and in his Tuscan cap
> A jewel of more value than the crown.
> Whiles other walk below, the king and he
> From out a window laugh at such as we,
> And flout our train, and jest at our attire.   [I iv 405–20]

The contrasts made by visual and verbal images in this opening
act are everywhere intensive. They are also ironic when
considered in the perspective of the entire play. Edward's frantic
and inconsistent behaviour, the profanity of his love, and his
inability to grasp political realities, culminate in the physical
horrors of Act v. The play's first movement is really a theme and
variations: Edward's weakness and frivolity are intensified and
reiterated by contrast with the stern demands of the more
aggressive barons, especially Mortimer, and by the interplay
between the natural pomp of kingship and the private erotic
pageantry of hedonistic self-satisfaction. Marlowe carefully
balances the public and the private, the political and the erotic,
motifs. . . .

SOURCE: extract from *Stage and Image in the Plays of Christopher Marlowe* (Salzburg, 1972), pp. 118–27.

NOTES

[Renumbered from the original – Ed.]

1. There is an interesting analysis of the speech, to which my discussion is partly indebted, by Bent Sunesen, 'Marlowe and the Dumb Show', *English Studies*, XXXV (1954), pp. 241–53.

2. It is used once by Isabella [I ii 67], once by Edward [I iv 73] and once by Gaveston [II ii 63].

3. See E. K. Chambers, *The Elizabethan Stage* (Oxford, 1923), I, pp. 122–212.

4. Ovid, *Metamorphoses*, III, 155ff.

5. Geffrey Whitney, *A Choice of Emblemes and Other Devices* (Leyden, 1586), p. 15. It is interesting that this moral interpretation of the Actaeon myth, imitative of Alciati as are many of Whitney's emblems, does not incorporate the religious allegory of the *Ovide moralisé*, in which Actaeon is Christ. See Jean Seznec, *Survival of the Pagan Gods*, p. 93.

6. Una Ellis-Fermor, *Christopher Marlowe* (London, 1927), p. 114.

7. For a discussion of the play as a 'tragedy of Elizabethan friendship ideas', see L. J. Mills, 'The Meaning of *Edward II*', *Modern Philology*, XXXII (1934), pp. 11–31.

8. Douglas Cole, *Suffering and Evil in the Plays of Christopher Marlowe* (Princeton, N.J., 1962), p. 167.

4. *THE JEW OF MALTA*

Harry Levin   More of the Serpent (1952)

What next? That has always been the crucial question for the creative mind. How can it continue to surprise the audience captured by its early boldness? The Renaissance could offer more in the way of unrealised potentialities, could open wider and smoother channels to innovation, than the age of Joyce, Picasso and Stravinsky. But Marlowe, like the most original artists of our century, strives to surpass himself with every effort. After his triumphant arrival with *Tamburlaine*, all his viceroys – Peele, Lodge, Greene and the rest – duly gained their contributory crowns. But Marlowe's own hyperbolic impetus had carried him as far as he could possibly go on the naïvely imperialistic plane. The next step he took, in whatever direction, would involve some kind of strategic retreat *pour mieux sauter*. Because his works were produced within so brief a span, we are not quite certain which of them came next. Each of them, however, introduces novelties of conception and execution which range them in a fairly logical order, proceeding from simplicity toward complexity and coinciding with the chronological sequence, as nearly as it can be inferred from the external evidence. *Tamburlaine*, the simplest, laid down the outline of a new dramatic genre, the tragedy of ambition – an ascending line propelled by the momentum of a single character, whose human relationships are incidental to his ulterior goal, and whose conflicts are literal, overt and invariably successful. If Tamburlaine had been more evenly matched against other characters, if his victims had been presented more sympathetically, if his path had been crossed by more effectual foes, if Callapine rather than heaven had avenged the death of Bajazeth, *Tamburlaine* would have fitted into a more elaborate and conventional genre, the tragedy of revenge.

That form arrived, not long after *Tamburlaine*, with Marlowe's gloomy colleague, Thomas Kyd, and his *Spanish Tragedy*. It gave to the enlarging repertory a role of comparable stature and much greater emotional range; for, while Tamburlaine threatened and acted, it remained for Hieronimo to lament and suffer, to 'shew a passion' [*Span. Trag.*, iii xiia, 145]. While Tamburlaine was a superhuman antagonist, driven by some sort of inner urge, Hieronimo is more of a human protagonist, responding to the outer situation; but since he is rather the challenged than the challenger, it is the situation that predominates – the vendetta thrust upon him when his son is murdered while seeking to avenge a previous murder. While Marlowe had been concerned with the individual who is a law unto himself, Kyd's concern was with the more general laws of God and man. *Tamburlaine* is an aesthetic spectacle, framed by an equivocal morality, which is flouted more emphatically than it is asserted. *The Spanish Tragedy*, though it is intermittently heroic, is consistently ethical; in subordinating love and war to revenge, it measures private motives against public sanctions. To take the law into one's own hands may be 'a kinde of Wilde Iustice', as [Francis] Bacon defined it [in his *Essays*]; but it implies an ethos, however primitive, which the hero imposes on others instead of rejecting. It was ambition that animated character, on the vast scale of Elizabethan drama; but it is revenge that motivates plot; and plot is the main thing, for technicians like Aristotle. For the Elizabethans, a plot was originally a piece of ground or the design of a house; and Shakespeare is fully conscious of the metaphor, when his plotters conspire in the Second Part of *Henry IV* [i iii 42]. Thence the term was used more abstractly for any scheme, especially for a conspiracy against the established order, as when 'the plot is laide' in *The Massacre at Paris* [i ii 107]. By a later extension, after many such intrigues had been hatched upon the stage, it was neutrally applied to the plan of a literary work.

Thus plot is a moral as well as a technical concept, which presupposes some responsible agent. As George Meredith, in *Modern Love*, discerned:

> In tragic life, Got wot,
> No villain need be! Passions spin the plot:
> We are betray'd by what is false within.

But when the heroine of *The Spanish Tragedy* cries out, 'We are betraide' [II iv 50], the hero is eminently justified in suspecting malice aforethought. So is Navarre, when the same cry goes up in *The Massacre at Paris* [I iii 34]. In short, we are in the presence of the villain – that ingenious theatrical figure who, by pulling the wires of the story, determines the structure of the play. Properly, his name has a low origin in the feudal term *villein*, a peasant or base fellow, which was easily transferred from a social to a moral context, and thence to the theatre. The role that it stigmatises is closely related to that of the Vice, the mischievous tempter in the moralities, or to the clever slaves and parasites who manipulated Roman comedy. Where Tamburlaine enacted the *Alazon* or proud man, your villain must enact the *Eiron* or sly man. The irony lies in the difference between his conduct upstage and his machinations behind the scenes, as it were. But what he conceals from the other characters must be revealed directly to the audience, and this convention tends to be less and less convincing. Thus Richard III, the Shakespearean heir of Marlovian invention, soliloquises at his first appearance:

> I am determined to prove a villain.   [I i 30]

Life would be considerably less tragic, God wot, if villainy announced itself in such resounding tones. The villains of actuality are readier to invest themselves, like Tamburlaine, with the sense of a lofty mission. Few, if any of them are cold-blooded hypocrites; what is false in our world is largely perpetrated by men who sincerely believe that it is true, and launch indignant countercharges at all who doubt the nobility of their intentions. The problem of evil would be no problem at all, if good and bad were clearly labelled in black and white. The difficulties of choice are the source of tragedy. 'In the twilight', Jean-Paul Sartre has reminded us, 'it takes sharp eyesight to distinguish God from the Devil'. To Macbeth, confounding the colours of good and evil, fair seems foul and foul seems fair. When Othello puts his trust in honest Iago, it is the blackamoor who is truly noble, the white man who is black-hearted. Yet when Shakespeare attempted his first tragedy, *Titus Andronicus*, he explicitly painted his Moorish villain as black as the traditional devil. By the time he came to *Julius Caesar*, he had acquired his comprehensive awareness of the endless jar between right and wrong. A contemporary witness, John Weever, tells us:

> The many-headed multitude were drawne
> By *Brutus* speach, that *Caesar* was ambitious,
> When eloquent *Mark Antonie* had showne
> His vertues, who but *Brutus* then was vicious?

Antony's vices would be shown up by Octavius, with the next revolution of Fortune's wheel; and Brutus, retrospectively, could claim to have been revenging Pompey's death. The question of war guilt can be pushed back indefinitely, and the blood feud is handed on from one generation to another. So it goes, with ambition and revenge acting as stimulus and reacting as response. The rising and falling lines are crisscrossed and paralleled in a symmetrical pattern of motivation. Sympathies shift when the erstwhile villain is hailed as a fallen hero, or when the revenger turns out to be a villain. With the give-and-take of injuries, gore is bound to flow in ever-increasing amounts. The ethic of revenge is the *lex talionis*, the Mosaic code of an eye for an eye, a thumb for a thumb. On the grim but equable assumption that 'blood asketh blood', *Gorboduc* sacrifices a life for a life, a Ferrex for a Porrex [IV Chorus 17]. But to right a grievous wrong by retaliating is to provoke the loss of further lives. Furthermore, revengers usually try to better the instruction, as Shylock would, if not for the intervention of a more merciful kind of justice.

> Thou never dost enough revenge the wronge,
> Except thou passe,

says Atreus in Jasper Heywood's translation of Seneca's *Thyestes*; and his cruelty to his brother's children is so surpassing that it brings down a curse upon the heads of his own. Warmed over by Shakespeare, it provides the cannibalistic catastrophe for *Titus Andronicus*. Though Kyd's Hieronimo is more punctilious, he cannot rest until he is 'reuenged thorowly' [IV iv 172]. And Kyd's Soliman, at a similar consummation, rejoices in having revenged a friend's death 'with many deaths' [v iv 148] – a total of thirteen in the play, *Soliman and Perseda*, as compared with eleven in *The Spanish Tragedy*. The fact that nine of the *dramatis personae* do not

survive the last act of *Hamlet* evinces Shakespeare's relative
moderation. There are sixteen corpses in the two parts of
Tamburlaine, not counting the casualty lists from the battlefields.
Apart from the offstage carnage in *The Massacre at Paris*, such as
the hundred Huguenots drowned in the Seine, twenty characters
are killed *coram populo* during an unusually abbreviated play – an
average of one killing for every sixty-three lines.

Numbers, at that rate, mean all too little; it is taken for granted
that an Elizabethan tragedy will terminate in many deaths; there
is more significance in the manner of them. Here the fine Italian
hand of Machiavellianism is discernible; and *The Jew of Malta* is
notable, not for its twelve fatalities – exclusive of the poisoned
convent and the exploded monastery – but for the perverse
ingenuity with which they are conceived and executed. Marlowe
might well be expected to outdo Kyd's theatricalism, to sharpen
the formula for the tragedy of revenge, to discipline its wallowing
emotions by his ruthless intellectuality. But, in the process, he
seems to have learned a good deal from *The Spanish Tragedy*: from
its complicated plotting, its interplay of motive, and above all its
moralistic tone. He was still too much of an intellectualist to let
himself be constricted by this framework, and too much of a hero-
worshipper to let his hero suffer very acutely. Barabas the Jew is
a man with a grievance, but his retaliation outruns the provocation. His revenges, augmented by his ambitions, are so
thorough-going that the revenger becomes a villain. He is not
merely less sinned against than sinning; he is the very incarnation
of sin, the scapegoat sent out into the wilderness burdened with
all the sins that flesh inherits. *Tamburlaine* dealt with the world
and the flesh, but not with the devil; that was to be the sphere of
Doctor Faustus. Somewhere between the microcosm of *Doctor
Faustus* and the macrocosm of *Tamburlaine* stands *The Jew of
Malta*. Contrasted with the amoral Tamburlaine, Barabas is an
immoralist, who acknowledges values by overturning them.
Contrasted with the devil-worshipping Faustus, he is more
consistently and more superficially diabolical. His is a test case
for the worldly logic, if not for the spiritual consequences, of the
Satanic decision: 'Evil be thou my Good' [*Paradise Lost*, IV 110].

In Shakespeare, as critics have noted, it is the villains who
expound free will and take a sceptical view of planetary
influences. In Marlowe the villains are heroes, by virtue – or

perhaps we should say *virtù* – of their unwillingness to accept misfortune. As soon as he is left 'to sink or swim' [i ii 274], Barabas defies his 'luckless stars' [266]. Like Tamburlaine and the rest, he considers himself to be 'fram'd of finer mould than common men' [224]. His attitude toward others is that of Lorenzo, the villain of *The Spanish Tragedy*:

> Ile trust my selfe, my selfe shall be my freend.
>
> [iii ii 118]

This fundamental premise of egoism is stated even more incisively by Richard III:

> Richard loves Richard. that is, I am I.   [v lll 184]

Barabas makes the same affirmation, somewhat more deviously, by misquoting slightly from the *Andria* of Terence:

> *Ego mihimet sum semper proximus.*   [i i 192]

[I am my own best friend.] The articles of his credo have been more bluntly set forth in the prologue, where Machiavel makes a personal appearance to bespeak the favour of the spectators for his protégé. It was a bold stroke, which undoubtedly thrilled them, with a different thrill from the one they felt at beholding Marlowe's resurrection of Helen of Troy. Marlowe based his speech on a Latin monologue by Gabriel Harvey, and both scholar-poets were in a position to know how grossly they distorted Machiavelli's doctrine and personality. Yet, in misrepresenting him, they voiced a state of mind which he anticipated and which Nietzsche would personify: the impatience with words and ideas, the special fascination with brutal facts, that marks the disaffected intellectual. Might could be right, snarls Machiavel, and fortification more important than learning. Marlowe must also have enjoyed the occasion for shocking the middle class, which wanted improving precepts from the drama. Instead, with Caesarian flourishes and Draconian precedents, he propounds a series of maxims which Blake might have included in his 'Proverbs of Hell'. These reflect the English suspicions of popery and of other Italianate observances,

recently intensified by the persecution of the French Protestants
and by the indictment that Gentillet had itemised in his *Anti-
Machiavel*.

> I count religion but a childish toy,
> And hold there is no sin but ignorance.   [14–15]

This last is a Machiavellian corollary to the Socratic equation of
knowledge and virtue. As for religion, it is dismissed by Atheism
with a peculiarly Marlovian monosyllable. Just as polysyllables
are a means of aggrandisement, 'toy' – which in Marlowe's day
meant trifle or frivolity – is the ultimate in belittlement.

  The Jew of Malta, continuing Marlowe's studies in *libido
dominandi*, emphasises conspiracy rather than conquest – or, in
the terms laid down by *Tamburlaine*, policy rather than prowess.
From the roaring of the lion we turn to the wiles of the fox.
'Policy', the shibboleth of political realism, is mentioned thirteen
times, and serves to associate Barabas with Machiavelli. Barabas
is well qualified to speak for himself, speaking more lines than any
of Marlowe's other characters, indeed, about half of the play.
Whereas Machiavel has his 'climbing followers', they have
theirs, from *Tamburlaine*'s viceroys to Edward's favourites; and
even Barabas, in his egoistic isolation, takes up with an alter ego.
The knight of Lope de Vega has his *gracioso*; the rogue of the
picaresque novel commonly squires a fellow-traveller; and
Barabas the Jew finds a roguish accomplice in Ithamore, the
Turkish slave. They are well aware, from their first encounter, of
what they have in common: 'we are villains both . . . we hate
Christians both' [II iii 219–20]. Barabas announces another key-
word when he asks Ithamore's profession, and the answer is 'what
you please' [171]. For 'profession', like 'vocation' or 'calling',
signified a way of life in a double sense: religious conviction and
practical employment. The ambiguity is the key to much
controversy, which dwelt with particular bitterness on what was
known as 'the profession of usury'. Barabas confides to Ithamore
what professions he has practised, starting in Italy as a Machiavellian doctor who poisoned his patients, carrying on the self-
appointed task of destruction as a military engineer in the wars of
the Empire, and reaching the climax of this protean and
predatory career as 'an Usurer'. After mastering all the shady

tricks of all the dubious trades, his culminating crime has been
the taking of interest. Later we learn the percentage: 'A hundred
for a hundred' [IV i 57].

The paradox of his notorious harangue is that it so crudely
expresses a vaunted subtlety:

> As for myself, I walk abroad a-nights,
> And kill sick people groaning under walls.
>
> [II iii 179–80]

And, in the same vein of horrific gusto, further revelations are
divulged. Reality is so callowly assailed that the modern reader
thinks of the so-called comic books. These, we think, are the
nightmares of spoiled children rather than the misdeeds of
wicked men. Yet we know how audiences were impressed, and
that Marlowe again was paid the compliment of imitation by
Shakespeare. The parallel monologue of Aaron the Moor in *Titus
Andronicus* throws light back upon *The Jew of Malta*, since it is
wholly preoccupied with pointless mischief:

> Tut, I have done a thousand dreadful things
> As willingly, as one would kill a fly.
>
> [*T. A.*, v i 141–2]

If this conveys any point it is an echo from an earlier scene, where
Titus objects to the killing of a fly. Though the cross-reference
seems to bring out the worst in both Shakespeare and Marlowe, it
manages to be characteristic of both. The real basis of distinction
is that, while Aaron is merely gloating over his macabre practical
jokes – including one which has been borrowed from an episode
in *The Jew of Malta* – Barabas is trenchantly satirising the
professions and institutions of his day. In sketching such a violent
self-portrait, he belatedly lives up to the introduction of his
Florentine patron and departs from the tragic dignity that he has
maintained throughout the opening scenes. There we hear the
note of lamentation that we heard in the threnodies of
Tamburlaine; but it has been transposed to the minor harmonics of
the Old Testament, notably the Book of Job. When the three
Jews fail to comfort Barabas, he invidiously compares himself
with Job, who, after all, lost a less considerable fortune; and

Marlowe even diminishes Job's five hundred yoke of oxen to two
hundred.

> For only I have toil'd to inherit here
> The months of vanity, and loss of time,
> And painful nights, have been appointed me.
>   [I ii 200–2]

By catching the lilt – and, in this case, the very language – of the
Bible, Marlowe has modulated and deepened his style. Barabas is
lighted with scriptural grandeur at the beginning of the second
act. There he is still in part what Edmund Kean was apparently
able to make him: a sympathetic figure, the injured party about
to seek redress, no Atheist, but an anti-Christian praying to the
wrathful deity of his tribe, a prophet imprecating the avenging
Jehovah. The darkness of the night is accentuated by the flicker
of his candle, and the heavy images are sustained by the tolling
rhythms:

> Thus like the sad presaging raven that tolls
> The sick man's passport in her hollow beak,
> And in the shadow of the silent night
> Doth shake contagion from her sable wings,
> Vex'd and tormented runs poor Barabas
> With fatal curses towards these Christians.
> The incertain pleasures of swift-footed time
> Have ta'en their flight, and left me in despair. [II i 1–8]

This is an extraordinary departure from the swiftness and
brightness of Tamburlaine's forensics. It has more in common
with the speeches of Dr Faustus – and with the lamenting Kyd,
the infernal Seneca, the nocturnal *Macbeth*. Shakespeare's puzzling reference to 'the School of Night' in *Love's Labour's Lost*
[IV iii, 255] may indeed be a side glance at such rhetorical
tendencies. But Marlowe looks upward, with the imprecations of
Barabas:

> Oh Thou, that with a fiery pillar ledd'st
> The sons of Israel through the dismal shades,
> Light Abraham's offspring; . . .   [II i 12–14]

Marlowe was never more the devil's advocate than when he chose a wandering Jew for his hero. His working model was less a human being than a bugbear of folklore, inasmuch as the Jews were officially banished from England between the reign of Edward I and the protectorate of Oliver Cromwell. In certain regions of the Mediterranean, Jewish financiers and politicians had risen to power in the sixteenth century; and Marlowe, whose play has no literary source, must have come across anecdotes about them. In his selection of a name there is a deeper significance, for Barabas was the criminal whom the Jews preferred to Jesus, when Pilate offered to release a prisoner. One of the witnesses against Marlowe's Atheism, Richard Baines, quotes his assertion: 'That Crist deserved better to dy then Barrabas and that the Jewes made a good Choise, though Barrabas were both a thief and a murtherer'. It could also be said that, if Christ died for all men, he died most immediately for Barabas; and that Barabas was the man whose mundane existence profited most immediately from Christ's sacrifice. From the perspective of historical criticism, Barabas actually seems to have been an insurrectionist. Marlowe, in instinctively taking his side, identifies his Jew with the Antichrist. Hence the crude cartoon becomes an apocalyptic monstrosity, whose temporal kingdom is the earth itself. It is no idle jest when Ithamore remarks of Barabas: 'The hat he wears, Judas left under the elder when he hang'd himself' [IV iv 89–90]. When Alleyn wore it with the accustomed gabardine, the red beard, and the hyperbolic nose, he must have seemed the exemplification of guile, acquisitiveness, and treachery.

Nature seemed to be imitating art when, a year after Marlowe's death, the Jewish physician, Roderigo Lopez, was executed for plotting against the Queen. This had some bearing on the success of the play; and, what is more, the play may have had some bearing on the outcome of the trial – where doubtful evidence was strengthened by prejudice. The animus that flared up on such occasions was kindled by the twofold circumstance that many Jews, forbidden to hold property, lived by trading in money; and that the profession of usury stood condemned by the orthodox tenets of Christianity. The gradual adaptation of Christian tenets to the rise of modern capitalism, through the diverging creeds of the Protestant Reformation, has been much scrutinised and debated by social historians. There seems to be little doubt that Jewish moneylenders, whose international connections enabled them to organise some of the earliest stock exchanges, performed an indispensable function in the developing European economy. The myth of the elders of Zion, controlling Europe from their treasuries, finds some degree of confirmation in Barabas.

> Thus trowls our fortune in by land and sea,   [I i 105]

he exults, cognisant that this blessing of Abraham entails the curse of anti-Semitism.

> Or who is honour'd now but for his wealth?   [I i 115]

he retorts, to the assumption that there have been other standards. Yet, as a self-made merchant prince, he speaks not so much for his race as for his epoch – an epoch when consumption was more conspicuous than it had ever been before. This timeliness keeps him from being quite alien in mercantile England. Though Malta was not to be a British colony for more than two centuries, it occupied a strategic position on the old trade routes and in the new struggle for markets. The polyglot Maltese, descended from the Phoenicians, mixed in their Levantine melting pot with Italians and Spaniards, were mainly Semitic in blood and Latin in culture. On their island, if anywhere, East met West. The Knights Hospitallers of Saint John – formerly of Jerusalem – had settled at Malta when Rhodes fell to the Turks in 1522, and successfully held out when besieged in 1565, presumably the period of the drama. Their baroque capital, with its bastioned port, was both an outpost of Christendom and a citadel against Islam; but the spirit of the crusaders who founded it had yielded to the emergent interests of the merchant adventurers.

The starting point of the play is the exit of Machiavel, who pulls back the arras that curtains the inner stage and thereby discovers Barabas in his counting-house. We are not asked to believe that this shallow recess is anything more than concretely strikes the eye. This is a back-room, not the façade of a palace. True, the stage direction indicates heaps of coins; but we are less impressed by them than by Barabas' gesture of dismissal.

Fie, what a trouble 'tis to count this trash!   [I i 7]

We are dazzled, not because riches are dangled before us, but because they are tossed aside; because precious stones are handled 'like pebble-stones' [23]. Not that Barabas is indifferent to them; soon enough he makes it evident that gold is to him what the crown is to Tamburlaine, 'felicity' [II i 51]; and he completes that blasphemy by marking his buried treasure with the sign of the cross. But it vastly increases the scale of his affluence to reckon it up so dryly and casually. Barabas out-Herods Tamburlaine by making hyperboles sound like understatements; he values the least of his jewels at a king's ransom. His will to power is gratified less by possession than by control. In this he does not resemble the conqueror so much as he adumbrates the capitalist; and Marlowe has grasped what is truly imaginative, what in his time was almost heroic, about business enterprise. To audit bills of lading for Indian argosies, to project empires by double-entry book-keeping, to enthrone and dethrone royalties by loans – that is indeed 'a kingly kind of trade' [v v 50]. In the succinct formulation of Barabas,

Infinite riches in a little room.   [I i 37]

Marlowe sublimates his expansive ideal from the plane of economics to that of aesthetics. The line itself is perfect in its symmetry; each half begins with the syllable 'in' and proceeds through antithetical adjectives to alliterative nouns; six of the ten vowels are short *i*'s; and nothing could be more Marlovian than the underlying notion of containing the uncontainable. It is hard to imagine how a larger amount of implication could be more compactly ordered within a single pentameter. Ruskin once categorically declared that a miser could not sing about his gold; James Russell Lowell, on the contrary, has described this line as 'the very poetry of avarice'; and if that be a contradiction in terms, it matches the contradictions of Marlowe's theme.

To pursue this theme, *libido dominandi*, we now take the fox's path through the realms of high finance. Barabas warns us that it is more complex, if less spectacular, than the lion's path across the battlefield:

Give us a peaceful rule make Christian kings,
That thirst so much for principality.   [1 i 136–7]

His policy spins a plot for *The Jew of Malta* which can be pursued
on three interconnecting levels. The conventions of English
drama prescribed an underplot, which is ordinarily a burlesque
of the main plot; clowns are cast as servants and play the zany to
their respective masters; and the stolen sheep is a symbolic
counterpart of the infant Jesus in the *Second Shepherds' Play* of
Wakefield. With the full development of tragedy, there is a
similar ramification upwards, which might conveniently be
called the overplot. That is the stuff of history as it impinges upon
the more personal concerns of the characters; thus the events of
The Spanish Tragedy are precipitated by wars between Spain and
Portugal. Thus, with *Hamlet*, the overplot is conditioned by the
dynastic relations of Denmark with Norway and Poland; while
the main plot concentrates upon Hamlet's revenge against
Claudius; and the underplot – which, in this instance, is more
romantic than comic – has to do with the household of Polonius,
and most particularly with Ophelia. *The Jew of Malta* is similarly
constructed, and probably helped to fix this triple method of
construction. The overplot, framed by the siege, is the inter-
relationship between the Christians and Jews, the Spaniards and
Turks. It is connected with the main plot through the peculations
of Barabas, who is caught up in the underplot through his
misplaced confidence in Ithamore. The bonds of self-interest
connect the central intrigue, which involves usury, with power
politics upon the upper level and with blackmail upon the lower.
Blackmail is the tax that Barabas pays on his ill-gotten hoards;
but his rear-guard actions against the blackmailers are more
successful than his efforts to beat the politicians at their own
game.

     Morally, all of them operate on the same level, and that is
precisely what Marlowe is pointing out. In order to sell a cargo of
Turkish slaves, the Spanish Vice-Admiral talks the Governor
into breaking the treaty between Malta and the Turks. It is not
merely in the slave market, but in the counting-house and the
senate chamber, that men are bought and sold. As for the traffic
in women, Ithamore becomes ensnared in it; soon after Barabas
buys him, he falls into the hands of the courtesan Bellamira and

her bullying companion, Pilia-Borza – whose name, meaning 'pick-purse', denotes the least sinister of his activities. The confidence game that this nefarious couple practises on Barabas, through their hold over Ithamore, was known in the Elizabethan underworld as 'cross-biting'. By whatever name it goes, it reduces eroticism to chicanery; it debases Marlowe's *libido sentiendi* to its most ignoble manifestation. Ithamore addresses Bellamira as if she were Zenocrate or Helen of Troy, instead of a woman whose professional habit is to do the persuading on her own behalf. The invitation to love, as he extends it, is sweetened for vulgar tastes; the classical meadows of Epicureanism now 'bear sugar-canes'; and rhetorical enticements sink into bathos with a couplet which burlesques 'The Passionate Shepherd':

> Thou in those groves, by Dis above,
> Shalt live with me, and be my love.   [IV ii 115–16]

The subversion of values is finally enunciated in *Tamburlaine* when, with the chorus of lesser kings, 'hell in heaven is plac'd' [*2*: v iii 41]. Here the confusion that exalts to the skies the god of Hades, and of riches likewise, is a final commentary upon an ethos turned upside down. When everything is ticketed with its price – an eye, a thumb, man's honour, woman's chastity – values turn inevitably into prices. The beauty of Helen herself is devalued, a decade after Marlowe's apostrophe, with the epic degradation of *Troilus and Cressida*:

> Why she is a pearl,
> Whose price hath launch'd above a thousand ships,
> And turn'd crown'd kings to merchants.
>   [*T. & C.*, II ii 81–3]

The principle of double-dealing, which prevails on all sides in Malta, is established in the scene where the Governor summons the Jews to raise funds for the Turkish tribute. Distinguishing somewhat pharisaically between his profession and theirs, he offers the alternative of conversion, which none of them accepts. When he mulcts them of half their estates, the other Jews comply at once; and since Barabas refuses, his wealth is entirely confiscated. To him, therefore, his co-religionists are Job's comforters; yet, from the outset, his devotion has centred less on his race than on his selfish interests. He finds a justification in observing that Christians preach religion and practise opportunism.

> What, bring you Scripture to confirm your wrongs?
> Preach me not out of my possessions.

[1 ii 114–15]

From one of the Knights, he picks up the catchword that seems to explain the disparity between what they profess and what they really do:

> Ay, policy? That's their profession.   [164]

In endeavouring to recover his lost fortune, he resolves to 'make bar of no policy' [279]. He justifies his next stratagem on the grounds that 'a counterfeit profession', his daughter's pretended conversion, is better than 'unseen hypocrisy', than the unexposed perfidies of professed believers. He admonishes his daughter that religion

> Hides many mischiefs from suspicion.   [291]

His cynicism seems altogether justified when the Knights break a double faith, refusing to pay the Turks the money they have seized for that purpose from Barabas. Their argument, the one that the Christians used in *Tamburlaine* when they violated their oath to their Mohammedan allies, proves a useful rationalisation for Barabas:

> It's no sin to deceive a Christian;
> For they themselves hold it a principle,
> Faith is not to be held with heretics.
> But all are heretics that are not Jews.   [1 iii 314–17]

Ithamore, going over to the other side, can quote this dangerous scripture against his master:

> To undo a Jew is charity, and not sin.   [IV iv 107]

After the Christians have broken their league with the Turks, Barabas leagues with the Turks against the Knights. His fatal mistake is to betray his new allies to his old enemies, the Christians, by whom he thereupon is promptly betrayed. He is repaid in kind; but his Turkish victims have been comparatively honourable; and he ends as an inadvertent defender of Christendom. Meanwhile, by craftily pitting infidels against believers, one belief against another, fanaticism against Atheism, Marlowe has dramatised the dialectics of comparative religion.

Is there, then, no such thing as sincere devotion? Perhaps some unfortunate person, Barabas is willing to allow,

> Haply some hapless man hath conscience. [i i 121]

If so, he does not appear on the Maltese horizon. But by chance, by that ironic destiny which Thomas Hardy calls 'hap', there is one woman,

> one sole daughter, whom I hold as dear
> As Agamemnon did his Iphigen. [139–40]

Though Agamemnon is less relevant than Jephtha might have been, the simile is an omen for Abigail, the single disinterested character in the play, who is characterised by the first four words she speaks: 'Not for my self . . .' [i ii 233]. Her father lovingly repeats her name, as David repeated the name of Absalom. His policy dictates her profession, when in filial duty she re-enters his former house, which has been converted into a nunnery. When she recognises that she has been the unwitting instrument of his revenge, 'experience, purchased with grief', opens her eyes to 'the difference of things'. She now experiences a genuine vocation, perceiving that

> there is no love on earth,
> Pity in Jews, nor piety in Turks.
> [iii iii 54–5]

By taking the veil, she extinguishes the latent spark of tenderness in Barabas, who retaliates by poisoning all the nuns. Stricken, she has the moral satisfaction of confessing that she dies a Christian.

But the pathos of these last words is undercut by the cynical dictum of her confessor:

> Ay, and a virgin too; that grieves me most.   [III vi 41]

Abigail's honesty, in the Elizabethan sense of chastity as well as sincerity, is confirmed by her death; but she finds no sanctuary among the religious. Her innocent lover, Don Mathias, has been slain while slaying the Governor's son, Don Lodowick, in a duel contrived by the vengeful Barabas. This contrivance gives a Marlovian twist to one of the strangest obsessions of the European consciousness: the legend of the Jew's daughter, who serves as a decoy in luring a Christian youth to his doom by her father's knife in their dark habitation. The story is deeply rooted in those accusations of ritual murder, which seem to result from mis-understandings of the Jewish Passover rite, and have left a trail of bloodier revenges – across whole countries and over many centuries – than could ever be comprehended within the theatrical medium. Created out of hatred to warrant pogroms, thousands of lurid effigies swing behind Barabas; and Abigail's sacrifice is one of millions, which have not yet atoned for the Crucifixion. In medieval versions the martyrdom commonly flowers into a miracle, as in the ballad of Hugh of Lincoln or the tale of Chaucer's Prioress. The latter points an old moral, 'Mordre wol out', which is expressly rejected by Marlowe's Machiavel:

> Birds of the air will tell of murders past;
> I am asham'd to hear such fooleries!   [Prol. 16–17]

But Barabas invokes the birds of the air, the raven before and the lark after Abigail has aided him to regain his moneybags. The night scene, in its imagery and staging, curiously foreshadows the balcony scene in *Romeo and Juliet*. When Abigail – who, like Juliet, is 'scarce fourteen years of age' [I ii 391] – appears on the upper stage, Barabas exclaims:

> But stay, what star shines yonder in the East?
> The loadstar of my life, if Abigail.   [II i 41–2]

When Shakespeare copies this picture, he brightens it, in accordance with the more youthful and ardent mood of Romeo:

> But soft, what light through yonder window breaks?
> It is East, and Juliet is the Sun.
>
> [II ii 2–3]

There is another moment which looks ahead to Shakespeare's romantic tragedy; and that comes after the duel, when the Governor eulogises the rival lovers and promises to bury them in the same monument. If this midpoint had been the ending, the drama might have retained its equilibrium; there would have been enough grievances and sufferings on both sides. With the disappearance of the fragile heroine and of the lyrical touches that cluster about her, tragedy is overshadowed by revenge. But we might have realised, when Abigail introduced herself to the Abbess as

> The hopeless daughter of a hapless Jew,   [I ii 328]

that Marlowe was shaping his play by the sterner conventions of *The Spanish Tragedy* and Kyd's Hieronimo,

> The hopeless father of a hapless son.
>
> [*Span. T.*, IV iv 84]

Between revenge and romance, between tragedy and comedy, *The Merchant of Venice* provides a Shakespearean compromise. It gives the benediction of a happy ending to the legend of the Jew's daughter; and it allows the Jewish protagonist, for better or for worse, his day in court. Legalism both narrows and humanises Shylock, in contradistinction to Barabas, who for the most part lives outside the law and does not clamour for it until it has overtaken him. In rounding off the angles and mitigating the harshness of Marlowe's caricature, Shakespeare loses something of its intensity. The mixed emotions of Shylock, wailing, 'O my ducats, O my daughter' [*M. of. V.*, II viii 15], are muted by being reported at second hand. We see and hear, we recall and recoil from the unholy joy of Barabas:

> O girl! O gold! O beauty! O my bliss!   [II i 57]

If the comparison is not with Shakespeare but with Marlowe's earlier writing, *The Jew of Malta* registers enormous gains in flexibility. Except when Barabas mutters to himself in a *lingua franca* of Spanish and Italian, the diction is plainer and much saltier. The average length of an individual speech in no more than 2.8 lines, as differentiated from the second part of *Tamburlaine*, where it runs to 6.3. This implies, theatrically speaking, more than twice as many cues in the later play, with a consequent thickening of the dialogue and a general quickening of the action. It follows that there are fewer monologues, although Barabas delivers a number of them – in that Biblical vein which transforms the basic modes of Tamburlaine's rhetoric, the threat and the plea, into the curse, the jeremiad, the prophecy. The Prophets had spoken English blank verse in Greene and Lodge's *Looking-Glass for London*, as had the Psalmist in Peele's *David and Bethsabe*. But *The Jew of Malta* requires some means of private comment, as well as public speech, to express the cross-purposes between policy and profession, deeds and words. It leans much more upon the soliloquy, which the extroverted Tamburlaine hardly needed, and its characteristic mode is the aside. Marlowe did not invent this simplistic device; actors had voiced their thoughts to audiences before they had exchanged them with each other; and characterisation of the villain was, for obvious reasons, peculiarly dependent upon that convention. It could not be disregarded by a playwright who had to guide introverted characters through the Machiavellian province of false declarations and unvoiced intentions. '*I must dissemble*', says Barabas [IV i 50], and the italics [of the Quarto] alert the reader to what the spectator feels when the spoken words are aimed at him in a stage whisper. The actor is professionally a dissembler, etymologically a hypocrite. The histrionics of Barabas are not confined to his role in the disguise of a French musician. Except for his unwarranted confidences to his daughter and to his slave, he is always acting, always disguised. We, who overhear his asides and soliloquies, are his only trustworthy confidants. We are therefore in collusion with Barabas. We revel in his malice, we share his guilt. We are the 'worldlings' to whom he addresses himself [V v 52].

This understanding is the framework of Marlowe's irony. When Barabas is first interrogated by the Knights, his replies are deliberately naïve; we know that he knows what they want from him; but he dissembles his shrewdness, plays the *Eiron*, and fences with the Governor. Often he utters no more than a line at a time, and engages in stichomythy – in capping line for line – with his interlocutors. Repartee is facilitated by Marlowe's increasing willingness to break off a speech and start upon another at the caesura, without interrupting the rhythm of the blank verse. Speeches of less than a line are still rather tentative, and prose is a more favourable climate than verse for the cultivation of pithy dialogue. Possibly the most striking advance beyond *Tamburlaine* is the transition from a voluble to a laconic style, from Ciceronian periods to Senecan aphorisms. Effects depend, not upon saying everything, but upon keeping certain things unsaid. The climax of ironic dissimulation comes with the scene where the two Friars 'exclaim against' Barabas [III vi 46]. In their association with the nuns, Marlowe has lost no opportunity for anti-clerical innuendo; now the 'two religious Caterpillars' hold the upper hand over Barabas, since they have learned of his crimes from the dying Abigail; but since they are bound by the seal of confession, they cannot lodge a downright accusation. He has both these considerations in mind, as do we, when he parries their hesitating denunciations.

> Thou art a – ,

says one Friar; and Barabas admits what is common knowledge, that he is a Jew and a usurer.

> Thou hast committed – ,

says the other, and again the admission is an evasion:

> Fornication? but that was in another country:
> And besides, the wench is dead.
>
> > [IV i 33, 42–4]

For anyone else there might be, for others there have been, romance and even tragedy in the reminiscence. For Barabas it is simply an alibi, a statute of limitations. He is content to remind the Friars, with a legalistic shrug, that the Seventh Command-

ment is not to be taken as seriously as the Sixth. Deploring his
callousness, we are tempted to admire his cheerful candour, and
are almost touched by the emotional poverty of his life.

At this impasse he takes the initiative, with the dissembling
announcement that he stands ready to be converted. His
renunciation is actually a temptation, to which the Friars easily
succumb, enticed by his Marlovian catalogue of the worldly
goods he professes to renounce.

> Warehouses stuff'd with spices and with drugs,
> Whole chests of gold in bullion and in coin,
> . . .
> All this I'll give to some religious house,
>
> > [IV i 67–8, 78]

Pretending to be persuaded, it is he who persuades and they who
do the courting. Their courtship is the most grotesque of
Marlowe's variations on the tune of 'Come live with me and be
my love'. The vistas of opulence that Barabas has just exhibited
contrast with the cheerless asceticism of their monkish vows.
While Barabas ironically aspires toward grace, they fall into the
trap of worldliness that he has so lavishly baited for them.

> You shall convert me, you shall have all my wealth,

he tells one. Whereupon the other tells him,

> Oh Barabas, their laws are strict!
> . . .
> They wear no shirts, and they go bare-foot too.

and is told in turn,

> You shall confess me, and have all my goods.   [84–9]

By playing off one monastic order against the other, he divides
and conquers. He murders one Friar and pins the blame on the
other, with a threadbare trick which Marlowe may have
encountered in a jestbook. The fact that the same trick occurs in a
play of Thomas Heywood's, *The Captives*, plus the fact that
Heywood sponsored the publication of *The Jew of Malta*, has led

some commentators to infer that he may have added these scenes to Marlowe's play. It would seem more probable that *The Jew of Malta* influenced *The Captives*. Clearly it influenced *Titus Andronicus*, where the jest of a leaning corpse is mentioned by Aaron in his imitative monologue. Since we owe the text of *The Jew of Malta* to Heywood's quarto of 1633, published more than forty years after the drama was written, it may well have been retouched here and there. But the Friars are integral to Marlowe's design; Abigail's death would go unrevenged without them, and Machiavel's contempt for the clergy would go undemonstrated. Furthermore, in the canon of Heywood's extant works, there is no passage which is comparably sharp in tone or audacious in matter. Closer affinities might be sought in the sardonic tragi-comedy of Marston, or in the baroque tragedy of Webster.

It seems wiser – and is certainly more rewarding – to accept *The Jew of Malta* as an artistic whole, noting its incongruities and tensions, than to take the easy course of ruling them out as interpolations by a later hand. Criticism is warranted in stressing the disproportion between the two halves of the play; but the very essence of Marlowe's art, to sum it up with a Baconian phrase, is 'strangeness in the proportions'. The 'extreme revenge' [III iii 48] of Barabas runs away with the play, egregiously transcending the norms of vindictiveness; but it is the nature of the Marlovian protagonist to press whatever he undertakes to its uttermost extreme. As Barabas progresses, the Old Testament recedes into the background, and the foreground is dominated by *The Prince*. Effortlessly, his losses of the first act are made good by the second; and the third repays, with compound interest, his grudge against the Governor. Here, with the disaffection of Abigail, he abandons any claim upon our sympathy and vies with his new accomplice, Ithamore, in the *quid pro quo* of sheer malignity. In the fourth act he is blackmailed, not only by Bellamira and her bravo, but by the pair of Friars. His countermeasures lead him, in the fifth act, upward and onward into the realms of the higher blackmail, where Turks demand tribute from Christians and Christians from Jews.

> Why, was there ever seen such villany,
> So neatly plotted, and so well perform'd? [III iii 1–2]

Ithamore asks the audience. Yet who should know better than he, that the performance of each plot somehow leaves a loose end? Murder is not postponed from act to act, as it is in the bungling *Arden of Feversham*; rather, as in a well-conducted detective story, every crime is its own potential nemesis. Barabas does not count on Abigail's love for Mathias when he calculates the killing of Lodowick. He does away with her and her sister religionists without expecting the Friars to inherit his guilty secret. When he silences them, he comes to grips with the complicity of Ithamore and with the extortions of Pilia-Borza. In settling their business, he incriminates himself; and, though he survives to betray the entire island, his next and final treason is self-betrayal.

To show the betrayer betrayed, the engineer hoist in his petard, the 'reaching thought' [I ii 226] of Barabas overreached, is the irony of ironies. Marlowe's stage management moves toward a *coup de théâtre*, a machine which is worthy of all the machination that has gone before. Barabas can kill with with a poisoned nosegay, can simulate death with 'Poppy and cold mandrake juice' [v i 81], and – thrown to the vultures from the walls of the town – can let the enemy in through the underground vaults, the subterranean corridors of intrigue. His hellish broth for the nuns is brewed from the recipes of the Borgias, seasoned with 'all the poisons of the Stygian pool' [III iv 103], and stirred with imprecations from the classics. 'Was ever pot of rice-porridge so saucy?' comments Ithamore [108]. The sauce of the jest is that poetic justice takes, for Barabas, the shape of a boiling pot. He is shown '*above*' – from which coign of vantage he likes to look down on the havoc he engineers – '*very busy*' in his 'dainty gallery' [v v 1–13, 35], explaining his cable and trap-door to the Governor. When the signal is given, and the monastery blown up with the Turks inside, it is Barabas who falls through the trap. The curtain below is flung open, '*A Caldron discovered*', and in it Barabas fuming and hissing his last. He implores the Christians to help him, but they are 'pitiless' [v v 75]. Once he merely professed 'a burning zeal' [II iii 91], but now he feels 'the extremity of heat' [v v 92]. He dies cursing. The steaming caldron in which he expires, like the 'hell-mouth' of *Doctor Faustus*, was a property in the lists of Alleyn's company. But, like the human pie in *Titus Andronicus*, today it excites more ridicule than terror. In the age of *Macbeth*, however, a caldron was no mere object of domestic utility. It was the standard punishment for the poisoner. It had betokened a city of abomination in the flaming vision of Ezekiel. And in the *Emblems* of Geffrey Whitney, printed in 1586, it illustrates the humbling of aspiration and amplifies the gospel of Luke [xviii 14], *Qui se exaltat, humiliabitur*:

> The boyling brothe, aboue the brinke doth swell,
>   And comes to naughte, with falling in the fire:
> So reaching heads that thinke them neuer well,
> Doe headlong fall, for pride hathe ofte that hire:
>   And where before their frendes they did dispise,
>   Nowe beinge falne, none helpe them for to rise.

Barabas stews in the juice of his tragic pride, foiled and foiled again, like the melodramatic villain he has become. Malta is preserved; murder will out; crime does not pay; the reward of sin is death; vengeance belongs to the Lord. This is exemplary but commonplace doctrine, and we have clambered through a labyrinth to reach it. Can Machiavel's introductory proverbs of hell be conclusively refuted by such copybook didacticism? Barabas is a consistent Machiavellian when, at the very pinnacle of his career, he soliloquises on Turks and Christians:

> Thus loving neither, will I live with both,
> Making a profit of my policy.   [v ii 113–14]

The words 'live' and 'love' jingle strangely amid this concentration of cold antipathy. Yet they are in character – or rather, Barabas steps out of it at the crisis, when he wilfully departs from the teaching of his master. Machiavelli, in his chapter on cruelty and pity, had counselled: 'Both dowbtlesse are necessarie, but seinge it is harde to make them drawe both in one yoake, I thinke it more safetie (seinge one must needes be wantinge) to be feared then loved, for this maybe boldlie sayde of men, that they are vngratefull, inconstante, discemblers, fearefull of dayngers, covetous of gayne.' This may unquestionably be said of Barabas, and he is all too painfully conscious of it; he is conscious of being hated, and wants to be loved. To be loved – yes, that desire is his secret shame, the tragic weakness of a character whose wickedness is otherwise unflawed. His hatred is the bravado of the outsider whom nobody loves, and his revenges are compensatory efforts to supply people with good reasons for hating him. Poor Barabas, poor old rich man! That he should end by trusting anybody, least of all the one man who wronged him in the beginning! He has authority now, but Malta hates him. Instead of playing upon the fear of the islanders, he proposes to earn their gratitude by ridding them of the Turks. As Governor, he is anxious to make his peace with the former Governor, to whom he says: 'Live with me' [v ii 99]. It is worse than a crime, as Talleyrand would say; it is a blunder.

The original miscalculation of Barabas was his failure to reckon with love. Then Abigail, sincerely professing the vows she had taken before out of policy, declared that she had found no love on earth. Having lost her, holding himself apart from the 'multitude' of Jews, Barabas must be his own sole friend: 'I'll look unto my self' [i i 176]. Yet he would like to win friends; he needs a confidant; and for a while he views Ithamore, much too trustingly, as his 'second self' [iii iv 15]. It is the dilemma of *unus contra mundum*, of the egoist who cannot live with others or without them. Since he conspires against them, they are right to combine against him, but their combinations frequently break down, for each of them is equally self-centred.

For, so I live, perish may all the world.   [v v 11]

When every man looks out for himself alone and looks with suspicion on every other man, the ego is isolated within a vicious circle of mutual distrust. The moral of the drama could be the motto of Melville's *Confidence-Man*, 'No Trust'. Without trust, sanctions are only invoked to be violated; men live together, not in a commonwealth, but in an acquisitive society, where they behave like wolves to their fellow men. Barabas, who is fond of comparing himself to various beasts of prey, announces in his most typical aside:

Now will I show myself to have more of the Serpent than the dove; that is, more knave than fool.   [ii iii 36–8]

This is taking in vain the injunction of Jesus, when he sent forth the Apostles 'as sheep in the middest of wovlves' [Matthew, x 16]. They were enjoined to remain as innocent as doves, but also to become as wise as serpents, so that they might distinguish between vice and virtue. Bacon amplified this precept in his *Meditationes Sacrae*, but in his career he did not exemplify it very happily. The innocence of the dove can scarcely preserve itself unless it is armed with the wisdom of the serpent; but it is difficult to acquire such worldly wisdom without being somewhat corrupted in the process. *Columbinus serpens: serpentina columba*, by whichever name Gabriel Harvey designates that hybrid creature, it is engendered in the humanist's mind by the crossbreeding of innocence and experience. Experience, as the dovelike Abigail discovers, is purchased with grief. The serpentine Barabas, too, comes to grief; and the difference between his caldron and Tamburlaine's chariot, between feeling pain and inflicting it, may well betoken Marlowe's advancing experience in the ways of the world. He is awakening to a vision of evil, though he innocently beholds it from the outside. The devil obligingly identifies himself by wearing horns and a tail.

But the devil is no diabolist; he sees through himself; he knows that men have invented him to relieve themselves of responsibility for those woes of the world which [the First Knight] attributes to 'inherent sin' [I ii 103]. The devil's disciple, Machiavel, holds that there is no sin but ignorance; and Machiavel's disciple, Barabas, prefers the role of the knave to that of the fool. Thus, in letting other knaves get the better of him, he commits the only sin in his calendar, the humanistic peccadillo of folly. He acts out the Erasmian object lesson of a scoundrel who is too clever for his own good, the cheater cheated, wily beguiled. In getting out of hand, his counterplots exceeded the proportions of tragedy, and his discomfiture is more like the happy endings of melodrama. T. S. Eliot endows the play with a kind of retrospective unity by interpreting it as a comedy, a 'farce of the old English humour'. Though the interpretation is unhistorical, it has the merit of placing *The Jew of Malta* beside the grotesquerie of Dickens and Hogarth and – most pertinently – Ben Jonson's *Volpone, or the Fox*. Jonson's comedy of humours begins where Marlowe's tragedy of humours leaves off; Volpone and Mosca continue the misadventures of Barabas and Ithamore; and the Fox of Venice has learned not a few of his tricks from the Jew of Malta. The atmosphere of both plays is conveyed, and both playwrights are linked together, by a couplet upon an earlier comic dramatist which Jonson revised from Marlowe's translation of Ovid:

> Whilst Slaues be false, Fathers hard, & Bauds be whorish,
> Whilst Harlots flatter, shall *Menander* flourish.
>
> [*Volp.*, I xv 17–18]

The hard-bitten types of New Comedy are perennially recognisable: miser, impostor, parasite, prostitute. Whether in Malta or Venice, Athens or London, their outlook is always a street and never a landscape. Social intercourse is, for them, a commercial transaction; self-interest is the universal motive; everything, every man's honesty and every woman's, has its price; all try to sell themselves as dearly, and to buy others as cheaply, as possible. The moral issue is the simple choice between folly and knavery – in Elizabethan terms, the innocence of the gull and the wisdom of the coney-catcher. The distance between these extremes, as *The Jew of Malta* demonstrates, can be precariously narrow. Barabas, for all his monstrous activism, inhabits a small and static world. Though Marlowe would not be Marlowe without a cosmic prospect, he seems to be moving centripetally through a descending gyre toward a core of self-imposed limitation. But, even as potentialities seem to be closing in, actualities are opening up. The room is little, the riches are infinite.

SOURCE: ch. 3 of *The Overreacher*: *A Study of Christopher Marlowe* (New York, 1952); text cited from British edition, *Christopher Marlowe: The Overreacher* (London, 1954), pp. 75–102.

Anonymous   'The Jew of Malta in Performance' (1964)

Arriving late in the Marlowe birthday year, this production at last gives it fitting recognition on the London stage. How wise of the Royal Shakespeare Company to have decided against a pious revival of *Dr Faustus* or *Edward II*, and to have chosen a work that has not been seen here professionally for over forty years and which can prompt no parrot references to the author's 'mighty line'.

Melodrama has a habit of dropping out of literary history (witness the blank page of the Victorian theatre) precisely because it only reveals its quality in action. Compared with Marlowe's better-known works *The Jew of Malta* is not an impressive text (though it has marvellous passages, such as Machiavel's prologue); but when played full out, with the assembled forces of the Knights of Malta and their white-robed Turkish enemies, and with the physical apparatus of Barabas's villainy – the arsenal of poisons, the fatal scaffolding over the boiling cauldron – its impact is overwhelming.

Nor are these empty effects. Much more deliberately than Shakespeare in *The Merchant of Venice*, Marlowe is using the figure of the Jew to attack hypocrisy in Christian society. The Knights of Malta seize on all his goods to pay their tribute to the Turks, and try to pass off this theft as an act of Christian evangelism.

Throughout the play, the Church and civil authorities are shown trying to live off Barabas's money and wits, while persuading themselves that they are conferring a favour on him; and when the Governor craftily drops the Jew into his own cauldron, he is careful not to interfere with the second part of Barabas's plot – thus conveniently ridding himself of the Turkish army (who fry to death in a nunnery according to plan). After this, the play's last couplet –

> let due praise be given
> Neither to Fate nor Fortune, but to Heaven.

– comes as an outrageous irony.

By showing the emergence of a clear-sighted opportunist within a society that would act in the same way if it dared, the play stands as a counterpart of the current Stratford [productions of Shakespeare's] history cycle. Marlowe's view, however, seems a good deal more subversive than Shakespeare's, and the textbook objections to the play's mixed form reflect no more than the theatrical camouflage masking the play's real purpose.

No one could accuse Marlowe of painting a flattering portrait of a Machiavellian Jew: and yet one grows a good more fond of him than of any other character. While his chilly epigrams on Christian duplicity strike home as justly as Shylock's ('Preach me not out of my possessions'), his villainous deeds are so preposterous that one cannot take them as anything but a huge and entirely deliberate joke.

No doubt this side of things is pointed up in Clive Revill's performance, generally inviting prospective victims home to supper and masquerading as a flamenco lute-player with a poisoned flower in his hat. But as the evening wears on, there is no doubt that the effects are Marlowe's own. The greatest master of excess in British drama, he here uses it for comedy, and its effects on last night's audience had to be heard to be believed: 'O brother, all the nuns are dead!' (*laughter*) – 'let's bury them' (*prolonged laughter*).

Clifford Williams has directed the play against a massive pair of sun-bleached walls which slide apart for indoor scenes and lock together for street settings; it is a neutral classical arrangement which can accommodate the moment-to-moment changes between pantomime, horror and wintry calm. The last mood is beautifully established in Derek Godfrey's flint-eyed prologue.

More riotous effects are secured by Glenda Jackson as a snake-haired courtesan, and the knockabout team of Ken Wynne and John Nettleton as two friars competing for Jewish donations. Ian Richardson is spell-binding as Barabas's villainous Moorish slave [Ithamore] who appears as a depraved Ariel or a Puck smitten with rabies.

SOURCE: unsigned review in *The Times* (2 October 1964) of the RSC production at the Aldwych Theatre, London.

5. MARLOWE'S SENSE OF TRAGEDY

Stephen J. Greenblatt   Marlowe and
Renaissance Self-Fashioning (1977)

On 26 June 1586, a small fleet, financed by the Earl of
Cumberland, set out from Gravesend for the South Seas. It sailed
down the West African coast, sighting Sierra Leone in October,
and at this point we may let one of those on board, the merchant
John Sarracoll, tell his own story:

The fourth of November wee went on shore to a towne of the
Negros, . . . which we found to be but lately built: it was of about two
hundreth houses, and walled about with mightie great trees, and stakes
so thicke, that a rat could hardly get in or out. But as it chanced, wee
came directly upon a port which was not shut up, where wee entred
with such fiercenesse, that the people fled all out of the towne, which we
found to bee finely built after their fashion, and the streetes of it so
intricate, that it was difficult for us to finde the way out, that wee came in
at. Wee found their houses and streets so finely and cleanly kept, that it
was an admiration to us all, for that neither in the houses nor streets was
so much dust to bee found, as would fill an egge shell. Wee found little in
their houses, except some matts, goards, and some earthen pots. Our
men at their departure set the towne on fire, and it was burnt (for the
most part of it) in a quarter of an houre, the houses being covered with
reed and straw.[1]

This passage is atypical, for it lacks the blood bath that usually
climaxes these incidents, but it will serve to remind us of what
until recently was called one of the glorious achievements of
Renaissance civilisation, and it will serve to introduce us to the
world of Christopher Marlowe.

What is most striking in Sarracoll's account, of course, is the
casual, unexplained violence. Does the merchant feel that the
firing of the town needs no explanation? If asked, would he have
had one to give? Why does he take care to tell us why the town

burned so quickly, but not why it was burned? Is there an aesthetic element in his admiration of the town, so finely built, so intricate, so cleanly kept? And does this admiration conflict with or somehow fuel the destructiveness? If he feels no uneasiness at all, why does he suddenly shift and write not '*we*' but '*our men*' set the town on fire? Was there an order or not? And, when he recalls the invasion, why does he think of rats? The questions are all met by the moral blankness that rests like thick snow on Sarracoll's sentences: 'The 17 day of November wee departed from Sierra Leona, directing our course for the Straights of Magellan.'

If, on returning to England in 1587, the merchant and his associates had gone to see the Lord Admiral's Men perform a new play, *Tamburlaine the Great*, they would have seen an extraordinary meditation on the roots of their own behavior. For despite all the exoticism in Marlowe–Scythian shepherds, Maltese Jews, German magicians – it is his own countrymen that he broods upon and depicts. If we want to understand the historical matrix of Marlowe's achievement, the analogue to Tamburlaine's restlessness, aesthetic sensitivity, appetite and violence, we might look, not at the playwright's sources, not even at the relentless power-hunger of Tudor absolutism, but at the acquisitive energies of English merchants, entrepreneurs and adventurers, promoters alike of trading companies and theatrical companies.

But what bearing does Marlowe actually have on a passage like the one with which I opened? He is, for a start, fascinated by the idea of the stranger in a strange land. Almost all of his heroes are aliens or wanderers, from Aeneas in Carthage to Barabas in Malta, from Tamburlaine's endless campaigns to Faustus's demonic flights. From his first play to his last, he is drawn to the idea of physical movement, to the problem of its representation within the narrow confines of the theater. Tamburlaine almost ceaselessly traverses the stage, and when he is not actually on the move, he is imagining campaigns or hearing reports of gruelling marches. The obvious effect is to enact the hero's vision of a nature that 'Doth teach us all to have aspiring minds' and of the soul that 'Wills us to wear ourselves and never rest' [*1 Tam.*, II vii 20, 26]. But as always in Marlowe, this enactment, this realisation on the level of the body in time and space, complicates, qualifies, exposes, and even mocks the abstract conception. For the

cumulative effect of this restlessness is not so much heroic as
grotesquely comic, if we accept Bergson's classic definition of the
comic as the mechanical imposed upon the living. Tamburlaine
is a machine, a desiring machine that produces violence and
death. Menaphon's admiring description begins by making him
sound like Leonardo's Vitruvian Man or Michelangelo's David
and ends by making him sound like an expensive mechanical
device, one of those curious inventions that courtiers gave to the
Queen at New Year's: a huge, straight, strongly-jointed creature
with a costly pearl placed between his shoulders, the pearl
inscribed with celestial symbols. Once set in motion, this *thing*
cannot slow down or change course; it moves at the same frenzied
pace until it finally stops.

One further effect of this unvarying movement is that,
paradoxically, very little progress seems to be made, despite
fervent declarations to the contrary. To be sure, the scenes
change, so quickly at times that Marlowe seems to be battering
against the boundaries of his own medium: at one moment the
stage represents a vast space, then suddenly contracts to a bed,
then turns in quick succession into an imperial camp, a burning
town, a besieged fortress, a battlefield, a tent. But then all of those
spaces seem curiously alike. The relevant contrast is *Antony and
Cleopatra*, where the restless movement is organised around the
deep structural opposition of Rome and Egypt, or *1 Henry IV*,
where the tavern, the court and the country are perceived as
diversely shaped spaces, spaces that elicit and echo different
tones, energies, and even realities. In *Tamburlaine*, Marlowe
contrives to efface all such differences, as if to insist upon the
essential meaninglessness of theatrical space, the vacancy that is
the dark side of its power to imitate any place. This vacancy –
quite literally, this absence of scenery – is the equivalent in the
medium of the theater to the secularisation of space, the abolition
of qualitative up and down, which for Cassirer is one of the
greatest achievements of Renaissance philosophy, the equivalent
then to the reduction of the universe to the co-ordinates of a
map:[2]

> Give me a map; then let me see how much
> Is left for me to conquer all the world,
> That these, my boys, may finish all my wants.
>
> [*2*: v iii 124–6]

Space is transformed into an abstraction, then fed to the appetitive machine. This is the voice of conquest, but it is also the voice of wants never finished and of transcendental homelessness. And though the characters and situations change, that voice is never entirely absent in Marlowe. Barabas does not leave Malta, but he is the quintessential alien: at one point, his house is seized and turned into a nunnery; at another, he is thrown over the walls of the city, only to rise with the words, 'What, all alone?' Edward II should be the very opposite: he is, by his role, the embodiment of the land and its people, but without Gaveston he lives in his own country like an exile. Only in *Doctor Faustus* does there seem to be a significant difference. Having signed away his soul and body, Faustus begins a course of restless wandering, but at the close of the twenty-four years, he feels a compulsion to return to Wittenberg.[3] Of course, it is ironic that when a meaningful sense of place finally emerges in Marlowe, it does so only as a place to die. But the irony runs deeper still. For nothing in the covenant or in any of the devil's speeches requires that Faustus has to pay his life where he originally contracted to sell it; the urge is apparently in Faustus, as if he felt there were a fatality in the study itself, felt it appropriate and even necessary to die there and nowhere else. 'O would I had never seen Wittenberg', he despairingly tells his friends. But the play has long before this exposed such a sense of place to radical questioning. To Faustus's insistent demands to know the 'where about' of hell, Mephistophilis replies:

> Hell hath no limits, nor is circumscribed
> In one self place. But where we are is hell,
> And where hell is there must we ever be.   [I v 124–6]

By implication, Faustus's feeling about Wittenberg is an illusion, one of a network of fictions by which he constitutes his identity and his world. Typically, he refuses to accept the account of a limitless, inner hell, countering with the extraordinary, and in the circumstances, ludicrous 'I think hell's a fable'. Mephistophilis's quiet response slides from parodic agreement to devastating irony: 'Ay, think so still, till experience change thy mind.'[4] The experience of which the devil speaks can refer not only to torment after death but to Faustus's life in the remainder of the play: the half-trivial, half-daring exploits, the alternating states of bliss and despair, the questions that are not answered and the answers that bring no real satisfaction, the wanderings that lead nowhere. The chilling line may carry a further suggestion: 'Yes, continue to think that hell's a fable, until experience *transforms* your mind.' At the heart of this mental transformation is the anguished perception of time as inexorable, space as abstract. In his final soliloquy, Faustus's frenzied invocation to time to stop or slow itself gives way to horrified clarity: 'The stars move still, time runs, the clock will strike'. And his appeal to nature – earth, stars, air, ocean – at once to shield him and destroy him is met by silence: space is neutral and unresponsive.

Doctor Faustus, then, does not contradict but, rather, realises intimations about space and time in Marlowe's other plays. That man is homeless, that all places are alike, is linked to man's inner state, to the uncircumscribed hell he carries within him. And this insight returns us to the violence with which we began: the violence of Tamburlaine and of the English merchant and his men. It is not enough to say that their actions are the expression of brute power, though they are certainly that. For experiencing this limitlessness, this transformation of space and time into abstractions, men do violence as a means of marking boundaries, effecting transformations, signalling closure. To burn a town or to kill all of its inhabitants is to make an end and, in so doing, to give life a shape and a certainty that it would otherwise lack. The great fear, in Barabas's words, is 'That I may vanish o'er the earth in air, / And leave no memory that e're I was' [1 ii 270–1]. As the town where Zenocrate dies burns at his command, Tamburlaine proclaims his identity, fixed forever in the heavens by his acts of violence:

> Over my zenith hang a blazing star,
> That may endure till heaven be dissolv'd,
> Fed with fresh supply of earthly dregs,
> Threatening a death and famine to this land.
>
> [*2*: III ii 6–9]

In the charred soil and the blazing star, Tamburlaine seeks literally to make an enduring mark in the world, to stamp his image on time and space. Similarly, Faustus, by violence not on others but on himself, seeks to give his life a clear fixed shape. To be sure, he speaks of attaining 'a world of profit and delight, / Of power, of honour, of omnipotence' [1 i 52–3], but perhaps the hidden core of what he seeks is the *limit* of twenty-four years to live, a limit he himself sets and reiterates. Time so marked out should have a quality different from other time, should possess its end: 'Now will I make an end immediately', he says, writing with his blood.

But in the tragic irony of Marlowe's world, these desperate attempts at boundary and closure produce the opposite effect, reinforcing the condition they are meant to efface. Tamburlaine's violence does not transform space from the abstract to the human, but rather further reduces the world to a map, the very emblem of abstraction:

> I will confute those blind geographers
> That make a triple region in the world,
> Excluding regions which I mean to trace,
> And with this pen reduce them to a map,
> Calling the provinces, cities and towns
> After my name and thine, Zenocrate.   [*1*: IV iv 81–6]

At Tamburlaine's death, the map still stretches out before him, and nothing bears his name save Marlowe's play (the crucial exception to which we will return).[5] Likewise at his death, pleading for 'some end to my incessant pain', Faustus is haunted by eternity: 'O no end is limited to damned souls' [v ii 181].

The reasons why attempts at making a mark or an end fail are complex and vary significantly with each play, but one critical link is the feeling in almost all Marlowe's protagonists that they are *using up* experience. This feeling extends to our merchant, John Sarracoll, and his men: they not only visit Sierra Leone, they consume it. Tamburlaine exults in just this power to 'Conquer, sack, and utterly consume / Your cities' [*2*: IV i 195–6]. He even contrives to use up his defeated enemies, transforming Bajazeth into his footstool, the kings of Trebizon and Soria into horses to be discarded, when they are broken-winded, for 'fresh horse' [*2*: v i 130]. In a grotesquely comic moment, Tamburlaine's son suggests that the kings just captured be released to resume the fight, but Tamburlaine replies, in the language of consumption, 'Cherish thy valour still with fresh supplies, / And glut it not with stale and daunted foes' [*2*: IV i 89–

90]. Valor, like any appetite, always demands new food.

Faustus's relationship to knowledge is strikingly similar; in his opening soliloquy he bids farewell to each of his studies in turn as something he has used up. He needs to cherish his mind with fresh supplies, for nothing can be accumulated, nothing saved or savored. And as the remainder of the play makes clear, each of these farewells is an act of destruction: logic, medicine, law and divinity are not so much rejected as violated. The violence arises not only from the desire to mark boundaries but from the feeling that what one leaves behind, turns away from, *must* no longer exist; that objects endure only for the moment of the act of attention and then are effaced; that the next moment cannot be fully grasped until the last is destroyed. Marlowe writes in the period in which European man embarked on his extraordinary career of consumption, his eager pursuit of knowledge, with one paradigm after another seized, squeezed dry and discarded, and his frenzied exhaustion of the world's resources:

> Lo, here, my sons, are all the golden mines,
> Inestimable drugs and precious stones,
> More worth than Asia and the world beside;
> And from th'Antarctic Pole eastward behold
> As much more land, which never was descried,
> Wherein are rocks of pearl that shine as bright
> As all the lamps that beautify the sky!
> And shall I die, and this unconquered?
>
> [2: v iii 152–9]

So fully do we inhabit this construction of reality that most often we see beyond it only in accounts of cultures immensely distant from our own:

The Nuer have no expression equivalent to 'time' in our language, and they cannot, therefore, as we can, speak of time as though it were something actual, which passes, can be wasted, can be saved, and so forth. I do not think that they ever experience the same feeling of fighting against time or of having to co-ordinate activities with an abstract passage of time because their points of reference are mainly the activities themselves, which are generally of a leisurely character. . . . Nuer are fortunate.[6]

Of course, such a conception of time and activity had vanished from Europe long before the sixteenth century, but English Renaissance works, and Marlowe's plays in particular, give voice to a radically intensified sense that time is abstract, uniform and inhuman. The origins of this sense of time are difficult to locate with any certainty. Puritans in the late sixteenth century were already campaigning vigorously against the medieval doctrine of the unevenness of time, a doctrine that had survived largely intact in the Elizabethan Church Calendar. They sought, in effect, to desacramentalise time, to discredit and sweep away the dense web of saints' days, 'dismal days', seasonal taboos, mystic observances and folk festivals that gave time a distinct, irregular shape; in its place, they urged a simple, flat routine of six days work and a sabbath rest.[7] Moreover, there seem, in this period, to have been subtle changes in what we may call family time. At one end of the life cycle, traditional youth groups were suppressed or fell into neglect, customs that had allowed adolescents considerable autonomy were overturned, and children were brought under the stricter discipline of the immediate family. At the other end, the Protestant rejection of the doctrine of Purgatory eliminated the dead as an 'age group', cutting off the living from ritualised communion with their deceased parents and relatives.[8] Such changes might well have contributed to a sense in Marlowe and some of his contemporaries that time is alien, profoundly indifferent to human longing and anxiety. Whatever the case, we certainly find in Marlowe's plays a powerful feeling that time is something to be resisted and a related fear that fulfilment or fruition is impossible. 'Why waste you thus the time away?' an impatient Leicester asks Edward II, whose crown he has come to fetch. 'Stay a while', Edward replies, 'let me be king till night' [v i 59], whereupon, like Faustus, he struggles vainly to arrest time with incantation. At such moments, Marlowe's celebrated line is itself rich with irony: the rhythms intended to slow time only consume it, magnificent words are spoken and disappear into a void. But it is precisely this sense of the void that compels the characters to speak so powerfully, as if to struggle the more insistently against the enveloping silence.

That the moments of intensest time-consciousness all occur at or near the close of these plays has the effect of making the heroes seem to struggle against *theatrical* time. As Marlowe uses the vacancy of theatrical space to suggest his character's homeless-ness, so he uses the curve of theatrical time to suggest their struggle against death, in effect against the nothingness into which all characters fall at the end of a play. The pressure of the dramatic medium itself likewise underlies what we may call the *repetition compulsion* of Marlowe's heroes. Tamburlaine no sooner annihilates one army than he sets out to annihilate another, no sooner unharnesses two kings than he hitches up two more. Barabas gains and loses, regains and reloses his wealth, while pursuing a seemingly endless string of revenges and politic murders, including, characteristically, two suitors, two friars, two rulers, and, in effect, two children. In *Edward II*, the plot is less overtly episodic, yet even here, after spending the first half of the play alternately embracing and parting from Gaveston, Edward immediately replaces the slain favorite with Spencer Junior and thereby resumes the same pattern, the wilful courting of disaster that is finally 'rewarded' in the castle cesspool. Finally, as C. L. Barber observes, 'Faustus repeatedly moves through a circular pattern, from thinking of the joys of heaven, through despairing of ever possessing them, to embracing magical dominion as a blasphemous substitute.'[9] The pattern of action and the complex psychological structure embodied in it vary with each play, but at the deepest level of the medium itself the motivation is the same: the renewal of existence through repetition of the self-constituting act. The character repeats himself in order to continue to be that same character on the stage. Identity is a theatrical invention that must be reiterated if it is to endure.

To grasp the full import of this notion of repetition as self-fashioning, we must understand that it is set against the culturally dominant notion of repetition as warning or memorial. In this view, patterns exist in the history of individuals or nations in order to inculcate crucial moral lessons, passing them from generation to generation.[10] Men are notoriously slow learners, but gradually, through repetition, the paradigms may sink in. Accordingly, Tudor monarchs ordered the formal reiteration of the central tenets of the religious and social orthodoxy, carefully specifying the minimum number of times a year these tenets were to be read aloud from the pulpit. Similarly, the punishment of criminals was public, so that the state's power to inflict torment and death could act upon the people as an edifying caution. The high number of such executions reflects not only judicial 'massacres'[11] but the attempt to teach through reiterated terror. Each branding or hanging or disembowelling was theatrical in conception and performance, a repeatable admonitory drama enacted on a scaffold before a rapt audience. This idea of the 'notable spectacle', the 'theatre of God's judgements', extended quite naturally to the drama itself, and, indeed, to all of literature, which thus takes its rightful place as part of a vast, interlocking system of repetitions, embracing homilies and hangings, royal progresses and rote learning.

Marlowe seems to have regarded the notion of drama as admonitory fiction, and the moral order upon which this notion was based with a blend of fascination, contemptuous amusement, and loathing. *Tamburlaine* repeatedly teases its audience with the *form* of the cautionary tale, only to violate the convention. 'The gods, defenders of the innocent, / Will never prosper your intended drifts' [*1*: 1 ii 68–9], declares Zenocrate and then promptly falls in love with her captor. With his dying breath, Cosroe curses Tamburlaine – a sure prelude to disaster – but the disaster never occurs. Bajazeth, the King of Arabia, and even Theridamas and Zenocrate have powerful premonitions of the hero's downfall, but he passes from success to success. Tamburlaine is proud, arrogant and blasphemous; he lusts for power, betrays his allies, overthrows legitimate authority and threatens the gods; he rises to the top of the wheel of fortune and then steadfastly refuses to budge. Since the dominant ideology no longer insists that rise-and-decline and pride-goes-before-a-fall are unvarying, universal rhythms, we undoubtedly miss some of the shock of Tamburlaine's career, but the play itself invokes those rhythms often enough to surprise us with their failure to materialise.

Having undermined the notion of the cautionary tale in *Tamburlaine, Part One*, Marlowe demolishes it in *Part Two* in the most unexpected way – by suddenly invoking it. The slaughter of thousands, the murder of his own son, the torture of his royal captives are all without apparent consequence; then Tamburlaine falls ill, and when? When he burns the Koran! The one action that Elizabethan churchmen themselves might have applauded seems to bring down divine vengeance. The effect is not to celebrate the transcendent power of Mohammed but to challenge the habit of mind that looks to heaven for rewards and punishments, that imagines human evil as 'the scourge of God'. Similarly, in *Edward II*, Marlowe uses the emblematic method of admonitory drama, but uses it to such devastating effect that the audience recoils from it in disgust. Edward's grisly execution is, as orthodox interpreters of the play have correctly insisted, iconographically 'appropriate', but this very appropriateness can only be established *at the expense of* every complex, sympathetic human feeling evoked by the play. The audience is forced to confront its insistence upon coherence, and the result is a profound questioning of the way audiences constitute meaning in plays and in life.

This questioning is pursued as well in *The Jew of Malta* and *Doctor Faustus*. In the former, Marlowe invokes the motif of the villain-undone-by-his-villainy, but the actual fall of Barabas is brought about in his confidence in Ithamore, his desire to *avoid* the actual possession of power, and his imprudent trust in the Christian governor of Malta – in short, by the minute shreds of restraint and community that survive in him. In *Doctor Faustus*, as Max Bluestone observes in an English Institute essay, the homiletical tradition is continually introduced only to be undermined by dramatic spectacle.[12] Moreover, in these plays Marlowe questions not only the traditional value system upon which the notion of literature as a cautionary tale was based but the radical *critique* of this value system. Barabas's Machiavellianism and Faustus's skepticism are subjected to relentless probing and are exposed as themselves inadequate conceptions of reality. Marlowe's brilliant demonstration of Faustus's shallowness has long been admired; the intelligence of his analysis of Machiavellianism has been less well understood. The heart of this analysis lies not in the Prologue nor even in the fact that Barabas is outfoxed by a cleverer Machiavel than himself; it lies rather in the sketchiness of characterisation that distinguishes this protagonist from Tamburlaine, Edward and Faustus. Where the titles of Marlowe's other major plays are proper names, *The Jew of Malta* deflects the focus from the hero as fully conceived individual to the hero as embodiment of a category. Of course, the Jew has a name, but he remains curiously vague and unreal; even his account of his past – killing sick people or poisoning wells – tends to de-individualise him, accommodating him to an ract, anti-Semitic fantasy of a Jew's past. In falling short of an stential identity, he approximates the shadowy status of Machiavelli's Prince; he is, to adapt Edward Said's characterisation of Freud's Moses or Nietzsche's Dionysus, more 'an idea of energy' than a man.[13] It is only as such a faceless being that the Machiavel can survive; by thrusting him in a drama and giving him a local habitation and a name, Marlowe demonstrates the inadequacy of the whole conception. Most dramatic characters – Shylock would be an appropriate example – *accumulate* identity in the course of their play; Barabas desperately tries to dispossess himself of such identity. But this steady erosion of himself is precisely what he has pledged himself to resist; his career, then, is in its very essence suicidal.

If the heart of Renaissance orthodoxy is a vast system of repetitions in which paradigms are established and men gradually learn what to desire and what to fear, the skeptics, Barabas and Faustus, remain embedded within this orthodoxy: they simply reverse the paradigms and embrace what the society brands as evil. In so doing, they imagine themselves set in diametrical opposition to their society where in fact they have already unwittingly accepted its crucial structural elements. For the issue is not man's power to disobey, but the characteristic modes of desire and fear produced by a given society, and the rebellious heroes never depart from those modes. With their passionate insistence on will, Marlowe's protagonists anticipate the perception that human history is the product of men themselves, but they fail to understand that this product is shaped, in Lukács's phrase, by forces that arise from their relations with each other and which have escaped their control.[14] As Marx writes in a famous passage in *The Eighteenth Brumaire of Louis Bonaparte* (1852):

Men make their own history, but they do not make it just as they please; they do not make it under circumstances chosen by themselves, but under circumstances directly found, given and transmitted from the past. The tradition of all the dead generations weighs like a nightmare on the brain of the living. And just when they seem engaged in revolutionising themselves and things, in creating something entirely new, precisely in such epochs of revolutionary crisis they anxiously conjure up the spirits of the past.[15]

Tamburlaine rebels against hierarchy, legitimacy, the whole established order of things, and to what end? To reach 'The sweet fruition of an earthly crown.' His will is immeasurably stronger, but it is essentially the same as the will of Mycetes, Cosroe, Bajazeth or any of the other kings that strut around the stage. *Part One* ends not in an act of revolt but in the supreme gesture of legitimacy, a proper marriage, with the Scourge of God earnestly assuring his father-in-law of Zenocrate's unblemished chastity. Similarly, the end of *The Jew of Malta* demonstrates how close Barabas has been all along to the gentile world he loathes and wishes to destroy. Barabas himself has said as much, but he somehow fails to make a connection between his perception of likeness and his violent hatred, until at the close he boils in the pot he has prepared for his enemy. Likewise, Faustus's whole career binds him ever more closely to that Christian conception of the body and the mind, that divinity, he thought he was decisively rejecting. He dreams of living 'in all voluptuousness' [II iii 92], but his pleasures are parodic versions of Holy Communion.[16]

Marlowe stands apart, then, from both orthodoxy and skepticism; he calls into question the theory of literature and history as repeatable moral lessons, and he calls into question his age's characteristic mode of rejecting those lessons. But how does he himself understand his characters' motivation, the force that compels them to repeat the same actions again and again? The answer, as I have already suggested, lies in self-fashioning. Marlowe's heroes struggle to invent themselves; they stand, in Coriolanus's phrase, 'As if a man were author of himself / And knew no other kin' [*Cor.*, v iii 36–7]. Shakespeare characteristically forces his very Marlovian hero to reach out and grasp his mother's hand; in Marlowe's plays, with the exception of *Dido Queen of Carthage*, we never see and scarcely even hear of the heroes' parents. Tamburlaine is the son of nameless 'paltry' Scythians, Faustus of 'parents base of stock' [Prol., 11], and Barabas, so far as we can tell, of no one at all. (Even in *Edward II*, where an emphasis on parentage would seem unavoidable, there is scant mention of Edward I). The family is at the center of most Elizabethan and Jacobean drama as it is at the center of the period's economic and social structure; in Marlowe, it is something to be neglected, despised, or violated. Two of Marlowe's heroes kill their children without a trace of remorse;

most prefer male friendships to marriage or kinship bonds; all insist upon free choice in determining their intimate relations. Upon his father's death, Edward immediately sends for Gaveston; Barabas adopts Ithamore in place of Abigail; Faustus cleaves to his sweet Mephistophilis; and, in a more passionate love scene than any with Zenocrate, Tamburlaine wins the ardent loyalty of Theridamas.

The effect is to dissolve the structure of sacramental and blood relations that normally determine identity in this period and to render the heroes virtually autochthonous, their names and identities given by no one but themselves. Indeed self-naming is a major enterprise in these plays, repeated over and over again as if the hero continues to exist only by virtue of constantly renewed acts of will. Augustine had written in *The City of God* that 'if God were to withdraw what we may call his "constructive power" from existing things, they would cease to exist, just as they did not exist before they were made.'[17] In the neutrality of time and space that characterises Marlowe's world, this 'constructive power' must exist within the hero himself; if it should fail for an instant, he would fall into nothingness, become, in Barabas's words, 'a senseless lump of clay / That will with every water wash to dirt' [I ii 221–2]. Hence the hero's tragic compulsion to repeat his name and his actions, a compulsion Marlowe links to the drama itself. The hero's re-presentations fade into the reiterated performances of the play.

If Marlowe's protagonists fashion themselves, they do not do so just as they please; they are, as we have seen, compelled to use only those forms and materials produced by the structure of relations in their particular, quite distinct worlds. We watch Tamburlaine construct himself out of phrases picked up or over-heard: 'And ride in triumph through *Persepolis*' [I: II v 50] or 'I that am term'd the Scourge and Wrath of God' [I: III iii 44]. Like the gold taken from unwary travellers or the troops lured away from other princes, Tamburlaine's identity is something *appropriated*, seized from others. Similarly, Barabas is virtually composed of hard little aphorisms, cynical adages, worldly proverbs – all the neatly packaged nastiness of his society. Even Edward II, with his greater psychological complexity, can only clothe himself in the metaphors available to his station, though these metaphors – the 'Imperial Lion', for example – often seem little applicable. And the most haunting instance in Marlowe of his self-fashioning by quotation or appropriation occurs in *Doctor Faustus*, when the hero concludes the signing of the fatal deed with the words '*Consummatum est*' [I v 73].

To unfold the meaning of this repetition of Christ's dying words, we would have to trace the entire, tortuous network of Faustus's fears and desires: his blasphemy is a wilful defilement of the sacred and, as such, the uncanny expression of a perverse, despairing faith; it is Faustus's appropriation to himself of the most solemn and momentous words available in his culture to mark this decisive boundary in his life; it is an ambiguous equation of himself with Christ, first as God, then as dying man; it is the culmination of his fantasies of making an end, and hence a suicide that demonically parodies Christ's self-sacrifice. And beyond all these, Faustus's use of Christ's words evokes the archetypal act of role-taking. To grasp this, we must restore the words to their context in the Gospel of John:

> After this, Jesus knowing that all things were now accomplished, that the Scripture might be fulfilled, saith, I thirst. Now there was set a vessel full of vinegar: and they filled a sponge with vinegar, and put it upon hyssop, and put it to his mouth. When Jesus therefore had received the vinegar, he said, It is finished [*Consummatum est*]: and he bowed his head, and gave up the ghost. [xix 28–30]

As it is written in Psalm 69, 'and in my thirst they gave me vinegar to drink' [21], so it is fulfilled: Christ's thirst is not identical to the body's normal longing for drink, but an *enactment* of that longing so that he may fully accomplish the role darkly prefigured in the Old Testament. The drink of vinegar is the final structural element in the realisation of his identity. Faustus's blasphemy then is a demonic re-enactment of the moment in which Christ acknowledges the fulfilment of his role, and the magician thereby hopes to touch upon the primal springs of identity itself.

But in the Gospel of John, as we have seen, the words 'Consummatum est' are a true end; they are spoken at the moment of Christ's death. In *Doctor Faustus*, they are, rather, a beginning, spoken at the moment Faustus is embarking on his bargain. Unlike Christ, who is his own transcendent object, and whose career is precisely the realisation of himself, Faustus, and all of Marlowe's self-fashioning heroes, must posit an object in order to exist. Naming oneself is not enough; one must also name and pursue a goal. The heroes do so with a splendid energy that distinguishes their words as well as their actions from the surrounding society. The Turks, friars and Christian knights may all be driven by 'The wind that bloweth all the world besides,/ Desire of gold' [*Jew*, III ii 3–4], but only Barabas can speak of 'Infinite riches in a little room' [I i 37]. Theridamas may declare that 'A god is not so glorious as a king', but when he is asked if he himself would be a king, he replies, 'Nay, though I praise it, I can live without it' [*1 Tam.*, II v 66]. Tamburlaine cannot live without it, and his reward is not only 'The sweet fruition of an earthly crown' but what Plato's rival Gorgias conceives as 'the magic violence of speech'.[18]

It is this Gorgian conception of rhetoric, and not the Platonic or Aristotelian, that is borne out in Marlowe's heroes. For Gorgias, man is forever cut off from the knowledge of being, forever locked in the partial, the contradictory and the irrational. If anything exists, he writes, it is both incomprehensible and incommunicable, for 'that which we communicate is speech, and speech is not the same thing as the things that exist.'[19] This tragic epistemological distance is never bridged; instead through the incantatory power of language, men construct magnificent deceptions in which and for which they live. It is precisely by means of this incantatory power that Faustus conjures up the Prince of Deceptions and that Tamburlaine makes his entire life into a project, transforming himself into an elemental, destructive force, driving irresistibly forward: 'For *Will* and *Shall* best fitteth Tamburlaine' [*1*: III iii 41]. He collapses all the senses of these verbs – intention, command, prophecy, resolution, and simple futurity – into his monomaniacal project.

All of Marlowe's heroes seem similarly obsessed, and the result of their passionate willing, their insistent, reiterated naming of themselves and their objects, is that they become more intensely real to us, more present, than any of the other characters. This is only to say that they are the protagonists, but once again Marlowe relates the shape of the medium itself to the central experience of the plays; his heroes seem determined to realise the Idea of themselves as dramatic heroes. There is a parallel in Spenser's Malbecco, who is so completely what he is – in this case, so fanatically jealous – that he becomes the allegorical incarnation of Jealousy itself. But where this self-realisation in Spenser is Platonic, in Marlowe it is Gorgian – that is, Platonism is undermined by the presence of the theater itself, the unavoidable distance between the particular actor and his role, the insistent awareness in audience and players alike of illusion.

Within the plays, this awareness is intensified by the difficulties the characters experience in sustaining their lives as projects, by that constant reiteration to which, as we have seen, they are bound. For even as no two performances or readings of a text are exactly the same, so the repeated acts of self-fashioning are never absolutely identical; indeed, as Gilles Deleuze has recently observed, we can only speak of repetition by reference to the difference or change that it causes in the mind that contemplates it.[20] The result is that the objects of desire, at first so clearly defined, so avidly pursued, gradually lose their sharp outlines and become more and more like mirages. Faustus speaks endlessly of his appetite, his desire to be glutted, ravished, consumed, but what is it exactly that he wants? By the end of the play it is clear that knowledge, voluptuousness, and power are each mere approximations of the goal for which he sells his soul and body; what that goal is remains maddeningly unclear. 'Mine own fantasy / . . . will receive no object', [1 i 102–3], he tells Valdes and Cornelius, in a phrase that could stand as the play's epigraph. At first Barabas seems a simpler case: he wants wealth, though there is an unsettling equivocation between the desire for wealth as power and security and desire for wealth as an aesthetic, even metaphysical gratification. But the rest of the play does not bear out this desire as the center of Barabas's being; he seeks rather, at any cost, to revenge himself on the Christians. Or so we think until he plots to destroy the Turks and restore the Christians to power. Well then, he wants always to serve his own self-interest: *Ego mihimet sum semper proximus* [*Jew*, 1 i 192]. But where exactly is the self whose interests he serves? Even the Latin tag betrays an ominous self-distance: 'I am always my own neighbor', or even, 'I am always *next* to myself.' Edward II is no clearer. He loves Gaveston, but why? 'Because he loves me more than all the world' [1 iv 77]. The desire returns from its object, out there in the world, to the self, a self that is nonetheless exceedingly unstable. When Gaveston is killed, Edward has within seconds adopted someone else: the will exists, but the object of the will is little more than an illusion. Even Tamburlaine, with his firm declaration of a goal, becomes ever more equivocal. 'The sweet fruition of an earthly crown' turns out not to be what it first appears – the acquisition of kingship – for Tamburlaine continues his restless pursuit long after this acquisition. His goal then is power, which is graphically depicted as the ability to transform virgins with blubbered cheeks into slaughtered carcasses. But when Tamburlaine views the corpses he has made and defines this object for himself, it immediately becomes something else, a mirror reflecting yet another goal:

> All sights of power to grace my victory;
> And such are objects fit for Tamburlaine,
> Wherein, as in a mirror, may be seen,
> His honour, that consists in shedding blood.
>
> [*1*: v ii 413–16]

It is Tamburlaine, [in his] 'What is beauty saith my sufferings then?' [*1*: v ii 97ff.], who gives the whole problem of reaching a desired end its clearest formal expression in Marlowe: beauty, like all the goals pursued by the playwright's heroes, always hovers just beyond the reach of human thought and expression. The problem of elusiveness is one of the major preoccupations of Renaissance thinkers from the most moderate to the most radical, from the judicious Hooker to the splendidly injudicious Bruno.[21] Marlowe is deeply influenced by this contemporary thought, but he subtly shifts the emphasis from the infinity that draws men beyond what they possess to the problem of the human will, the difficulty men experience in truly wanting anything. Kenneth Burke remarks that for Saint Augustine the essence of evil is that anything should be 'sought for itself, whereas things should be sought only in terms of the search for god'. Marlowe's heroes seem at first to embrace such evil: they freely proclaim their immense hunger for something that takes on the status of a personal absolute, and they relentlessly pursue this absolute. The more threatening an obstacle in their path, the more determined they are to obliterate or overreach it: I long for, I burn, I will. But, as we have seen, we are never fully convinced by these noisy demonstrations of single-minded appetite. It is as if Marlowe's heroes wanted to be wholly perverse, in Augustine's sense, but were incapable of such perversity, as if they could not finally desire anything for itself. For Hooker and Bruno alike, this inability arises from the existence of transcendent goals – it is a proof of the existence of God; for Marlowe, it springs from the tragic fact that all objects of desire are fictions, theatrical illusions shaped by the characters. And those characters are themselves fictions, fashioned in reiterated acts of self-naming. The problem is already understood in its full complexity by Montaigne, but, as Auerbach observes, 'his irony, his dislike of big words, his calm way of being profoundly at ease with himself, prevent him from pushing on beyond the limits of the problematic and into the realm of the tragic'.[23] Marlowe, whose life suggests the very opposite of that 'peculiar equilibrium' that distinguishes Montaigne, rushes to embrace the tragic with a strange eagerness.

Man can only exist in the world by fashioning for himself a name and an object, but these, as Marlowe and Montaigne understood, are both fictions. No particular name or object can entirely satisfy one's inner energy demanding to be expressed or fill so completely the potential of one's consciousness that all longings are quelled, all intimations of unreality silenced. Throughout the sixteenth century, Protestant and Catholic polemicists demonstrated brilliantly how each other's religion – the very anchor of reality for millions of souls – was a cunning theatrical illusion, a demonic fantasy, a piece of poetry. Each conducted this unmasking, of course, in the name of the *real* religious truth, but the collective effect upon a skeptical intellect like Marlowe's seems to have been devastating. And it was not only the religious 'deconstruction' of reality to which the playwright was responding. On the distant shores of Africa and America and at home, in their 'rediscovered' classical texts, Renaissance Europeans were daily confronting evidence that their accustomed reality was only one solution, among many others, of perennial human problems. Though they often tried to destroy the alien cultures they encountered, they could not destroy the testimony of their own consciousness. 'The wonder is not that things are', writes Valéry, 'but that they are *what* they are and not something else.'[24] Each of Marlowe's plays constitutes reality in a manner radically different from the plays that preceded it, just as his work as a whole marks a startling departure from the drama of his time. Each of his heroes makes a different leap from inchoate appetite to the all-consuming project: what is necessary in one play is accidental or absent in the next. Only the leap itself is always necessary, at once necessary and absurd, for it is the embracing of a fiction rendered desirable by the intoxication of language.

Marlowe's heroes *must* live their lives as projects, but they do so in the midst of intimations that the projects are illusions. Their strength is not sapped by these intimations: they do not withdraw into stoical resignation or contemplative solitude, nor do they endure for the sake of isolated moments of grace in which they are in touch with a wholeness otherwise absent in their lives. Rather, they derive a tragic courage from the absurdity of their enterprise, a murderous, self-destructive, supremely eloquent courage.

In his turbulent life and, more importantly, in his writing, Marlowe is deeply implicated in his heroes, though he is far more intelligent and self-aware than any of them. Cutting himself off from the comforting doctrine of repetition, he writes plays that spurn and subvert his culture's metaphysical and ethical certainities. We who have lived after Nietzsche and Flaubert may find it difficult to grasp how strong, how courageous Marlowe must have been: to write as if the admonitory purpose of literature were a lie, to invent fictions only to create and not to serve God or the state, to fashion lines that echo in the void, that echo more powerfully because there is nothing but a void. Hence Marlowe's implication in the lives of his protagonists and hence, too, his transcendence of this implication in the creation of enduring works of art. For the one true goal of all these heroes is to be characters in Marlowe's plays; it is only for this, ultimately, that they manifest both their magnificent energy and their haunting sense of unsatisfied longing. And they alone survive a life that was violent, sordid and short.

SOURCE: essay in Alvin Kernan (ed.), *Two Renaissance Mythmakers: Christopher Marlowe and Ben Jonson – Selected Papers from the English Institute, 1975–6*, new series, 1 (Baltimore, Md, and London, 1977), pp. 41–69.

NOTES

[Abbreviated and renumbered (with some revision) from the original – Ed.]

1. John Sarracoll's account, in Richard Hakluyt, *The Principall Navigations, Voyages, Traffiques & Discoveries of the English Nation* (1589), enlarged to 3 vols (1598–1600); the text cited here is that of the Glasgow edition (1904), II, pp. 206–7.

2. See Ernst Cassirer, *The Individual and the Cosmos in Renaissance Philosophy*, trans. Mario Domandi (New York, 1963), esp. ch. 1, 'Nicholas Cusanus'.

3. Here, as elsewhere in my discussion of *Doctor Faustus*, I am indebted to conversations with my colleague Edward Snow and to his essay, 'Marlowe's Doctor Faustus and the Ends of Desire.'

4. 'Experience' may also have the sense of 'experiment', as if Faustus's whole future were a test of the proposition that hell is a fable.

5. The futility of naming cities after oneself was a commonplace in the period; see, for example, Ralegh's *History of the World* (1614): v v 2, p. 646: 'This was that *Seleucia*, whereto *Antigonus the great* who founded it, gave the name of *Antigonia*: but *Seleucus* getting it shortly after, called it *Seleucia*; and *Ptolemie Evergetes* having lately won it, might, if it had so pleased him, have changed the name into *Ptolemais*. Such is the vanitie of men, that hope to purchase an endless memoriall unto their names, by workes proceeding rather from their greatnesse, than from their vertue; which therefore no longer are their owne, than the same greatnesse hath continuance.'

6. E. E. Evans-Pritchard, *The Nuer* (Oxford, 1940), p. 103; quoted in E. P. Thompson, 'Time, Work-Discipline and Industrial Capitalism', *Past and Present*, 38 (1967), ch. 5.

7. See Keith Thomas, *Religion and the Decline of Magic* (London, 1971), p. 621; likewise Christopher Hill, *Society and Puritanism in Pre-Revolutionary England* (1964; 2nd edn London, and New York, 1967), ch. 5.

8. See Natalie Zemon Davis, 'Some Tasks and Themes in the Study of Popular Religion', in Charles Trinkhaus and Heiko A. Oberman, *The Pursuit of Holiness in Late Medieval and Renaissance Religion* (Leyden, 1974), pp. 307–36.

9. C. L. Barber, ' "The Form of Faustus' Fortunes Good or Bad" ', *Tulane Drama Review*, VIII, 4 (1964), p. 99.

10. For a typical expression of this view, see Ralegh's *History*: II xix 3, pp. 508–9: 'The same just God who liveth and governeth all thinges for ever, doeth in these our times give victorie, courage, and discourage,

raise, and throw downe Kinges, Estates, Cities, and Nations, for the
same offences which were committed of old, and are committed in the
present: for which reason in these and other the afflictions of *Israel*,
alwaies the causes are set downe, that they might bee as precedents to
succeeding ages.'

11. This characterisation of the period's legal procedure is Christo-
pher Hill's: 'The Many-Headed Monster in Late Tudor and Early
Stuart Political Thinking', in Charles H. Carter (ed.), *From the
Renaissance to the Counter-Reformation: Essays in Honor of Garrett Mattingly*
(New York, 1965), p. 303.

12. Max Bluestone, '*Libido Speculandi*: Doctrine and Dramaturgy in
Contemporary Interpretations of Marlowe's *Doctor Faustus*', in Norman
Rabkin (ed.), *Reinterpretations of Elizabethan Drama* (New York, 1969), p.
82.

13. Edward Said, *Beginnings* (New York, 1975), p. 58. As *The Prince,
The Courtier, The Governor* and *The Schoolmaster* bear witness, these
intermediate beings fascinated the Renaissance. See Stephen J.
Greenblatt, *Sir Walter Ralegh: The Renaissance Man and His Roles* (New
Haven, Conn., 1973), ch. 2.

14. See Georg Lukács, *History and Class Consciousness*, trans. Rodney
Livingstone (Cambridge, Mass., 1971), p. 15. The fountainhead of all
modern speculation along these lines is Vico's *New Science* [1725].

15. In Robert C. Tucker (ed.), *The Marx-Engels Reader* (New York,
1972), p. 437.

16. See C. L. Barber, op. cit., esp. p. 107.

17. Augustine of Hippo, *The City of God*, trans. Henry Bettenson
(London, 1972), II, xii 26, p. 506. See Georges Poulet, *Studies in Human
Time*, trans. Elliott Coleman (Baltimore, Md, 1956), p. 19.

18. See Mario Untersteiner, *The Sophists*, trans. Kathleen Freeman
(Oxford, 1954), p. 106.

19. Kathleen Freeman, *Ancilla to the Pre-Socratic Philosophers*
(Cambridge, Mass., 1948), p. 129.

20. Gilles Deleuze, *Différence et Répétition* (Paris, 1968), p. 96. The
idea originates with Hume.

21. (a) Richard Hooker, *Of the Laws of Ecclesiastical Polity* (1594–7);
cf. Everyman edition (London, 1954), I, I xi 4, pp. 257–8:

For man doth not seem to rest satisfied, either with fruition of that
wherewith his life is preserved, or with performance of such actions as
advance him most deservedly in estimation; but doth further covet,
yea oftentimes manifestly pursue with great sedulity and earnestness,
that which cannot stand him in any stead for vital use; that which
exceedeth the reach of sense; yea somewhat above the capacity of

reason, somewhat divine and heavenly, which with hidden exultation it rather surmiseth than conceiveth; somewhat it seeketh, and what that is directly it knoweth not, yet very intentive desire thereof doth so incite it, that all other known delights and pleasures are laid aside, they give place to the search of this but only suspected desire. . . . For although the beauties, riches, honours, sciences, virtues, and perfections of all men living, were in the present possession of one: yet somewhat beyond and above all this there would still be sought and earnestly thirsted for.

(b) Giordano Bruno, *Degli Eroici Furori* (1585); cf. *The Heroic Frenzies*, trans. Paul E. Memmo Jnr – *University of North Carolina Studies in Romance Languages and Literatures*, No. 50 (1964), pp. 128–9:

Whatever species is represented to the intellect and comprehended by the will, the intellect concludes there is another species above it, a greater and still greater one, and consequently it is always inpelled toward new motion and abstraction in a certain fashion. For it ever realises that everything it possesses is a limited thing which for that reason cannot be sufficient in itself, good in itself, or beautiful in itself, because the limited thing is not the universe and is not the absolute entity, but is contracted to this nature, this species or this form represented to the intellect and presented to the soul. As a result, from that beautiful which is comprehended, and therefore limited, and consequently beautiful by participation, the intellect progresses towards that which is truly beautiful without limit or circumscription whatsoever.

[Details of original publication of Hooker and Bruno works inserted – Ed.]

22. Kenneth Burke, *The Rhetoric of Religion* (Berkeley, Cal., 1961), p. 69.

23. Eric Auerbach, *Mimesis: The Representation of Reality in Western Literature*, trans. Willard R. Trask (Princeton, N.J., 1953; new edn 1968), p. 311.

24. Paul Valéry, *Leonardo, Poe, Mallarmé*, trans. Malcolm Cowley and James R. Lawler, vol. VIII of *The Collected Works of Paul Valéry*, ed. Jackson Mathews (Princeton, N.J., 1972), p. 93.

SELECT BIBLIOGRAPHY

TEXTS

Editions of single plays are available in the New Mermaid series (Benn, London) and in the Revels Plays series (Manchester University Press, and Methuen, London). Neither series is as yet complete. *Tamburlaine* is also available in the Regents Renaissance Drama series, edited by J. D. Jump (University of Nebraska Press, Lincoln, Neb., and Edward Arnold, London, 1967); and *Dr Faustus* in a critical edition by W. W. Greg (Oxford University Press, 1950).

For reference to editions of the Complete Plays, see Note on Text, page 19, above.

CRITICAL STUDIES

All the books and articles in the following list are mentioned in the Introduction to this volume, with the exception of those which have a brief descriptive note.

Books or articles excerpted or reprinted in this volume are *not* listed below, and the reader is referred to the relevant Source citation.

This volume is a companion to the Casebook on *Dr Faustus*, edited by John D. Jump.

W. A. Armstrong, *Marlowe's 'Tamburlaine': The Image and the Stage* (Hull, 1966): an account of Marlowe's dramaturgy.
J. Bakeless, *The Tragicall History of Christopher Marlowe*, 2 vols (Cambridge, Mass., 1942).
Roy W. Battenhouse, *Marlowe's 'Tamburlaine': A Study in Renaissance Moral Philosophy* (Nashville, Tenn., 1941; rev. edn, 1964).
David M. Bevington, *From 'Mankind' to Marlowe: Growth of Structure in the Popular Drama of Tudor England* (Cambridge, Mass., 1962).
Nicholas Brooke, 'Marlowe the Dramatist', in J. R. Brown and B. Harris (eds), *Stratford-upon-Avon Studies, 9: Elizabethan Theatre* (London, 1966).
Douglas Cole, *Suffering and Evil in the Plays of Christopher Marlowe* (Princeton, N.J., 1962).
Ian Duthie, 'The Dramatic Structure of *Tamburlaine the Great, Parts One*

and Two', in *English Studies, 1948* (Essays and Studies, New Series), I
(1948): Duthie argues for a single concept governing both Parts,
against the usual opinion that *Part Two* is an after-thought. (See, for
example, F. P. Wilson, cited below.)

T. S. Eliot, 'Notes on the Blank Verse of Christopher Marlowe' (1919),
collected in *The Sacred Wood: Essays on Poetry and Criticism* (London,
1920); reprinted in *Selected Essays* (London, 1932).

Una Ellis-Fermor, *Christopher Marlowe* (London, 1927).

Leslie Hotson, *The Death of Christopher Marlowe* (London, 1925): a study
of the documents relating to the playwright's death.

L. C. Knights, 'The Strange Case of Christopher Marlowe', in his
Further Explorations (London, 1965).

P. H. Kocher, *Christopher Marlowe: A Study of His Thought, Learning and
Character* (Chapel Hill, N.C., 1946).

Clifford Leech, 'Marlowe's Humor', in Richard Hosley (ed.), *Essays on
Shakespeare and Elizabethan Drama in Honor of Hardin Craig* (Columbia,
Miss., 1962).

Alexander Leggatt, 'Tamburlaine's Sufferings', *Yearbook of English
Studies*, III (1973).

Mollie M. Mahood, 'Marlowe's Heroes', in her *Poetry and Humanism: An
Analysis of Seventeenth-Century English Poetry* (London, 1950).

Brian Morris (ed.), *Christopher Marlowe*: Mermaid Critical Commentary
series (London, 1968); contains essays on Marlowe and the early
Shakespeare; Marlowe and Brecht; Marlowe's orthodoxy, humour
and naturalism; *The Jew of Malta* in the theatre; and *The Tragedy of
Dido*.

Michael Quinn, 'The Freedom of Tamburlaine', *Modern Language
Quarterly*, XXI (1960).

Tulane Drama Review, VIII, 4 (1964); besides the essays mentioned in
the Introduction to this Casebook, there are accounts of the
'Structure of *Tamburlaine*'; 'Innocent Barabas' in *The Jew of Malta*;
Marlowe's use of spectacle and stage devices; a director's comments
on the staging of *Edward II*; and a review of twentieth-century
criticism.

Eugene M. Waith, *Ideas of Greatness: Heroic Drama in England* (New
York, and London, 1971).

F. P. Wilson, *Marlowe and the Early Shakespeare* (Oxford, 1954).

NOTES ON CONTRIBUTORS

JOHN RUSSELL BROWN: Professor of English, University of Sussex, and Associate Director of the National Theatre, London. He has published books on Shakespeare and Renaissance Drama, and on contemporary theatre; among the volumes edited by him are the Casebooks on *Antony and Cleopatra* and on *Much Ado About Nothing & As You Like It*. His *Discovering Shakespeare* (1981) sets out a new way of studying the plays.

J. S. CUNNINGHAM: Professor of English, University of Leicester. His publications include work on Alexander Pope and on modern literature, as well as on Renaissance drama.

EDWARD DOWDEN (1843–1913): appointed Professor of English Literature at Trinity College, Dublin, in 1867; a noted Shakespearean scholar and literary critic, his publications include *Shakspere: His Mind and Art* (1875).

MICHAEL DRAYTON (1563–1631): pastoral and historical poet, his greatest work is the topographical poem on England, *Polyolbion* (1622). He also wrote sonnets and religious verse, and collaborated on some plays.

STEPHEEN J. GREENBLATT: Associate Professor of English, University of California at Berkeley.

ROBERT GREENE (c.1558–92): prolific poet, playright and pamphleteer. He died in poverty after twelve years in which he wrote about 35 works for publication; two of his plays, *James IV* and *Friar Bacon and Friar Bungay*, still give pleasure in performance today.

JOSEPH HALL (1574–1656): poet, essayist and, subsequently, bishop. One of the earliest verse-satirists in English, writing in imitation of Juvenal, he was also one of the first to compose short prose 'characters' in the tradition of Theophrastus.

WILLIAM HAZLITT (1778–1830): critic, essayist and political writer; his works include *Characters of Shakespeare's Plays* (1817–18), *Lectures on the English Poets* (1818–19) and *A View of the English Stage* (1818–21). In *The Spirit of the Age: or, Contemporary Portraits* (1825) he gives a vivid account of the ideas of his own times.

LEIGH HUNT (1784–1859); political journalist, essayist and poet; he wrote a great deal of dramatic criticism, as well as occasional essays, historical studies and 3 volumes of autobiography.

BEN JONSON (1572–1637): playwright and poet. Besides his own works – including two supreme comedies: *Volpone* (1606) and *The Alchemist* (1609) – he was influential as a critic and counsellor of younger writers.

CHARLES LAMB (1775–1834): essayist; his *Specimens of the English Dramatic Poets who Lived about the Time of Shakespeare* (1808) was the product of wide reading and very personal taste. He was happiest in occasional essays and books for children.

CLIFFORD LEECH (died 1977): successively Professor of English at the University of Durham and at the University of Toronto; he was the first general editor of the Revels Plays series, and wrote books on Shakespeare, Webster, Ford and other dramatic subjects.

HARRY LEVIN: appointed Irving Babbitt Professor of Comparative Literature at Harvard University in 1960, having previously held a chair in English there. He has published studies on Shakespeare and James Joyce as well as Marlowe, and on comparative literature.

JOHNSTONE PARR: Professor Emeritus of English, Kent State University; his article on Marlowe (1944) became the title-essay in a collection of studies (Tuscaloosa, 1953).

GEORGE PEELE (c.1558–c.1597): actor, playwright and poet.

IRVING RIBNER: at the time of his death in 1972 he was Professor of English, State University of New York at Stony Brook. In addition to his comprehensive study of English history plays, he published a book on Jacobean tragedy and edited numerous play-texts.

JOHN ADDINGTON SYMONDS (1840–93): man of letters; he wrote extensively about the Italian renaissance, and published books on Shelley and Whitman, and translated Benvenuto Cellini's autobiography.

EUGENE M. WAITH: Professor of English at Yale University; his publications include a study on Tragi-comedy and several editions of plays.

A. W. WARD (1837–1924): appointed Professor of History and English Language and Literature at Owens College, Manchester, he was subsequently Vice-Chancellor of the new university there. He edited Pope, Crabbe and Mrs Gaskell, and published books on Chaucer and Dickens. For many years he was drama critic for *The Manchester Guardian*.

ROGER WARREN: Lecturer in the English Department, University of Leicester.

THOMAS WARTON (1728–90): Professor of Poetry at Oxford (1757–67) and subsequently Camden Professor of History there; he was appointed Poet Laureate in 1785. His works of literary criticism include *Observations on the 'Faerie Queene' of Spenser* (1754) and *A History of English Poetry* (1774–81).

JUDITH WEIL: Assistant Professor of English, University of Manitoba, Winnipeg.

DAVID HARD ZUCKER: his study of Marlowe was published by the Institute of English Language and Literature, University of Salzburg.

INDEX

For this Casebook character-names are not indexed. Page numbers in *italics* denote essays or extracts in the selection; those in **bold type** indicate major discussion of a play.